LIBRARY/NEW ENGLAND INST. OF TECHNOLOGY

3

P9-ASD-446

GAME PROG
IN C.

QA 76.76 .C672 Y98 2006

Yuzwa, Erik.

Game programming in C++

INCLUDES CD

NEW ENGLAND INSTITUTE OF TECHNOLOGY
LIBRARY

LIMITED WARRANTY AND DISCLAIMER OF LIABILITY

THE CD-ROM THAT ACCOMPANIES THE BOOK MAY BE USED ON A SINGLE PC ONLY. THE LICENSE DOES NOT PERMIT THE USE ON A NETWORK (OF ANY KIND). YOU FURTHER AGREE THAT THIS LICENSE GRANTS PERMISSION TO USE THE PRODUCTS CONTAINED HEREIN, BUT DOES NOT GIVE YOU RIGHT OF OWNERSHIP TO ANY OF THE CONTENT OR PRODUCT CONTAINED ON THIS CD-ROM. USE OF THIRD-PARTY SOFTWARE CONTAINED ON THIS CD-ROM IS LIMITED TO AND SUBJECT TO LICENSING TERMS FOR THE RESPECTIVE PRODUCTS.

CHARLES RIVER MEDIA, INC. ("CRM") AND/OR ANYONE WHO HAS BEEN INVOLVED IN THE WRITING, CREATION, OR PRODUCTION OF THE ACCOMPANYING CODE ("THE SOFTWARE") OR THE THIRD-PARTY PRODUCTS CONTAINED ON THE CD-ROM OR TEXTUAL MATERIAL IN THE BOOK, CANNOT AND DO NOT WARRANT THE PERFORMANCE OR RESULTS THAT MAY BE OBTAINED BY USING THE SOFTWARE OR CONTENTS OF THE BOOK. THE AUTHOR AND PUBLISHER HAVE USED THEIR BEST EFFORTS TO ENSURE THE ACCURACY AND FUNCTIONALITY OF THE TEXTUAL MATERIAL AND PROGRAMS CONTAINED HEREIN. HOWEVER WE, MAKE NO WARRANTY OF ANY KIND, EXPRESS OR IMPLIED, REGARDING THE PERFORMANCE OF THESE PROGRAMS OR CONTENTS. THE SOFTWARE IS SOLD "AS IS" WITHOUT WARRANTY (EXCEPT FOR DEFECTIVE MATERIALS USED IN MANUFACTURING THE DISK OR DUE TO FAULTY WORKMANSHIP).

THE AUTHOR, THE PUBLISHER, DEVELOPERS OF THIRD-PARTY SOFTWARE, AND ANYONE INVOLVED IN THE PRODUCTION AND MANUFACTURING OF THIS WORK SHALL NOT BE LIABLE FOR DAMAGES OF ANY KIND ARISING OUT OF THE USE OF (OR THE INABILITY TO USE) THE PROGRAMS, SOURCE CODE, OR TEXTUAL MATERIAL CONTAINED IN THIS PUBLICATION. THIS INCLUDES, BUT IS NOT LIMITED TO, LOSS OF REVENUE OR PROFIT, OR OTHER INCIDENTAL OR CONSEQUENTIAL DAMAGES ARISING OUT OF THE USE OF THE PRODUCT.

THE SOLE REMEDY IN THE EVENT OF A CLAIM OF ANY KIND IS EXPRESSLY LIMITED TO REPLACEMENT OF THE BOOK AND/OR CD-ROM, AND ONLY AT THE DISCRETION OF CRM.

THE USE OF "IMPLIED WARRANTY" AND CERTAIN "EXCLUSIONS" VARIES FROM STATE TO STATE, AND MAY NOT APPLY TO THE PURCHASER OF THIS PRODUCT.

GAME PROGRAMMING IN C++

ERIK YUZWA

NEW ENGLAND INSTITUTE OF TECHNOLOGY
LIBRARY

CHARLES RIVER MEDIA, INC.
Hingham, Massachusetts

3-06

\# 62290568

Copyright 2006 by THOMSON DELMAR LEARNING. Published by CHARLES RIVER MEDIA, INC. All rights reserved.

No part of this publication may be reproduced in any way, stored in a retrieval system of any type, or transmitted by any means or media, electronic or mechanical, including, but not limited to, photocopy, recording, or scanning, without *prior permission in writing* from the publisher.

Cover Design: Tyler Creative

CHARLES RIVER MEDIA, INC.
10 Downer Avenue
Hingham, Massachusetts 02043
781-740-0400
781-740-8816 (FAX)
info@charlesriver.com
www.charlesriver.com

This book is printed on acid-free paper.

Erik Yuzwa. *Game Programming in C++: Start to Finish*
ISBN: 1-58450-432-3

Library of Congress Cataloging-in-Publication Data

Yuzwa, Erik.
    Game programming in C++ : start to finish / Erik Yuzwa.
        p. cm.
    Includes index.
    ISBN 1-58450-432-3 (pbk. with cd : alk. paper)
    1. Computer games—Programming. 2. C++ (Computer program language)   I. Title.

    QA76.76.C672Y98 2005
    005.13'3—dc22

                                        2005032754

All brand names and product names mentioned in this book are trademarks or service marks of their respective companies. Any omission or misuse (of any kind) of service marks or trademarks should not be regarded as intent to infringe on the property of others. The publisher recognizes and respects all marks used by companies, manufacturers, and developers as a means to distinguish their products.

Printed in the United States of America
05 7 6 5 4 3 2 First Edition

CHARLES RIVER MEDIA titles are available for site license or bulk purchase by institutions, user groups, corporations, etc. For additional information, please contact the Special Sales Department at 781-740-0400.

Requests for replacement of a defective CD-ROM must be accompanied by the original disc, your mailing address, telephone number, date of purchase and purchase price. Please state the nature of the problem, and send the information to CHARLES RIVER MEDIA, INC., 10 Downer Avenue, Hingham, Massachusetts 02043. CRM's sole obligation to the purchaser is to replace the disc, based on defective materials or faulty workmanship, but not on the operation or functionality of the product.

Contents

Acknowledgments

Where to begin on something like this? This project would not have happened without the help and assistance of many individuals. I really thank God for blessing my life thus far and presenting many wonderful opportunities for me to explore. Although I've taken many risks of my own through this life, He's been helping out on the other end to provide some light on my journey.

A special "I love you" to my beautiful wife, Eliza, and our two sons, Noah and Isaac. Although I was able to get most of this book done after everyone went to bed, there was still the occasional weekend that was eaten up with me attached to the machine. Thanks to all of you who sacrificed our time together. To Noah, who insisted on keeping me company on some nights by teaching me the mambo thanks to his favorite show, *Dora the Explorer,* and to Isaac, who loves to stuff his face and call everything "nana" (banana).

To my mom, dad, and sister who've put up with me all these years despite my obvious obsessive need to play video games, combined with my ability to remember complete dialogue from every *Doctor Who* episode; yet I can't remember a few birthdays. I love you all and am blessed to have such a great family. I'm still shocked that I was allowed to possess an *Apple IIe* machine in my room through my formative years. How blessed art thou, *Ultima IV?*

To Jenifer Niles, Lance Morganelli, Bryan Davidson and all the wonderful people at Charles River Media/Thomson Delmar Learning: This book would not have happened without your guidance, persistence, and the opportunity for us to work together. Many heartfelt thanks!

To Scott Tidwell and Randi Rost over at 3Dlabs. You guys went above and beyond the call of duty by helping me with my GLSL questions and providing me with a loaner Realizm 100 video card for some testing. Many thanks for everything.

To the wonderful developer support staff at ATI who have been readily available to help me pinpoint problems in my code and troubleshoot any driver related issues I've had.

Another much appreciated "Thank You" to Avi Shapiro and the people over at Graphic Remedy for answering me with my gDEBugger problems.

To Bernie Wieser and John Brimacombe, who have helped me with sections of this material, along with continuing to open my eyes in the field of game development and software engineering in general. Somewhere along the way, you guys also helped test some code. Thanks!

To Steve Ford who did a tremendous job on the music included in the Super-AsteroidArena project and to Benjamin Wong who put in a lot of late nights putting the artwork together. Thanks, guys, the check is in the mail. (No, really, I mean it.)

To Martin Piper for all of his support and help getting things running using the ReplicaNet networking solution for this book.

Thanks to the developers who hang around the gamedev.net, indiegamer.com, flipcode.com (R.I.P.), devmaster.net, and garagegames.com forums. Through the years there have been so many golden posts on these boards, which have helped me grind through code.

A final thanks goes to you, the reader. Game programming is not an easy field or subject, even with the current level of software and hardware that we have at our disposal. However, with this work comes many rewards. The reward of any completed game is the first step on a greater journey.

Preface

Welcome to the exciting world of game programming! This text was born from a desire to help others educate themselves on some of the popular techniques and practices behind creating games today. To some, the magic behind moving an image across the screen is taken for granted when playing a new game purchased on the Internet or at a store.

To others, however, moving their first visible object across the screen is a rite of passage into a larger, more exciting world—a world that usually responds to their every command provided it is formed correctly; a world that can come to life with dragons, space ships, submarines, and a host of infinite possibilities.

This book will help you pursue the knowledge behind making your computer game fantasies a reality.

WHO SHOULD USE THIS BOOK

If you are already familiar with the C/C++ programming language and want to enter the exciting world of game programming, then this book is for you. Over the course of this material, you will learn many interesting and exciting concepts behind the magic of game creation on the PC. Not only will you add a lot of theory to your game programming toolkit, you will also create a small basic game from scratch; a fun and exciting game of *Asteroids* called *SuperAsteroidArena*.

While you will focus on using the SDL and the OpenGL libraries to learn game programming, you can also apply the concepts and fundamentals presented here to create just about any kind of game with any other language.

BOOK HIERARCHY AND LAYOUT

This book is structured to enable you to learn about game programming and creation in a natural progression. Each chapter and subsection builds upon previous chapters and topics, which will help you sort through the vast amount of material available on game programming. The text is presented in a tutorial format that allows you to progress at your own pace.

The following brief overview can help you chart your path through this book:

Chapter 1:   This is an introduction into the world of game programming on the PC. This chapter focuses on providing an overview of the existing technologies available to the game developer today.

Chapter 2:   This chapter introduces you to some of the concepts behind the design of a game.

Chapter 3:   This chapter focuses on introducing you to some basic concepts surrounding the popular SDL library and Windows programming in general.

Chapter 4:   This chapter introduces you to some of the objects that you will be developing throughout the rest of this book. You will make a small engine known as Peon, which will contain some small but useful objects for nearly any game you make.

Chapter 5:   This chapter introduces you to some of the mathematics behind working with 3D graphics.

Chapter 6:   This chapter introduces you to the world of OpenGL, which is a cross-platform graphics library.

Chapter 7:   This chapter expands upon the OpenGL introduction provided in Chapter 6.

Chapter 8:   This chapter is an introduction to some of the popular methods of organizing the objects in your game world. Scenegraphs, BSP trees, and OctTree algorithms are discussed here.

Chapter 9:   This chapter contains the graphics segment of the *SuperAsteroidArena* project.

Chapter 10:   This chapter focuses on introducing you to working with input devices through SDL.

Chapter 11:   This chapter introduces you to working with the popular SDL_ Mixer library and OpenAL to load and playback some high-quality music and sound effects for your games.

Chapter 12:   This chapter focuses on the segment of the *SuperAsteroidArena* project that deals with handling input and sound.

Chapter 13:   This chapter focuses on introducing you to principles of collision detection and physics.

Chapter 14:   This chapter focuses on providing an introduction to basic networking principles and techniques with source code in SDL_Net.

Chapter 15:   This chapter introduces you to the segment of the *SuperAsteroidArena* game which focuses on multiplayer communication.

Chapter 16:   This chapter introduces you to using models created in an external modeling tool. It also demonstrates one way to handle a model animation format.

Chapter 17:   This chapter focuses on providing an introduction to various techniques you can use for special effects within your game.

Chapter 18:   This chapter provides an introduction to the world of shader programming provided by the OpenGL ARB in the GLSL specification.

Chapter 19:   This chapter focuses on some ways of incorporating scripting support into your application or engine using Lua.

Chapter 20:   This last segment for the *SuperAsteroidArena* game focuses on applying some final polish to the game.

Chapter 21:   The final chapter of this book discusses other things to think about when finishing your game and delivering it to your customers.

No matter how small a game is, the art and practice of creating that game involves a rather large amount of work. For this reason, not every aspect of game programming or development is presented in these pages. Topics and items that are outside the focus of this book are noted where possible.

PROGRAMMING STYLE

Although this book makes an assumption that you are somewhat versed in the C/C++ language, the accompanying code for this material is meant to be as small and clean as possible. Feel free to have your favorite C++ reference book and material accompany you on the journey through the code for this book.

FURTHER SUPPORT

ON THE CD

Although the source code presented throughout this book is available on the accompanying CD-ROM, updates naturally accompany any software. Please be sure to visit either the publisher's Web site at *http://www.charlesriver.com* or the site devoted to this book at *http://book.wazooinc.com* for updates.

1 Game Technologies

Chapter Goals

- Introduce and cover some of the popular license agreements.
- Discuss existing and useful game technologies that are currently available for game developers.
- Introduce the Concurrent Versioning System (CVS).
- Introduce creating HTML-friendly documentation with Doxygen.
- Discuss some helpful C++ components provided by the Standard Template Library (STL).

For the beginner game developer, plenty of useful game technologies already exist and are worth discussing. Because some games might require a different approach (in either the technical or design aspects), an in-depth evaluation of the strengths and weaknesses of each is presented in this chapter so that you can better minimize the risks involved in developing your game.

COMMON LICENSE AGREEMENTS

Some of the more common license arrangements are also worth mentioning; you need to understand the limitations surrounding any technology you decide to use. There tends to be a lot of misinformation about what a license means, even though most agreements give you a lot of flexibility.

Lesser GNU public license: Most game development libraries are released under the LGPL license, which allows you to use the software in any application—commercial or otherwise. The only restriction is that if you modify any of the source code of the LGPL'd software, you only need to make those particular modifications public. It is not necessary to release the source code for the rest of your project. Software libraries such as the SDL and the Peon engine used in this book are released under this license arrangement. You need to make sure that the modified source code is publicly accessible, whether this is through a published link on your Web site, in public documentation (such as a game manual), or on an FTP server.

GNU public license (GPL):   Some software falls under this category. It is a popular choice for some of the industry's leading released source code (also known as AAA), such as code from Id Software. GPL is similar in many ways to LGPL in that you must include copyright notices with your project, and you can charge money for projects created using GPL'd modules. However, any project using GPL-protected software then automatically becomes a derivative project and is bound by the GPL terms and conditions. In other words, if you create a game using the Quake2 or Quake3 code released by Id Software under the GPL, then you are allowed to charge money for it but must make the source code to your project publicly accessible.

The BSD license: Some projects are also released under this license, which allows you to do just about whatever you want with the software. The only restriction is that you keep the original licensing copyright notice with your distribution, and you cannot use the original creator of the software to endorse your project without express written consent. Apart from those restrictions, you can modify the source code any way you want.

Creative Commons license: A rising star among open source licenses is the Creative Commons license. As more game assets are created and released to the Internet, such as a texture set created by one artist, some background music created by another, and maybe a collection of 3D Studio Max models, the common GPL or LGPL structures do not always make sense for their creations. As such, the Creative Commons license was developed for these types of terms and conditions. The official site is listed in Appendix F, but it brings you to a Web page that is in the form of a License Wizard. Using this wizard, you can walk through a series of questions pertaining to how exactly you want to protect your work. When it is finished, the wizard will produce the terms and conditions in the form of legalese that you can distribute with your project or advertise on your Web site.

In standard practice with your own library or project, it is usually a good idea to cut and paste your copyright into every header file in your project. At the very least, you should have some kind of a text file that you distribute with your project that clearly outlines with what type of license you are releasing your project. Most projects have an accompanying README or COPYING text file explaining the license in the root folder of the project.

SOME HELPFUL TECHNOLOGIES

On the Internet today are many entertainment or multimedia-related projects, and you should become familiar with some of the popular choices for game programming on the Windows platform.

The following engines or technologies are ranked in alphabetical order, not by any special preference. Do not forget to thoroughly understand the license agreements surrounding each package or toolkit before going forward with your project.

Blitz3D/Max: Mark Sibly launched the Blitz3D game engine kit in 2000. This kit is used by some programmers for their success. The engine comes with an editor that allows you to work with scripting code in order to interface with the *Blitz* engine. Although the scripting language is called *BlitzBasic* and looks similar to the old *QBasic* syntax, it provides a powerful interface to the underlying engine, which will run on any Windows system supporting DirectX7 or higher. As of this writing, an updated cross-platform version of *Blitz3D* (called *Blitz-Max*) has been released; this version is now capable of supporting both the MacOS and Win32 platforms. It offers an improved code base over its predecessor, and the rendering engine has been altered to support OpenGL in order to function in the cross-platform environment. Although larger projects can sometimes be difficult to manage with the Blitz IDE, this family of development software does target the beginner game developer with little-to-no skill in graphics programming. There also is a very large and supportive community from which you can draw experience should you encounter any difficulties creating your game.

DirectX: With their DirectX software development kit, Microsoft has been involved with games programming on Windows virtually since the release of Windows 95. The goal of DirectX was to unify the interface design of input, sound, and graphics devices, in order to push the onus of device driver certification on the hardware vendor. As long as the hardware is DirectX certified, then it should function with any DirectX application. Now on version 9.0c of the SDK, DirectX is slowly migrating itself in preparation for the upcoming release of Windows Vista. It is still a popular development platform for Windows game programmers; however, it is now only supporting the Windows XP family of products. Microsoft has also recently announced the XNA initiative, which is an attempt to lessen the gap between game developers and the gaming audience for whom they are developing. Although the XNA Studio product (or family of products) is not due to ship until 2006, Microsoft is pledging that XNA offers a better way to make game development a faster process.

FMOD: A cross-platform audio library, FMOD has secured a strong foothold within the game development community by providing a fast and easy interface to your audio effects and music. Started in 1992 by Brett Paterson, FMOD began life as a Gravis Ultrasound mod player for DOS. Ten years and many revisions later, Brett has continued on with FMOD under the newly created company of Firelight Technologies. His team has since added support for the PS2, PSP, PS3, Xbox, and Xbox360 consoles. The license cost has a simple and fair scaling algorithm to provide FMOD for any project, from the small hobby or shareware title up to an AAA commercial venture such as Blizzard's *World of Warcraft*.

OGRE: Initially starting this project in late 2001, Steve Streeting wanted to create a cross-platform, scene-structured, and graphics-independent rendering engine that was labeled the *Object-Oriented Graphics Rendering Engine* (OGRE). Throughout the years in development, it has matured to quite an amazing rendering package/suite for your own graphics needs. It has multiple rendering capabilities supporting the Direct3D7, OpenGL, or the latest Direct3D9 interfaces. Among other features, it includes a way of presenting GUI controls, scene management organization, and some handy importers for using modeling data from some popular modeling packages. The OGRE team and surrounding community is friendly and ready to give some direction for any issues or concerns about using OGRE in your project.

OpenAL: Beginning in roughly 1998 as an open source audio library alternative to the DirectSound3D API established by Microsoft, the OpenAL library was envisioned as a cross-platform 3D audio library for any project, both commercial and hobby. The library or specification did not really begin to mature until Loki Software and Creative Labs teamed together to expand the interfaces in 2000. The OpenAL engine has driven quite a few successful game titles such as *Jedi Knight* by Lucasarts, the U.S. Army's *America's Army*, Epic's *Unreal Tournament 2003/2004* series, *Marble Blast* developed by GarageGames, and a host of others. OpenAL has a nice, clean interface that provides the developer with an easy-to-implement audio solution to their project, with the added benefit of a software mixer to fall back on. The design of the library is similar in nature to the OpenGL specification in regard to how audio properties are assigned to an object, as well as an extension mechanism to support updates to the OpenAL specification. You will learn more about using OpenAL in Chapter 12, "Input and Sound Timebox."

Popcap framework: One of the most successful publishing companies for shareware games is the Popcap game online portal, which launched in 2000. They have published a long list of successful titles through the years and are now contributing back to the small-time game developer with the release of their toolkit, which is used in most of their developed products. Popcap was among the first online publishing companies that have specialized in making small, but addictive, titles such as *Bookworm, Bejeweled,* and *Zuma.* The framework is a kick start to creating small, but exciting games on the Windows platform. It is not meant for any 3D graphics, however, as it focuses on providing a strong software sprite library.

RakNet: The most common hurdle in any multiplayer project is properly dealing with networking sockets. The DirectPlay networking middleware component of the DirectX SDK was available free of charge, but it was only available on Windows. Other developers also did not like the way it was implemented. One such developer, Kevin Jenkins, decided to create the RakNet cross-platform library in 2001 based on a reliable-UDP packet delivery method, which is a popular protocol of choice for fast network and Internet gaming. RakNet is released under the LGPL and is a popular networking middleware component.

ReplicaNet: In late October 2000, while working for (the now defunct) Argonaut Games, Martin Piper was charged with writing a multiplayer Jet Ski demo for the Xbox platform. Instead of taking the typical network coding approach, Martin opted for a solution that involved creating a virtual database, which maintained itself across each node in the network. With much research into distributed technologies such as CORBA, DIVE, NPSNET and VIRTUS, Martin crafted a solution that described the data used by the game entities in such a way that the game logic would not need to concern itself with serialization. The database copy on each node would manage and replicate itself across every node when necessary. ReplicaNet is a cross-platform library, capable of running on Windows, Linux, and some game consoles. Martin has graciously offered the freeware license of ReplicaNet for use for this book. It is discussed in further detail in Chapter 15, "Networking Timebox."

Quake2 and Quake3:   Although these game(s) are several years old, John Carmack and the rest of Id Software have been more than generous in making the source code available under the GPL. This code can help point you in the right direction on a wide variety of common game programming issues, such as networking or graphics-related problems. Being among the first companies to release any source code to an actual AAA-quality game, Id Software has always been generous in helping the struggling developer.

SDL: While working at the now defunct Loki Software, Sam Lantinga created and launched a cross-platform toolkit in 1997 known as Simple DirectMedia Layer (SDL). Released under the LGPL, the SDL provides a thin interface to the underlying video, sound, and input components across each platform, which allows you to focus more on developing higher level game logic rather than worrying about creating windows, initializing input hardware, or other low-level device tasks. With the ability to integrate itself quite seamlessly with OpenGL, it is another popular choice among beginner programmers and independent game professionals alike, and it is the library with which you will be making a simple engine throughout the rest of this book.

Torque: Jeff Tunnell and Rick Overman, along with a few others from the game company Dynamix, decided that they wanted to go into business for themselves after leaving Sierra. They created their own publishing company called GarageGames, which was launched in 2000. GarageGames is an independent (indie) friendly publishing house that is becoming a popular gateway for game development. They offer a license to their proprietary game engine, *Torque*, for use for your own projects. *Torque* is a huge, impressive, cross-platform game engine that has not only powered the *Tribes2* game, but is also behind several successful projects such as *MarbleBlast* and *Orbz*. Although a license fee provides you with the source code to the mature and commercially proven engine itself, chances are high that you will not need to modify it. Instead, your game interfaces with the engine via *TorqueScript*, a scripting language similar in nature to JavaScript, to leverage the power and flexibility of the engine. Although there is a bit of a learning curve, the sheer amount of useful resources available on the Web site and through the *Torque* community can help you through the initial hurdles. Since the Torque engine hides a lot of the lower-level programming from you, it generally takes some tinkering with the engine in order to understand the relationship between the scripts you create and how they interact with the underlying components.

As you can see, there are a large number of engines and game toolkit technologies available to help complete the difficult task of designing and implementing a game. Although they are all excellent resources, some require more programming knowledge than others. Although some packages are more productive in the long run, they might have a much higher learning curve in the beginning, which can cause unexpected delays to the project. However, there are enough game resources available to satisfy the needs of anyone at any skill level and using just about any programming language.

Before you plunge into the world of game programming, you need to have some tools handy for creating your adventures. Throughout the remainder of this chapter, you will learn about some important tools that can apply to not only your own game development, but also to just about any software project upon which you embark.

Concurrent Versioning System (CVS)

"Time is money" is a common business mantra, and now more than ever companies are trying to cut down their expense overhead to improve their shareholder ranking and profit margins. As in regular software development, game development houses usually have very little room for error. The code developed by the team becomes part of the lifeblood of the company. To lose the code would have a catastrophic impact on the project and in a worst-case scenerio could even sink the company itself. Although having a regular software backup schedule is essential to keeping a physical history of the project, version control is also of primary importance as it allows you or any team member to view the history of the code base you are all developing. Since a team of developers, scripters, documentation writers, and so on, are all involved in the project, the code base can be a constantly shifting entity that can change hourly. As you might imagine, not having a working snapshot of the latest code base can cause problems and unneccessary delays. Without the ability to view a history of the resources involved, you might experience unneccessary delays and frustration if you and your team are trying to track down any bugs that have suddenly appeared in your game.

Anything can be dumped into a version control system, from the artwork created by the artists, the code of your game, the sound and music effects created by the sound engineers, and even the HTML code that contains the Web site for your product.

One of the most popular version control systems is the Concurrent Versioning System (CVS). Originally created for the Unix platform, CVS has gained worldwide popularity as the version control system of choice. For the purposes of this book, you will be using a Windows flavor of CVS, called *CVSNT*.

Installing CVSNT

ON THE CD

Browse to the /tools_install folder included on the CD-ROM and launch the CVSNT setup binary. You do not need to change any of the default settings with the installation, so just allow it to install. When the installation is completed, it will be necessary for a machine reboot.

When finished, you can now create your own code repository. Go into the system control panel and launch the CVSNT control panel applet, denoted by the green fish (see Figure 1.1).

Automatic Updates	Set up Windows to automatically del
CVS for NT	Configure the CVS NT Service
Date and Time	Set the date, time, and time zone fo
DirectX	Changes properties for DirectX

FIGURE 1.1   CVSNT applet.

You are now presented with the main CVSNT panel. Click on both of the Stop buttons to stop the CVS services. In a File Explorer window, create a folder on the working drive to house a repository as shown in Figure 1.2.

cvs_repository	File Folder	3/12/2005 6:08 AM
cvs_temp	File Folder	3/12/2005 6:07 AM

FIGURE 1.2   Local repository folder.

In the Repositories tab, click the Add button to create a new repository. In the Location field, be sure to select the cvs_repository that you created previously. Then enter the name /projects in the Name field. This name is your key to accessing your repository, as shown in Figure 1.3 so do not forget it .

A message dialog box should appear inquiring whether you want to initialize the folder. Press Yes. Select OK, go back to the main tab, and start up the services again using the Start buttons. That is all you need to create a CVS repository server that houses your project.

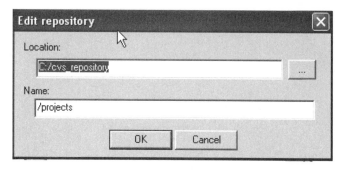

FIGURE 1.3   Name the repository.

Using CVS

Now that you have your central repository server created, it is time to learn how to use it for development purposes. Although you can use the command line to interact with the CVSNT server, it is easier for beginners to use a tool with a graphical user interface. For this book, you are using the TortoiseCVS Windows Explorer shell interface to work with CVSNT.

ON THE CD
    Available on the accompanying CD-ROM in the /tools_install folder, the TortoiseCVS GUI hooks itself right into the Windows Explorer shell menus, making it much easier to interact with your CVS repository. In practice, you only need to remember a few important concepts regarding a repository system: how to work with a module (that is, checkout), how to update files, and how to put them back into the repository (that is, checkin).

CREATING THE *SUPERASTEROIDARENA* PROJECT

Now you will begin preparation for creating the *SuperAsteroidArena* game. First, you will create a new project within the repository system that you have just finished installing. Create a new blank folder called c:\cvs_working_folder. Within this folder, create another folder called *SuperAsteroidArena*. Right-click on this folder and select the Make New Module of the CVS menu option (see Figure 1.4).

    You next need to fill out some important information to define the project properly within the repository. You might want to read up on implementing security on your repository; for now there is none. The fields should be filled out as they appear in Figure 1.5.

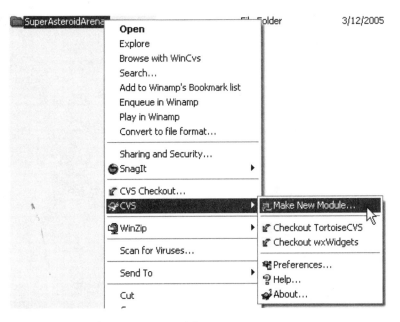

FIGURE 1.4   Make New CVS module.

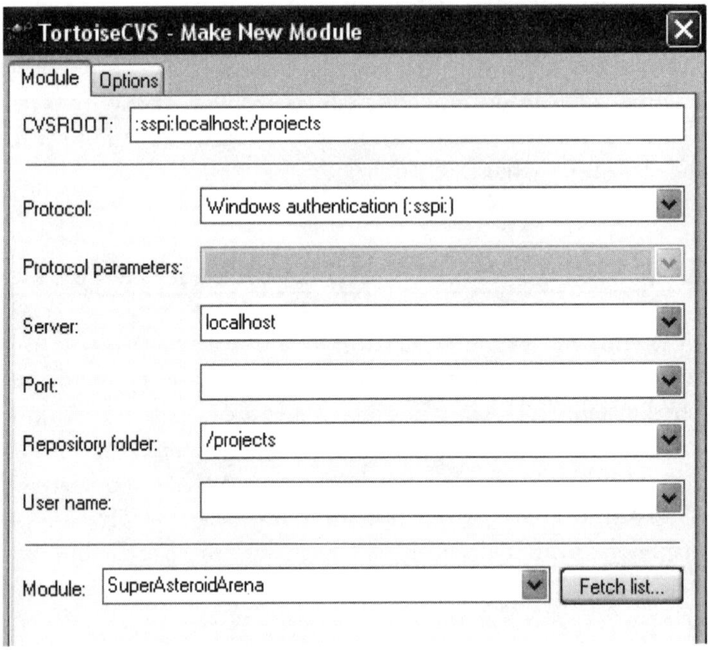

FIGURE 1.5   CVS project definition.

When finished, select OK, and you should see a results window informing you whether the creation was successful or not. You should see a message similar to Figure 1.6.

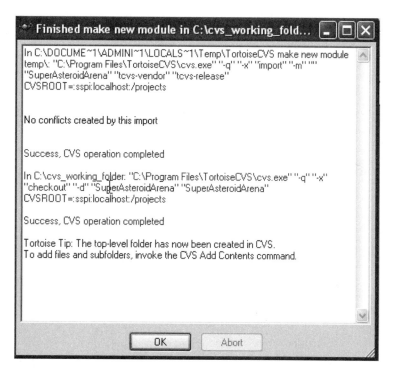

FIGURE 1.6 Project creation status.

Working with Files

Although there is no source code to play with just yet, you can practice using CVS by working with a simple text document.

Within the *SuperAsteroidArena* folder, create a new text file todo.txt and open it with Notepad. Type some text such as `Create game here` and save/close the file. You should notice that in Windows Explorer, the file now has a blue question mark icon on it. This signals that it is a file that does not yet exist within the repository as shown in Figure 1.7.

FIGURE 1.7 Unexisting file in the project.

You can fix that by right-clicking on the file and selecting the CVS Add. . . . option seen in Figure 1.8.

FIGURE 1.8 CVS Add dialog.

Select OK on the dialog box that pops up, and then CVS will try to add this new file into your project in the repository. The operation should result in a success message, and the file should now have a new icon on it. This is a visual cue that it has been added, but not committed to the repository, as demonstrated in Figure 1.9.

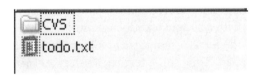

FIGURE 1.9 File added to repository.

To fix this, simply right-click the file again and select the CVS Commit menu option visible in Figure 1.10.

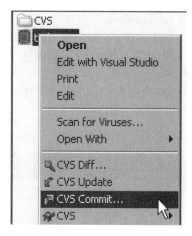

FIGURE 1.10　Commit file.

Select OK, and you should see another success message generated by CVS.

 Note by default that when an object is added to the repository, it is automatically assigned a version number of 1.0 by CVS.

Checking Out Objects

To demonstrate the process of checking out a project/file, move to a different folder on your computer. Right-click somewhere in the File Explorer window and select the CVS Checkout menu option. The CVS settings should remain the same, so you should be fine just selecting the OK button. CVS will do some work, and you should end up with a results window like Figure 1.11.

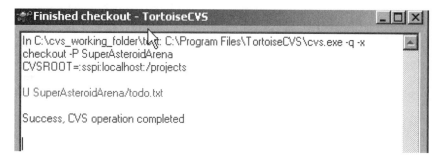

FIGURE 1.11　Status of checkout.

Now that you have got the todo.txt file to work with again, update it with some other text. Again, type whatever you want and save/close the file. It should now be a different color (red), which again is a visual cue that the file was modified. If you use the CVS Commit dialog as outlined previously, CVS will update the version that you have in the repository with this new one. Notice again the updated version numbers shown in Figure 1.12.

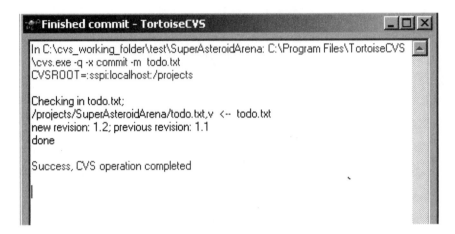

FIGURE 1.12   Commit status.

Introduction to Doxygen

ON THE CD

If you have team members touching the same modules often enough, or even if you are the lone developer, any code can get complex and unreadable. Documentation becomes critical as the developer should understand what each module is attempting to actually do. Not only that, but sometimes it is necessary to update code that has not been touched in a long time, and you probably will not remember the reasons behind why you implemented the code the way you did. Available on the CD-ROM in the /tools_install folder, *Doxygen* is a powerful and handy tool that generates Web page-friendly documents from the commented source code that provides an overview to the project. Listing 1.1 demonstrates a sample class header file with Doxygen-friendly commenting, available on the CD-ROM in /chapter_source/chapter_01/HealthObj.h.

LISTING 1.1 Sample Doxygen-Friendly Class Definition

```
/*!
* \brief This object modifies an entity's hit points
*
* The purpose of this object is to hang around in your game world
* until the Player picks it up. Depending upon how much health
* points the instance of this object is worth, it is added or
* subtracted to the player's overall health score
*/
class HealthObj : public ObjA
{
  public:
  /*!
  * constructor
  */
  HealthObj();

  /*!
  * destructor
  */
  virtual ~HealthObj();

  //comment blocks can also begin with...
  /**
  * This method places our object in the game world along
  * with assigning it a health value
  * @param x - x position
  * @param y - y position
  * @param z - z position
  * @param h - health
  * @return true or false if this object was allowed
  */
  bool setPosition( float x, float y, float z, int h );

  //snip!
};
```

The Doxygen tool comes with a nice and friendly graphical user interface to help you choose which options you would like to incorporate into the generation of the documentation. For example, you can specify your own cascading stylesheet (.css) files for the header and footer area of the document. After installing the utility, to launch the Doxygen tool you need to execute the Doxywizard menu item from your Start menu. You will be presented with a main dialog as shown in Figure 1.13.

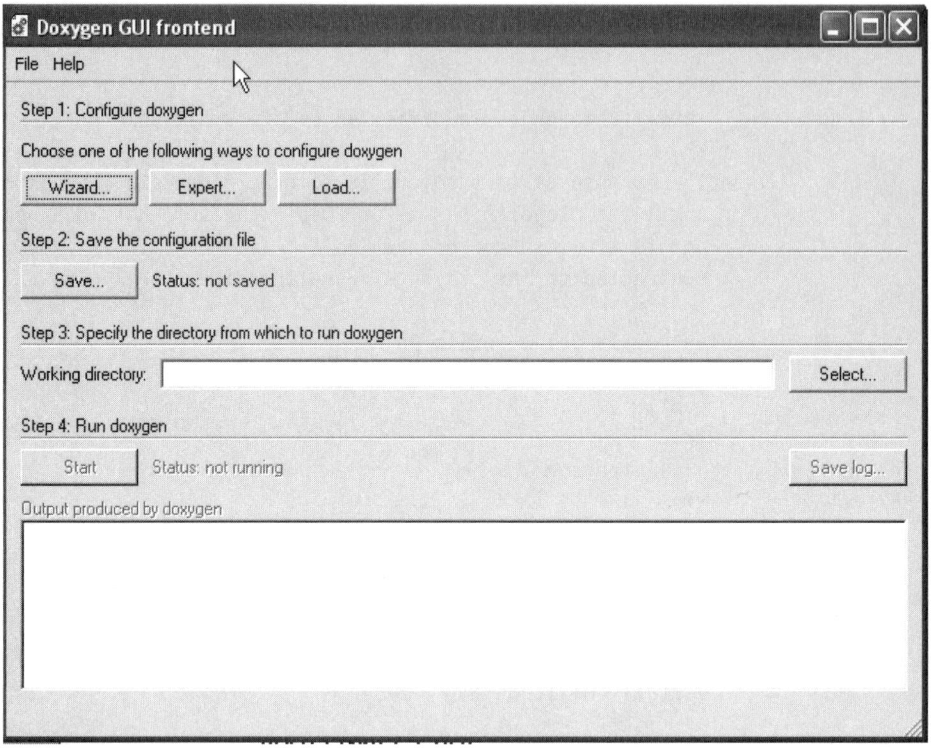

FIGURE 1.13   Doxywizard.

The use of the Wizard button will guide you through the basics of creating a Doxygen-compatible configuration file. When it is time to generate the HTML-friendly documentation, you launch Doxygen by pressing the Start button.

Within the specified target folder, if you then launch the html\index.html file in your browser, you will see the HealthObj object created from the Doxygen tool.

For further examples of using Doxygen in a real world situation, be sure to inspect the documentation or the source code files that accompany the *SuperAsteroidArena* or the *Peon* project contained on the accompanying CD-ROM.

Introduction to InnoSetup

The very first thing a potential customer will see before playing or buying your product is usually one of the final tasks the game developer tackles during the lifetime of the project. The goal of the installation procedure is to make the process of installing your game as painless as possible for the player.

There are many friendly installer tools on the market, but one of the easier systems to use is InnoSetup. It can handle simple installation requirements such as file copying and registry key creation, along with providing an easy uninstall procedure. It is also available on the CD-ROM in the /tools_install folder.

ON THE CD

Remember who your target player is when creating the installation procedure, as some players might have no idea what kind of system they are running, or which version of DirectX or OpenGL video drivers are installed. With this in mind, keep the language simple by not using a lot of technical jargon during the process.

NOTE

Re-running an installation procedure of an existing successful product is a good start to perfecting your own installation appearance. In order to maintain an atmosphere of "positive transfer" among other applications that the player is accustomed to installing, try to use the same installation language that other well-known products use.

The documentation provided with InnoSetup is incredibly detailed and makes it very easy to accomplish the basic necessities of an installer package. Listing 1.2 details a sample InnoSetup script used to install some files and create an icon.

LISTING 1.2   InnoSetup Sample Script Taken from the InnoSetup Examples

```
; – Example1.iss –
; Demonstrates copying 3 files and creating an icon.

; SEE THE DOCUMENTATION FOR DETAILS ON CREATING .ISS SCRIPT FILES!

[Setup]
AppName=My Program
AppVerName=My Program version 1.5
DefaultDirName={pf}\My Program
DefaultGroupName=My Program
UninstallDisplayIcon={app}\MyProg.exe
Compression=lzma
SolidCompression=yes

[Files]
Source: "MyProg.exe"; DestDir: "{app}"
Source: "MyProg.hlp"; DestDir: "{app}"
Source: "Readme.txt"; DestDir: "{app}"; Flags: isreadme

[Icons]
Name: "{group}\My Program"; Filename: "{app}\MyProg.exe"
```

After installing the InnoSetup application, you will need to launch the In-noSetup Compiler option from the Start menu. You will be presented with a Welcome Wizard dialog as shown in Figure 1.14.

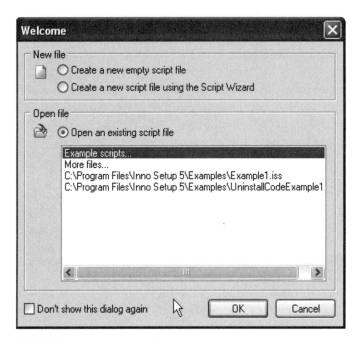

FIGURE 1.14   InnoSetup Compiler.

You have the choice of either starting with a blank compilation script or using the wizard to automatically generate your own.

For the purposes of the *SuperAsteroidArena* project, you will run through a quick setup here.

Start by selecting the option to use the wizard to generate your own setup script. Enter the application information relevant to the project as shown in Figure 1.15.

The entry fields are self explanatory. For the version number field, feel free to start off with a small number such as 0.1 and gradually increase it with each release of your game. The standard practice is to mark the version you present to the public as the 1.0 version.

After pressing the Next button, you will be presented with the Next dialog as shown in Figure 1.16.

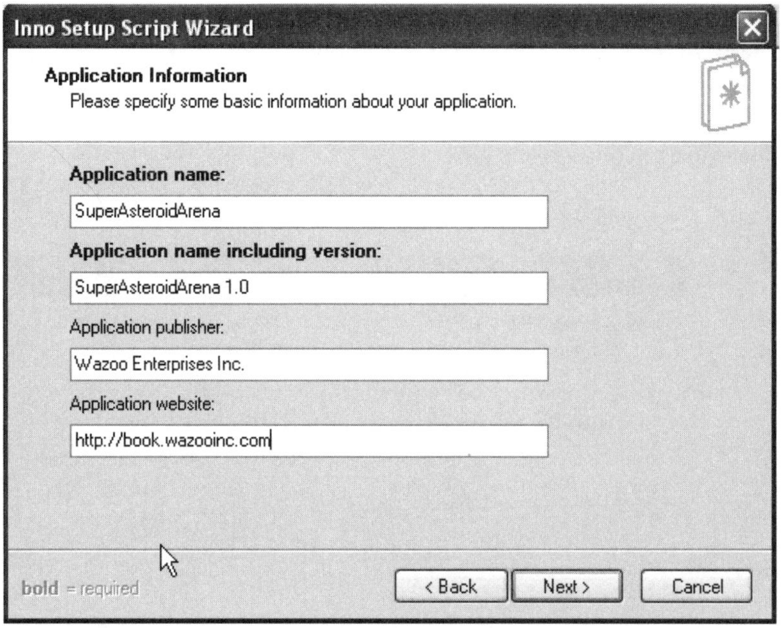

FIGURE 1.15 *SuperAsteroidArena* application information.

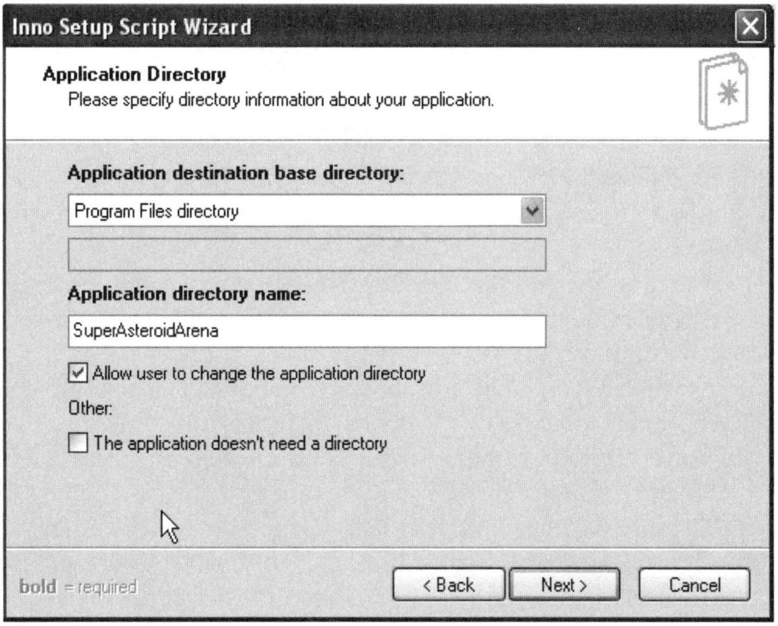

FIGURE 1.16 *SuperAsteroidArena* application directory.

Most of the retail games today choose to install their game within the `c:\Program Files` folder structure. You can either choose this as the default location or allow the player to select their own. After moving to the Next dialog, you can specify where the application binary is located within your folder structure. This is demonstrated in Figure 1.17.

FIGURE 1.17   *SuperAsteroidArena* application files.

The next phase of the installation generation wizard is to specify which icons are created for your application and where they will reside. Figure 1.18 details the available options.

As you can see, you have the ability to create an icon for your application on the Quick Launch toolbar along with one on the desktop. You can also choose whether you want everyone on this machine to have your game created in their respective Start menu folders.

The next dialog page in the Install Generation wizard contains the all-important information regarding the license of your game. This is an important step as you are detailing what kind of permissions the player has with your software. This is detailed in Figure 1.19.

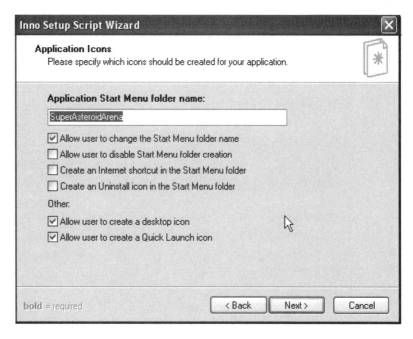

FIGURE 1.18   *SuperAsteroidArena* icon configuration.

If you are specifying a license file for use with a game you are trying to sell, consider putting your company's return policy in this license file. Detail explicitly the terms and conditions under which you may (or may not) refund the customer.

The final input dialog that you have available in InnoSetup is to specify any additional compiler settings. Figure 1.20 provides a screenshot of this Compiler Settings dialog.

When you are satisfied with your input decisions, the InnoSetup compiler will then generate the installation script for you. The compiler will then ask whether you want to create this new installation binary.

To see a real-world InnoSetup script in action, be sure to inspect the /SuperAsteroidArena/ArenaMain/installer.iss file contained within the *SuperAsteroidArena* project on the CD-ROM. You will also learn more about installation

tips in Chapter 21, "Finishing Tips and Tricks."

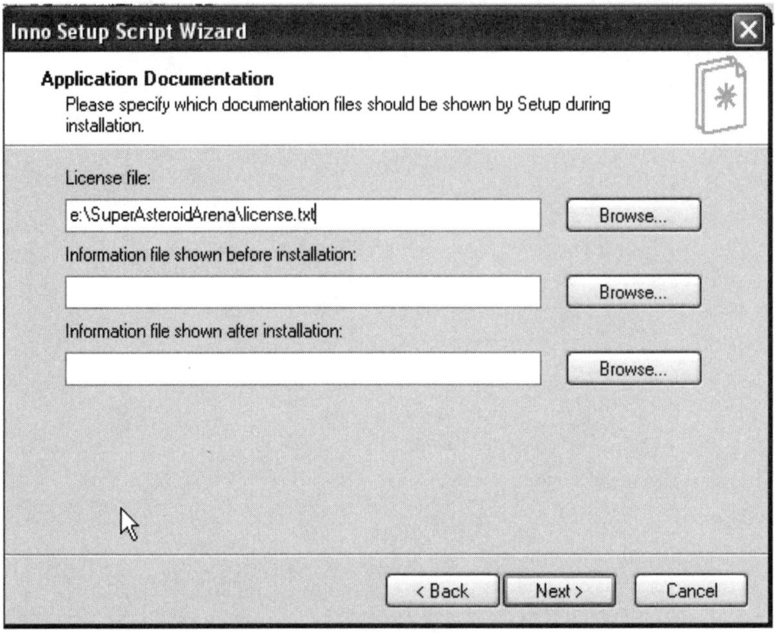

FIGURE 1.19 *SuperAsteroidArena* application documentation.

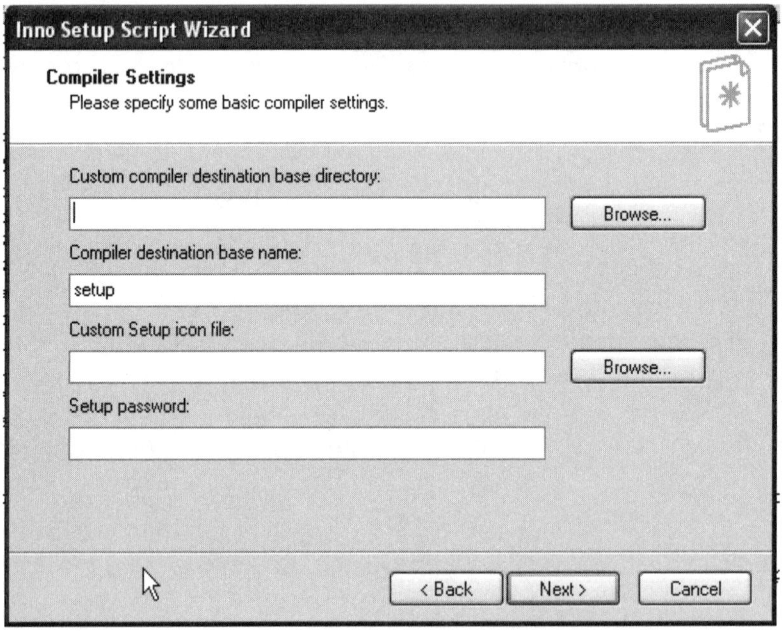

FIGURE 1.20 *SuperAsteroidArena* compiler settings.

THE STANDARD TEMPLATE LIBRARY

The STL programming library is another important and valuable tool that will save you a lot of time and troubleshooting. Despite the underground rumors that seem to persist in questioning the use of an STL within a game (or any other high-performance application), the fact of the matter is that the STL was originally created and optimized for speed. It is used on many past and present game projects on Windows, MacOS, and even some of the consoles. The STL is built around the concept of *containers*. In other words, the majority of the classes developed within the library are fast and efficient objects to store other objects. The three most commonly used containers from the STL that game programmers typically use are the Vector, String and Map container objects.

std::string

The STL string container represents an optimized safe array of characters that provides you with an easy-to-use container for storing string data. When working with char arrays, there is always a small chance that you might try to access an element in the array that is out of bounds. You might also come across problems with using strcat or strcpy to copy one large character array into a slightly smaller one. To handle these cases, you normally need to create blocks of tests to ensure that the string operations completed successfully. Instead, the STL string container gives you some easy ways of manipulating string data, without worrying about illegal operations such as those mentioned previously. Listing 1.3 demonstrates a simple sample.

LISTING 1.3   An std::string Example

```
//specify that you want to use objects defined in the
//std namespace.
using namespace std;

int main( int argc, char* argv[])
{
  //define a string object..can also be defined as std::string
  string text_string;

  //instead of strcpy we can use the = operator
  text_string = "Hello World";

  //instead of strcat we can use += operator
  text_string += " I am a std::string";
```

```
//when needing a pointer to the character string buffer,
//always use the .c_str() method
cerr << text_string.c_str() << endl;

return 0;
}
```

std::vector

Another popular container of choice for the game programmer is the STL `vector` object, which can be used as a dynamic array for any object you want to store. As with the `std::string` container, the `vector` container is one way of avoiding out of bounds errors. As elements are inserted into the container, the `vector` first ensures that there is enough room for the new element. If there is not, then it will create a large enough space for the new object. Listing 1.4 gives you a small sample of the power of the STL `vector`.

LISTING 1.4 An `std::vector` Example

```
//specify that you want to use objects in the std namespace
using namespace std;

int main(int argc, char* argv[])
{

  //define a vector container to store integers
  //can also be defined as std::vector
  vector<int> oVecInteger;

  oVecInteger.push_back( 9 );
  oVecInteger.push_back( 6 );

  //an iterator is an STL object used to enumerate or
  //process the contents of a container
  for( vector<int>::iterator it = oVecInteger.begin();
    it != oVecInteger.end(); it++)
  {

      //it is a pointer to the element in the iterator,
      //so *it dereferences it so we can get the value
      cout << "displaying value: " << *it << endl;
  }
```

```
        return 0;
    }
```

std::map

The last STL container object you will learn about here is the STL map container, which creates and stores objects in a key value-pair format. This object is especially useful when you need to quickly reference a collection of game objects. Listing 1.5 provides a sample of using STL map.

LISTING 1.5 An std::map Sample

```
//to demonstrate how simple it is to store objects in a map
//container, define a simple monster object
struct sMonster
{
  std::string monster_name;
  int monster_health;
};

int THAL_KEY = 1;
int KALED_KEY = 2;

//specify that you want to use objects from the std namespace
using namespace std;

int main(int argc, char* argv[])
{

  map<int, sMonster*> oMonsters;
  sMonster* mon1 = new sMonster();
  sMonster* mon2 = new sMonster();

  //set some basic properties for the monsters
  mon1->monster_name = "Thal";
  mon1->monster_health = 100;
  mon2->monster_name = "Kaled";
  mon2->monster_health = 50;

  //insert them into the map container using a key
  //value that we can use to find them later
  oMonsters.insert(make_pair(THAL_KEY, mon1));
```

```
//the following assignment is also legal
oMonsters[KALED_KEY] = mon2;

//we want to find the Thal monster so we need an
//iterator object to enumerate the map elements
map<ing, sMonster*>::iterator iter;

//find the element matching the key value
iter = oMonsters.find(THAL_KEY);
if (iter == oMonsters.end())
{
  //can't find it!
  cerr << "The Thal has been exterminated!" << endl;
}else
{
  cerr << "The Thal has " << iter->second->monster_health
  << " health left. " << endl;
}

//clean up. Note that since you are storing pointers to sMonster
//objects which are allocated on the memory heap, you need
//to clean up and deallocate this memory before calling the
//clear() method of the container.

sMonster* pObj;
for(map<int, sMonster*>::iterator it = oMonsters.begin();
  it != oMonsters.end(); it++)
{
  delete it->second;
    it->second = NULL;


    }
}

//clear the map of the sMonster pointers
oMonsters.clear();

return 0;
}
```

If you are considering using STL with a version of Visual Studio earlier than .NET 2003, then be sure to check out the STLPort project, which fixes many bugs and memory leaks detected in earlier versions of the STL packaged with Visual Studio 6.0. It is included in the accompanying CD-ROM under /tools_install. Another option for using the STLPort libraries is to ensure that you are working with the latest version of the Platform SDK available from Microsoft.

CHAPTER EXERCISES

1. This chapter only touched on the large amount of tools available to the game developer today. Do some of your own research with the help of your favorite search engine to find your own favorite sites and resources.
2. Take some time to study some of the technologies and tools listed in this chapter. When planning which to use, it helps to have a matrix created with the strengths and weaknesses of each one to help the decision-making process. Do not forget to include your own skills in order to help create or rank the feature list you require that best matches the game you want to create.
3. Be sure to practice using TortoiseCVS to interact with the CVS server. Get comfortable with manipulating and tracking many resources within a project.
4. Inspect the documentation accompanying CVSNT to add a layer of security to your source code repository. Create an update account that has permission to checkout, update, and checkin files, along with a read account, which only has enough permission to checkout the files.
5. Practice using the STL with some other small programs, with an attempt to use the map and vector containers often. Check in these small samples to your CVS repository, be sure to comment the code, and use the Doxygen tool to generate some documentation to accompany them.

SUMMARY

In this chapter you were introduced to some of the more common license arrangements under which game software tends to be bound. You were given a brief overview of the GPL, the LGPL, and the Creative Commons license arrangements. This chapter also introduced and provided an overview of some of the game technologies that exist for the game developer today. You were also introduced to some commonly used development tools that can save you from many hours of struggling and frustration. Regardless of whether you are a lone-wolf developer or are working in a team, ensuring that there is a proper backup schedule and source code repository system can help save your project from certain doom should you experience any unfortunate events. You were next shown how the Doxygen tool helps with generating HTML-friendly documentation from source code comments. You also were briefly introduced to the InnoSetup installation system, which is a terrific package for creating user-friendly installation binaries. You also covered some of the basics involved in using the common container objects of the Standard Template Library, including how to use the `string`, `vector` and `map` containers.

When you have the toolset needed to create your own fantastic adventures, you need to learn how to take the necessary steps to design your project, which you will learn about in the next chapter.

2 Design Fundamentals

Chapter Goals

- Introduce some common software design methods.
- Introduce software reusability techniques.
- Introduce the Unified Modeling Language (UML).
- Describe and cover the basic game phases.
- Describe and develop a design document using the Agile design process.

A basic understanding of some common design fundamentals can radically improve your project, but it is most often overlooked by beginning game developers. It can help to reduce the amount of development time for your game by minimizing some of the risks involved and enabling you to better plan the development stages.

WHAT IS A GAME DESIGN?

At the highest level of your game project, the game design details and defines how your game operates and responds to the player. The game design acts as a blueprint or structure that you and your team will use to work through to the completion of your game. It provides everyone with a central, single definition of what should occur within the game world, depending on what conditions exist or what input is received by the player. Design helps you map from the basic concepts of your game through to the implementation. It is also the central document that aids in coordinating tasks between team members. Design literally describes and entails the last word on everything involved with the game.

Skipping the game design process can contribute to massive delays in the project in the later stages. Programming by trial and error is not a manageable process. Not only is it much more difficult to maintain a single vision without a central document or design, but it can be nearly impossible to recruit any help without providing something the potential team member can browse through.

To help bring your gaming projects to fruition, you can take advantage of software design principles that the professional programmers use: the classic waterfall approach or an iterative design.

CLASSIC WATERFALL SOFTWARE DESIGN

You might already be familiar with this type of approach, since the *classic waterfall* method has been in use since the early days of software design. The waterfall model focuses on each phase of the design flowing into the next. This means that as you complete one phase of the design, you move into the next through implementation and testing phases, cascading down through the creation process like a waterfall. Figure 2.1 demonstrates this method.

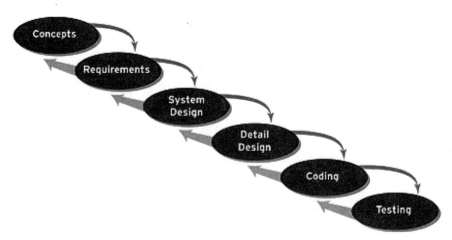

FIGURE 2.1 Classic waterfall design process.

Some programmers and software engineers working on applications will swear by this design method in the real world, but it is not always the best model to follow for game development. During the implementation phase of a project, for example, you might realize that there are some flaws in the design based upon some earlier (now erroneous) assumptions. After being perhaps months in development, it is often far too late to return to your client and/or project manager to ask for more time to rebuild a section of the code base.

The waterfall method also fails in some regards, as any software development project is more of a fluid body of work than one that is developed in isolation. What if the current target market demographic suddenly changes, and your marketing team demands some alterations to the game? What if technology changes much more quickly than anticipated, and new hardware or effects become available to implement in your game?

These are only a few of the pitfalls that you or your team can encounter during the project; therefore, you should have one or more contingency scenarios defined.

ITERATIVE SOFTWARE DESIGN

Because of some of the problems associated with the waterfall design approach, most game programmers (some unknowingly) tend to follow a much more iterative design process. This style of the design allows for much more fluidity and adaptation to the project if necessary.

Most of your gameplay is iterative in nature and is difficult to envision without the benefits of building tests to see how the different rules of your game and/or universe interact with each other. If, after testing, you decide that some of the rules need more tweaking or need to be removed altogether, the iterative method allows you to adjust the design as necessary. In the waterfall method, objects within each phase are pretty much set in stone as they depend upon objects created in the previous phase; therefore, any real tweaking is never allowed or even acceptable. Figure 2.2 provides an overview of the iterative process.

The "spiral" process underscores the continued process of requirements gathering, making adjustments, and client feedback, which forms the heart and soul of iterative design.

As you begin the overall design process, you are responsible for setting a schedule that represents the timeline of the project to the best of your knowledge at the present time. Along the way, you should mark project *milestones*, in which you and your team have the opportunity to do a mini-evaluation on the project so far. If you need to make any alterations or adjustments because of recommendations by the marketing department or if you discover any serious problems with the design in

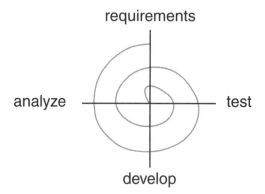

FIGURE 2.2 Iterative "spiral" design process.

general, this is a feasible approach to follow. Each milestone should have a subset of goals that you and your team are looking to accomplish. Again, during each milestone period, the team can also readjust any or all of the upcoming goals.

Principles of Agile Design

During the 1990s, the forming of Agile design methodologies was a direct response to models such as the waterfall approach, which were regarded by some as cumbersome, bureaucratic, and slow processes of creating useful software. Initially the methods proposed by the Agile designers were collectively known as "lightweight" techniques. In 2001 some prominent members of the iterative software design community met to form the Agile Alliance. Their first task was to create the Agile Manifesto, which grouped these lightweight principles under the universal Agile brand. This has become an extremely popular design process within the industry and benefits software designers of nearly every type of application. The core principles behind the Agile design methodology are as follows:

1. Minimize project risk by developing your software in short iteration periods, known as *timeboxes*, which last between one and four weeks.
2. Each timebox of the project is within itself a project of its own and includes all of the tasks behind releasing any updates to the main project. This includes new planning, new requirements, gathering and analysis, coding, implementation, and updating documentation.
3. The Agile method emphasizes personal communication involving face-to-face discussions with the client. Agile stresses the fact that meetings or discussions with the client should always overshadow the written documentation on the project. Agile teams are usually formed within close proximity to their

actual clients. For Agile purposes, *clients* are defined as the people who have defined the project to begin with. External customers and project managers are some good examples.

4. The progress of an Agile project is measured by the amount of functioning code at the end of every timebox.

5. Agile welcomes requirement changes by the client, even late in the project, in order for the client to maximize any competitive advantage.

To the newcomers of this type of software design methodology, there is sometimes confusion between an Agile design approach and a pure *ad-hoc* practice in which the developers simply work through the project in any direction they choose with little restrictions. Since Agile methods emphasize continuous feedback along with rigorous and disciplined processes, however, they create a successful environment with a clear direction and target.

Agile methods are focused around minimizing risk in the project. You are still working from a larger picture but can prune any features from the project based on your timebox progress.

NOTE

One of the foundation principles of Agile is that the design is test driven in nature. Agile developers create small tests to iteratively drive the project forward. Although it is one of the principles of proper Agile design, creating a test framework is out of the scope of this book. Please be sure to reference the Agile links contained in Appendix F for further information.

When to Use Agile

Although this highly iterative process is eagerly accepted for quite a few projects, in some cases the Agile methods might not work as well. The Alliance recommends that teams using Agile techniques are no larger than roughly 10 developers in size. These design techniques are also successful when used in projects that are extremely volatile or contain rapidly changing requirements. A project as volatile as a game makes Agile a perfect design candidate for you to learn and use to develop your game software.

INTRODUCTION TO THE UNIFIED MODELING LANGUAGE

As you are learning about software design techniques, it should be apparent that rarely does the project immediately shift into implementation and/or coding. Regardless of which software design model you prefer, after you have created the design document, it can save you a lot of time and hassle to transcribe your document into a modeling language. The Unified Modeling Language (UML) is an attempt to bring the concept of blueprints to the world of software design and implementation. The language of UML consists of a number of different graphical components that can be used to describe the architecture of your software. The benefit of this technique is that you now have a common graphical representation of your application that you and your team can follow. It becomes immediately apparent which component relies on which other component; this can alert you to any possible problems that might occur during the development phase of your project.

Although the UML is not the only modeling language, it is becoming the most widely accepted standard. In other words, this has major communication benefits with the other developers on your team in regards to understanding the overall design and architecture of your system.

Basic Class Notation

Within UML, a simple rectangle is the basic notation for representing a class. The rectangle is usually segmented into three sections. The uppermost section contains the class name, usually bolded. The middle section contains any attributes for the class, and the lowermost section contains any operations that the class can perform. Figure 2.3 demonstrates this.

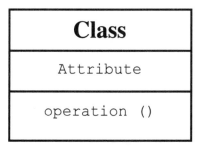

FIGURE 2.3   UML class notation.

 UML has a fairly strict differentiation between operations and methods of the class. Within a UML context, an operation is a service that you can request from any object of a class, and a method is a specific implementation of the operation.

Visibility Notation

Within UML you can also provide an overview of the *visibility* of any attribute or operation of the class. Since you are working with C++ for this book, this is equivalent to the usage of the public, private, and protected declarations. The characters -, #, and + declare the attribute or operation as private, protected, or public. Figure 2.4 details visibility.

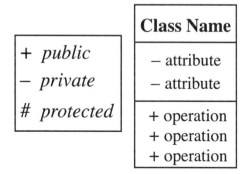

FIGURE 2.4 UML visibility notation.

Comment/Note Notation

Within the UML there is also a notation convention used to display or provide any additional comments the designer might have. This is provided via the Note model, which can also be referred to as a *comment*. Figure 2.5 details a comment notation in action.

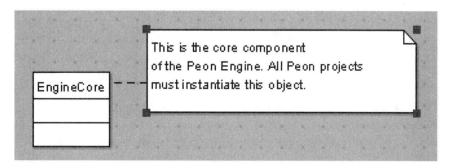

FIGURE 2.5 UML comment notation.

Modeling Class Relationships

As you are well aware, classes never exist by themselves in a vacuum. They are interconnected with other objects within the system. UML provides several *relationships* between objects, which are defined as connections between two or more notational elements. Within UML, there are three relationship types provided: a *dependency*, an *association*, and a *generalization*.

Dependency Relationship

One of the simpler relationships to model, the dependency provides a mechanism for one object to depend upon another object's interface.

Association Relationship

A relationship that runs a little deeper than the dependency, the association provides a mechanism for one object to contain another object. The UML provides two types of associations to further help define your relationships: aggregation and composition.

Aggregation Association

An aggregation association is responsible for modeling a "has-a" relationship among peer objects. The *has-a* wording means that one object contains another. A *peer* means that one object in the association is no more important than the other. Figure 2.6 provides the UML notation of an aggregation association.

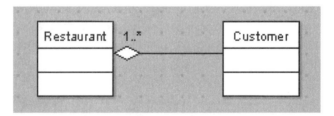

FIGURE 2.6   UML aggregation association.

A real-world example of an aggregation association can be the relationship between a franchise such as any fast food restaurant and the everyday customer. In this relationship, clearly the fast food outlet and the customer can operate independently of each other. If the franchise outlet goes out of business, the customer will still exist and can buy their favorite food product from another store. Likewise, if the customer no longer purchases from the outlet, the store will still remain in business.

Composition Association

Composition associations are more rigid than the aggregate. The difference between the two is that a composition is not a relationship among peer objects. In other words, the objects are not interdependent upon each other. Figure 2.7 provides the UML of a composition.

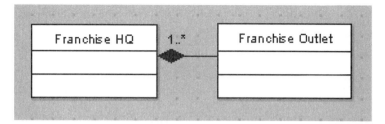

FIGURE 2.7   UML composition association.

A real-world example of a composition association is any typical food franchise such as *FastFoodInc*. There is a central office that oversees and manages every *Fast-FoodInc* franchise outlet. These outlets cannot exist independently of the central office. The composition association signals to you that if *FastFoodInc*'s central office goes out of business, then so must each franchise outlet (since they can no longer represent the *FastFoodInc* brand). However, the converse is not true. If a franchise outlet closes, the central office might still remain operational.

Generalization Relationship

The generalization relationship models the inheritance of one object to another. In other words, it is a relationship between the general (interface) and the specific. For this reason, you can substitute any child object for the parent class. Figure 2.8 details the UML representation of a generalization.

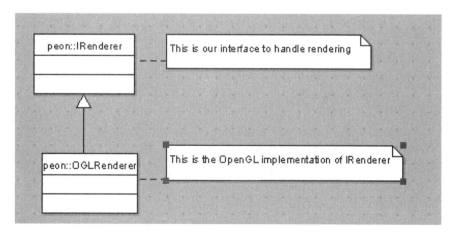

FIGURE 2.8   UML generalization relationship.

The generalization is a physical manifestation of the *is-a* relationship that you should be familiar with in C++.

SOFTWARE REUSABILITY

Reusability is another important concept to understand in all areas of development including games. For the purposes of this chapter, reusability can be defined as both *code reuse* and *design reuse.*

Code Reuse

Code reuse is a fairly obvious concept for most game programmers, but it is nevertheless an important aspect of reusability that can save you months of work.

As you build your experience in game programming, you will usually encounter situations in which you are redeveloping the same functions, methods, or objects. All of this code needs to be properly tested before being migrated into your game, and so you should only be redeveloping what is necessary in any new project. Generic modules, such as interfacing with the operating system, creating a window, and so on, should be coded and tested one time and placed into a central library or code repository for future projects. The small engine that you will create in this book makes use of the STL, which is a good example of code reuse.

It can be typical for your first game to take longer than any subsequent ones. After all, you might just be learning how to do things for the first time, along with building a small set of common functions and objects with which to work. Subsequent titles can take advantage of these objects, which allows you to focus more quickly on implementing the higher level objects in your game. The only caveat here is to be careful of over specification. Reuse done properly should reduce the amount of code size and complexity. Reuse done incorrectly can lead to heavyweight frameworks in which only a small fraction of objects are used.

Design Reuse

Although not as obvious as the code reuse aspect of software, *design reuse* refers to the common problems of software engineering that are solved a repeated number of times. This is evident in most game programming circles or newsgroups, in which the same types of questions are discussed again and again. If you abstract the approaches to solve these repeatable problems, you will get what are known as *design patterns*. Design patterns aid in describing the optimal design solution to a common problem. You will learn some of the more common design patterns that can help you get past any hurdles in your game. Only a small selection of helpful design patterns will be presented for use with your project. You should take the time to find some other quality design patterns that can be implemented as well.

With the Internet at your fingertips, there is no need to reinvent the wheel.

NOTE

Pattern 1: The Object Factory

The object factory is a class whose sole purpose is to allow the creation of families of objects. This usually implies that all of the objects that can be instantiated by the factory are derived from the same abstract base class. Listing 2.1 demonstrates one example of an object factory pattern.

LISTING 2.1   Using an Object Factory

```
//BaseObject - this is the lowest level object that we derive
//others from for this design pattern.
//In other words, an ABC (Abstract Base Class).
class BaseObject
{
public:
  BaseObject(){};            //constructor
  virtual ~BaseObject(){};   //virtual destructor
  float x, y, z;             //arbitrary member data
  virtual void doMethod(){}; //arbitrary method
};

//This is the ObjectA derived from BaseObject
class ObjectA : public BaseObject
{
  public:
    ObjectA(){};      //constructor
    ~ObjectA(){};     //destructor
    void doMethod(){}; //do some arbitrary thing
};

//This is the ObjectB derived from BaseObject
class ObjectB : public BaseObject
{
  public:
    ObjectB(){};      //constructor
    ~ObjectB(){};     //destructor
    void doMethod(){}; //do some arbitrary thing
};
```

```
//snip
//This demo ObjectFactory is used to generate new BaseObject
//instances.
//OBJECT_A - identifier for the ObjectA class
//OBJECT_B - identifier for the ObjectB class
BaseObject* ObjectFactory::create_object( int type )
{
  BaseObject* pObj = NULL;
  if( type == OBJECT_A)
  {
    pObj = new ObjectA();
  }else if(type == OBJECT_B)
  {
    pObj = new ObjectB();
  }

  if(pObj){ pObj->doMethod(); } //if object exists, call doMethod

  return pObj; //return our new object
}
```

Pattern 2: The Singleton

The singleton pattern ensures that one and only one instance of a particular object can exist in your application. This is helpful when you want to guarantee that you have only one instance of an object, such as the object encapsulating your audio or video hardware. Listing 2.2 details this design pattern that is implemented within the Peon engine.

LISTING 2.2 /PeonMain/include/ISingleton.h

```
/**
 * Template class for creating single-instance global classes.
 * The code in this file is taken from Article 1.3 in the the book:
 * Game Programming Gems from Charles River Media with the
 * copyright notice going to Scott Bilas.
 */
template <typename T> class ISingleton
{
protected:

  /** The static member object */
  static T* ms_Singleton;
```

```
public:

  /**
   * Constructor
   */
  ISingleton( void )
  {
    assert( !ms_Singleton );
    ms_Singleton = static_cast< T* >( this );
  }

  /**
   * Destructor
   */
  ~ISingleton( void )
  {   assert( ms_Singleton );   ms_Singleton = 0;   }

  /**
   * This method just returns the internal member by
   * reference
   * @return T& - reference to internal abstract Type
   */
  static T& getSingleton( void )
  { assert( ms_Singleton );   return ( *ms_Singleton ); }

  /**
   * This method just returns the internal member by
   * a pointer
   * @return T* - pointer to the internal abstract Type
   */
  static T* getSingletonPtr( void )
  { return ms_Singleton; }
};


//snip
//Now to use it in your code.
//The FileLogger object in the Peon engine just dumps info
//to a text file. You will learn about it later on, but here's
//a sample of its use (since it's derived from an ISingleton).
new FileLogger( PEON_LOG_DEBUG );
//Physically open the log file
FileLogger::getSingleton().openLogStream("PeonMain.log");
```

```
//Within any other module, you can grab the handle to the
//logfile by using the proceeding code.
FileLogger::getSingleton().logDebug("Necronomicon", "Klaatu Verata
  Nikto");
```

Pattern 3: The Publisher–Subscriber Pattern

This design pattern is useful for keeping the state of objects synchronized using a one-way propagation of change notification. Normally, this means that you have one or more objects designated as *subscribers* who register themselves with a central object known as the *publisher*. When the state of the publisher is modified, it then proceeds to notify each of the known subscribers who can decide what to do with the information. Listing 2.3 demonstrates one way this could be done.

LISTING 2.3   Using a Publisher–Subscriber Pattern

```
//This object is the subscriber object which just
//contains a method that allows it to be notified by
//the Publisher.
class Sub
{
public:
  Sub(){};              //constructor
  virtual ~Sub(){};     //destructor

  //notification method
  virtual void onNotification( Pub* the_publisher ){};
};

//This object is the publisher object which has a container
//to store the list of Subscriber objects.
class Pub
{
private:
  std::list<Sub*> m_oSubscribers; //list of subscribers

public:
  Pub(){}; //constructor
  ~Pub(){}; //destructor
  bool registerSubscriber( Sub* pSub ); //add a new Sub to the list
  void notifySubscribers() //iterate through the subscribers
  {
    std::list<Sub*>::iterator it;
```

```
          for( it  = m_oSubscribers.begin();
               it != m_oSubscribers.end(); ++it )
       {
          (*it)->onNotification(this);
       }
    }
};
```

Pattern 4: The Façade Pattern

Known most of the time as a type of *manager* class, the façade design pattern enables you to provide a single object, which behaves as an interface to a group of similar related objects. One example of this pattern is to use a façade interface to communicate with your input or graphics subsystems. This object is especially useful at reducing the amount of *coupling*, or object interdependencies, in your application. By minimizing the amount of coupling in your code design, you reduce the amount of time spent on replacing any subsystems should there be a necessity to do so. Listing 2.4 provides some background behind the façade design pattern.

LISTING 2.4   Façade Design Pattern

```
//This object contains our graphics device – say OpenGL.
class GraphicsDevice
{
public:
  bool loadGraphics();

};

//This object encapsulates the texture resources used by our
//game.
class TextureManager
{
public:
  bool loadTextures();
};

//This object encapsulates the font resources used by our game
class FontManager.
{
public:
  bool loadFonts();
};
```

```
//This "parent" object encapsulates the graphics device,
//texture manager and font manager objects. When you need
//access to one of those objects, you have to go through
//THIS one first.
class GraphicsSubsystem
{
private:
  GraphicsDevice m_oDevice;
  TextureManager m_oTexManager;
  FontManager m_oFontManager;

public:
  //This method demonstrates how useful the Façade pattern is.
  //We use it to indirectly work with lower-level objects.
  bool loadGraphicsSubsystem()
  {
    bool value = true;
    value = m_oDevice.loadGraphics();
    value = m_oTexManager.loadTextures();
    value = m_oFontManager.loadFonts();
    //Obviously proper error checking is skipped. We're
    //just trying to demonstrate the design pattern here!
    return value;
  }
};
```

ANATOMY OF A GAME

Although games are incredibly complex and performance-intensive pieces of software, they can all be abstracted to some common runtime phases that will be outlined and described here.

These phases are meant to outline the operational lifetime of your game while it is running for the player. This is not an abstraction to the entire process of creating a game in terms of management, product life cycle, support, and so on.

Initialization Phase

The *initialization phase* is the first phase involved in your game and obviously the most important. Within this phase your program attempts to create interfaces to the underlying hardware available on the machine and attempts to perform any or all of the following list of actions:

- Your video card is located and initialized to any desired resolution.
- An interface to your sound hardware is created and opened.
- Interfaces to your keyboard, mouse, and, optionally, the joystick are created.
- Networking interfaces are loaded and initialized.
- Any game-specific objects or data structures are loaded and initialized.
- Game-specific graphics and audio resources are loaded and initialized.

When this phase is completed successfully, the game then proceeds to the *process phase.*

It is normally a good practice to load as many objects and resources as possible for your game in this phase.

Process Phase

Throughout the course of the process phase, the game is responsible for updating all of the game world objects, along with rendering (that is, drawing) them to the screen. You can, therefore, subdivide this phase into two subphases: *updating* and *rendering.*

Updating Phase

The updating phase is responsible for a host of actions along the lines of the following:

- Updating all the game world objects for the current map, location, or level.
- Processing any collision-detection calculations to test which objects have hit other objects to determine which ones are active or inactive within the game world.
- Gather and process any input from the player to determine what your object (that is, the Avatar) is attempting to do.
- Gather and process any network events to determine your relation to other players in the game.
- Process any artificial intelligence routines for computer-controlled objects or players.
- Start or stop any appropriate audio file.

Rendering Phase

The rendering phase is responsible for drawing all of the game world objects to the screen. You must perform many chores here in terms of video object management, but the primary goal of this phase is to get everything on the screen as quickly as possible.

The game continues in the process phase until it has received a signal or message that you want to quit the game. It will then move into the *destruction phase*.

Destruction Phase

The overall goal of the destruction phase of your game is to clean up any object or hardware device used during the lifetime of your game. You will need to perform tasks like the following:

- Clean up all of the audio resources and the audio hardware.
- Deallocate all of the video resources and the video hardware.
- Clean up all of the input devices used.
- Shut down and cancel any further network communication and/or device interfaces.
- Clean up any object memory allocated during the lifetime of the game.

Just about every game moves through these phases in one fashion or another, and understanding these basics will help to provide an overview to how things are supposed to work in your game projects.

THE *SUPERASTEROIDARENA* DESIGN DOCUMENT

Design documents created using the waterfall model often can be notoriously large and complex in nature. One immediate problem with this approach is that as the document grows to encompass the project, not everyone in the team will properly update it. Another issue with these large design documents is that some team members might not even reference it because they feel that some objects or design decisions that are documented might already be outdated. In an attempt to create a design document that is both usable and maintainable, you can benefit from some of the Agile design techniques to create the *SuperAsteroidArena* project's design documentation. Although the Agile design approach is tailored for working with a customer to keep the project moving and updated, you will need to wear two hats during development of *SuperAsteroidArena* as you are your own client.

Drafting a Project Overview

The initial project overview should contain a one- or two-line sentence describing the overall game. This should be an exciting description of the whole purpose of the game, which will attract any potential customers or players. Listing 2.5 details the project overview.

LISTING 2.5   *SuperAsteroidArena* Project Overview

```
Project Overview: The overall goal of this game is to annihilate
your opponents in space arena combat. Using your laser guns, you
need to maneuver your ship to rack up the most kills, while
avoiding death as long as possible.
```

What Type or Genre of Game Is It?

Now that you have defined an overview of what is taking place in your game, you need to decide what type or *genre* of game you are creating. Although this small list of game genres is an attempt to categorize or classify existing software, there are many examples of mutated types of games that blend together several different genres.

Action/Arcade: This type of game usually involves the player being really involved in the game world in order to win. Usually an action game has the player performing a lot of fast and repetitive actions such as shooting a lot of enemies while simultaneously dodging hails of lasers or bullets.

Strategy: A strategy game gives the player the ability to plan out his moves, which usually centers on directing your resources to defeat the other players. For strategy games, you can usually spot two subgenres of this game type:

Real-Time: This type of strategy game forces the player to make quick decisions where they cannot spend too much time planning out their empires. Although they start out slowly, most real-time strategy (or RTS) games quickly ramp up the action, forcing the player to frantically move their units around the game world.

Turn Based: These types of strategy games are much slower than RTS experiences and give the player as much time as they need to decide what action to perform next. These games usually work by dividing the play into rounds or turns. Usually at the start of each round, the player is given a certain number of resources with which to work. After the player has used up these resources, the turn usually ends.

Adventure: Although these types of games are not released as often anymore, adventure games revolve around the player experiencing a story through the game. They usually involve some type of quest for the player to accomplish. For the most part, they are single-player games that involve the player interacting with the environment to complete tasks or quests which reveal clues to proceed within the adventure toward the final goal.

Puzzle: Puzzle games are very popular among the crowd of players who enjoy being presented with a problem they must solve. They are enjoyed by a wide range of players and typically have a difficulty of play that ranges from beginner to advanced as the player moves through the game. Puzzle games vary tremendously in gameplay, as some are slow paced but others build the action at a frantic pace.

Platform: Platform games are another popular category, where the goal of the game is to complete a journey or quest of some nature. You move your character through the game world by negotiating different levels or maps and usually must collect items along the way to help you continue onward.

For the *SuperAsteroidArena* project, you can note in the documentation that it should be considered an action/arcade game.

Deciding upon a game genre will also help describe the project to your friends and any other potential customers.

NOTE

Who Is Your Audience?

This is a very important and critical question that needs to be answered as clearly and as early as possible in your project. The more detail that you can provide here, the easier it will be to create a list of requirements for the game itself along with providing some direction through the rest of the project. You need to decide who will benefit the most from your game. Within most people or companies who are developing their own games, the audience can be broken into two basic categories:

The casual gamer: Depending upon whom you ask, this type of gamer composes the bread and butter of the audience who typically supports a lot of shareware titles on the Internet today. They represent an audience who enjoys playing games, but also has other priorities in their lives such as work or family. In other words, they are the type of player who wants to jump into the action for shorter periods of time. This type of gamer is also typically not very computer savvy. They are usually not very knowledgeable about upgrading any computer hardware, or even the basic risks or benefits behind upgrading their core software. In other words, to target a more casual type of player, you need to ensure that your game will run on older hardware with little to no configuration required to execute your game. They should be able to double-click on the icon to launch your game. Period.

The hardcore gamer: This type of gamer is usually more computer savvy and enjoys the types of games that push their machine slightly harder than a casual game would (on average). This type of gamer would be more willing to sit down and play your software for a longer period of time or at the very least, invest more into your game. They are usually not afraid to update any core software components, such as applying new video drivers and so on, to play your game properly. With the more hardcore crowd, you can afford to use slightly later technology, such as OpenGL extensions or a newer version of DirectX.

Why Make the Game?

Another critical question to answer at the beginning of the project is why you want to make this game. Instead of answering with a vague (and unmeasurable) response such as, "to make money" or "to have fun," it might be more useful to describe why someone will choose your game over a similar product even if you have no intention of selling the game. There are many different clones of *Asteroids* available on the Internet, for example, so you should be prepared to discuss why a player might want to choose your version of *SuperAsteroidArena* over another clone game. This is a very important part of the design process, as you will need to demonstrate to anyone that your game is different.

What Do You Want To See?

Although this can change during the project development or testing stages, describe here what you are envisioning as the outcome of your project. When the player launches the finished product, what should he see?

For example, in *SuperAsteroidArena*, the player should be able to fly around in a section of space with the ability to blow up the other players to win the round. The player should be viewing the game world from an overhead bird's eye vantage point as they fly through a quadrant in space inhabited by asteroids and the other players.

What Does It Offer?

If a player were to download and purchase your *Asteroids* clone (or any game), what features does your game offer that separates it from the others? This is definitely a follow-up question to the previous two. To help decide on a feature list that you want to promote for the game, begin by doing some basic market research. Now that you have chosen the genre of your game, along with what type of player you are targeting, you can spend some time on the Internet to find other comparable products and create a document detailing how they are similar and how they differ. Although you can find more resources in Appendix F, "Further Resources," game portal sites such as *RealArcade.com* or *BigFishGames.com* provide a common gateway to hundreds of downloadable games. Although it is tough (that is, impossible) to find actual sales figures for these games, most of the game portal sites will have a ranking of some kind, which can help discern what is a popular sell. Select a few of the top-selling games, which more or less match the type of game you want to create. Study the games themselves from a more analytical approach. What type of system requirements do they have? Is the gameplay between them all similar, or do they try to make a different experience?

DRAFT AN INITIAL LIST OF TIMEBOXES

After you finish answering the preliminary questions for your design document, you will then segment the project into several timeboxes to accomplish the overall goal of creating the *Asteroids* clone. At the end of each timebox, you can evaluate how the subsection fits into the overall project as well as verifying that it does not need any modifications.

For this project, you will be working with five timeboxes:

Foundation and state timebox: The goal of this segment is to create the underlying objects to launch the game. This segment should also have some rudimentary states defined for the game, which you will fill in as the project progresses.

Graphics timebox: The goal of this segment of the project is to create the underlying objects necessary to create and display some of the basic graphics of the game including any graphical user interface components. This is covered in Chapter 10, "Working with Input Devices."

Input and sound timebox: The goal of this segment is to create and add the components necessary to the game to provide audio feedback and properly communicate with your input devices. This is covered in Chapter 12, "Input and Sound Timebox."

Networking timebox: The goal of this segment is to ensure that proper network communication is taking place between the game world and every player involved in the game. This is covered in Chapter 15, "Networking Timebox."

Special effects timebox: The goal of this timebox is to add some special effects to the game to make it far more visually appealing. These aspects are covered in Chapter 20, "Polish Timebox."

As you work through the timeboxes in this project, you will be constantly evaluating or updating the design document. This is a piece of the project that should definitely be added into your CVS repository.

The design document might seem a little on the lighter side, but you will be adding only what you need as you work through each timebox. This is a bit of a chicken-egg scenario—if this is your first game project, you will not really be aware of what kind of components are needed in the game you are trying to design. This is the reason behind learning an iterative design approach for this book. As you work through each timebox or phase of implementation, you can make iterative adjustments to the design.

WHO IS INVOLVED?

Although not a specific part of a game design document, but more of a project management aspect of the development, it is still important to decide on who is involved in the project and what roles they are to play. Although this book is assuming you are virtually the single stakeholder, you might eventually decide to incorporate extra help where or when it is needed. For example, you might decide to purchase your sound and art assets from an artist over the Internet, and so on. This all depends on where your strengths of the project lie along with how much time and energy you can invest into the game.

BUDGET CONCERNS

Even if you are creating (or planning) your game "for fun," it might be wise to consider developing a budget. The day may come where you might be creating a project for actual commercial sale and would definitely need to have a grasp on the budget surrounding your game. (How else do you calculate profit margins?)

Budget planning involves tracking the financial cost of the project (in strict dollars) along with the "effort" cost (in terms of time). Some developers argue that both are one and the same, but it might help to consider them separate entities for now.

If this is your first "serious" project, or indeed the first project you want to use tracking measures on, then it would help to create a spreadsheet to act as a logbook for the project. Although at first it might seem like a chore, try to keep an updated account of the time and money spent on the project. Even if you are only able to spend 30 minutes a day on "project-related" issues, put it in the log. It will be only as accurate and detailed as you keep it.

When the project is over, you can better understand how and where you are spending your time and money. This can be one method of pinpointing any mysterious sinkhole problems, but it also will help you better estimate your effort on future projects.

As you gain more experience, you will become better at gauging how long it will take you to implement certain types of modules, and so on. This can be a critical factor in deciding on a project to invest your efforts.

Even if you are the only developer involved in the project, you should not be under the impression that working on your own time is "free." For the first few projects, grant yourself an arbitrary salary or hourly wage. When the project is finished, use this wage value to determine how much your own project cost you if you were to pay yourself. This can be another determining factor in the type of projects you will embark upon.

DEMO VERSUS REGISTERED FEATURES

In nearly every game released on the Internet today, the standard approach for most companies or developers is to produce a demo version of the software, which provides the player with a small insight into the game world. It gives the player a chance to test out the game's basic gameplay along with any other features you want to expose to the player to further entice or convince him into buying the full version of your product, the registered version. In this design phase, you have already created a list of features that your game will have. Depending upon how serious you are about the project, you should also break this list into features that are included in the demo (or shareware) version of the game and which ones are featured in the registered version. Within the demo version of the game, it is also a common approach to present the player with a friendly screen describing why they should bother to register your product by sending you money. Also known as a *nag* screen, this gives you a chance to advertise the features that you restricted to the registered version of the game. Perhaps you include more weapons for the player or more maps and levels to enjoy. Perhaps the registered version allows up to 16 players to participate in a multiplayer session, whereas the demo version might only allow 2 or 4. These lists of features are obviously dependent upon the type of game you are creating, so do not forget what you learned from your basic market research. Within the group of products you are competing with, for example, they might all include dozens or hundreds of maps to the player after they register.

CHAPTER EXERCISES

1. Within the UML, how do you design a class or method that is abstract?
2. Understand the advantages and disadvantages of the classic waterfall design method compared to the iterative process. Further investigate the design methodologies such as eXtreme Programming (XP) or Pair Programming techniques.
3. Although the waterfall process might not seem ideal for most game projects, discuss any situations in which the waterfall method might be necessary.
4. Take some time to research other useful design patterns that can help your code practices. Although not always the "magic bullet," design patterns can simplify many aspects of your application and can improve your design and programming skills.

SUMMARY

You were introduced to a wide variety of common software engineering topics within this chapter. You learned the differences between the classic waterfall and iterative design methods. You were also introduced to the concept of software reusability along with a short list of design patterns that are useful in solving some of the common design problems facing most developers. Although brief, the introduction you were given covered using the Unified Modeling Language to learn more about documenting and designing your software. You also were provided with an introduction behind the fundamentals of how a game operates and functions. Finally, you were also introduced to the design document and how to create one that will help decrease the amount of time spent actually implementing your game. In the next chapter, you learn how to develop the foundation of your game engine using the SDL.

3 Introduction to SDL and Windows

Chapter Goals

- Introduce the SDL toolkit.
- Demonstrate how to startup, run, and shutdown SDL.
- Provide an overview of the SDL event queue.
- Introduce some file logging and INI file reading mechanisms.
- Explore the Component Object Model.
- Introduce a Dynamically Linked Library.

For creating games on the PC today, several dozen options are available, as you saw listed in Chapter 1, "Game Technologies." On the Windows platform, not only are there different versions of the Microsoft DirectX API from which to choose, but many open source libraries and game development toolkits spanning many different programming languages are also available.

INTRODUCTION TO THE SIMPLE DIRECTMEDIA LAYER

For this book, you will be using the *Simple DirectMedia Layer* (SDL) created and maintained by Sam Lantiga and a great community of helpful programmers. By using the SDL as the base toolkit for your projects, you are ensuring that your game can function on a wide array of the Windows operating systems as well as making your programs more portable to other systems such as Linux or the MacOS.

Besides having the ability to create cross-platform code, another benefit of using the SDL is that it assumes the lower-level responsibilities of window creation and management, which can become an unnecessarily daunting and tedious process for the beginner Windows programmer. Most of the skills and concepts that you will learn by using SDL can also be directly applied to any future DirectX project.

For setting up and configuring your C++ compiler to work with the SDL, please refer to the instructions listed in Appendix A, "Setting Up the SDL and the Compiler."

NOTE

Why Use SDL Instead of DirectX?

Although some of today's AAA (that is, big budget) game projects developed on the PC use DirectX, this book focuses on using the SDL (and OpenGL) toolkit for creating your game. Not only are previous versions of Visual Studio not supported in the latest version of the DirectX SDK, there are platform restriction considerations as well. Users of the DirectX 9.0c SDK will be able to use only the Windows XP and higher family of products to develop games, whereas SDL and OpenGL support nearly every version of Windows since NT along with major platforms such as MacOS and Linux. In other words, using SDL and OpenGL allows you to expand the potential audience of your game, which can lead to more interest and more sales. SDL is also a proven commercially viable toolkit for the shareware development community. Many successful independent projects have been released using this library.

SDL "Hello World"

The convention among learning nearly any programming language is to create a skeleton application that displays the text "Hello World" to the screen or console. Even though this book focuses on game programming, it will not deviate from this convention.

After you have configured your favorite IDE/compiler according to the instructions given in Appendix A, you can begin with your first SDL application. Listing 3.1 presents you with a basic SDL program located on the CD-ROM in

ON THE CD   \chapter_source\chapter_03\HelloWorld.cpp.

LISTING 3.1   SDL "Hello World"

```
#include <SDL.h>

int main(int argc, char* argv[])
{
  //initialize SDL and the video subsystem
  if(SDL_Init( SDL_INIT_VIDEO ) < 0)
    return -1;

  //signal SDL to change the text of the main window
  //to "SDL Hello World"
  SDL_WM_SetCaption("Hello World", "Hello World");

  //create an SDL_Surface object which represents the
  //game window
  SDL_Surface* screen = SDL_SetVideoMode(640, 480, 0, 0);

  //load the SDL logo bitmap to a temporary surface
  SDL_Surface* temp = SDL_LoadBMP("data\\textures\\sdl_logo.bmp");

  //create the working SDL_Surface which matches the
  //display format of the temporary surface
  SDL_Surface* bg = SDL_DisplayFormat(temp);

  //free the memory allocated to the temporary SDL_Surface
  SDL_FreeSurface(temp);

  SDL_Event event;
  bool quit = false;

  //This is the main message loop of the game
  while(!quit)
  {
    //check the message queue for an event
    if (SDL_PollEvent(&event))
    {
      //if an event was found
      switch (event.type)
      {
        //check to see if the window was closed via the "X"
        case SDL_QUIT:
```

```
              //set the quit flag to true
              quit = true;
          break;

          //check the keyboard to see if the ESC key was pressed
          case SDL_KEYDOWN:
            switch (event.key.keysym.sym)
            {
              case SDLK_ESCAPE:
                //set our quit flag to true
                quit = true;
              break;
            }
          break;
        }
      }

      //draw the background sprite
      SDL_BlitSurface(bg, NULL, screen, NULL);

      //update the current window
      SDL_UpdateRect(screen, 0, 0, 0, 0);
    }

    //free the allocated memory for the background surface
    SDL_FreeSurface(bg);

    //quit SDL and allow it to clean up everything
    SDL_Quit();

    //return control to Windows with no errors
    return 0;
  }
```

Do not forget to link your project to the sdl.lib *and the* sdlmain.lib *libraries.*

NOTE

After you compile and run the application, you should see a window appear similar to Figure 3.1.

FIGURE 3.1   HelloWorld output.

The approach taken by the HelloWorld application is to demonstrate how easy it is to get a simple SDL application up and running. The first task is to initialize the SDL subsystem and internal components, which is accomplished by one function call: SDL_Init. Next, you use SDL to generate the main window for your application. In this case, the window size and video resolution is 640 pixels wide by 480 pixels high (also known as 640 × 480). The next step is to load the SDL logo bitmap onto a structure that SDL can internally manipulate, the SDL_Surface. After the bitmap is loaded into memory properly, the main application enters the main loop. Until you exit the application by killing the main window, the program is in an infinite loop and is constantly flipping the window device buffers in order to present the SDL logo image onto the screen. You will learn more about this whole process as you begin to add components to the Peon engine, which is built upon the SDL toolkit.

Creating the `EngineCore`

One of the main components of the *Peon* engine, which is the game engine that you will be using throughout this book, is the `EngineCore` object that is responsible for starting up and initializing the important subsystems. It is also responsible for processing the SDL message queue, which receives event notifications from both events generated by the player and the underlying operating system. Although you will learn more about this object in the next chapter, it contains most of the backbone that is responsible for communicating with the operation system. Listing 3.2 documents the `EngineCore` object definition.

LISTING 3.2 `Peon::EngineCore` Definition

```
//This is the main core object of the Peon library which
//internally initializes the SDL components and puts the
//application into the main loop. Ignore the PEONMAIN_API for
//now. It is just signaling that you are marking this object
//to be exported from the PeonMain.DLL
class PEONMAIN_API EngineCore : public ISingleton<EngineCore>
{
public:
    /**
    * default destructor
    */
    ~EngineCore();

    /**
    * Default Constructor */
    EngineCore();

    static EngineCore& getSingleton(void);

    static EngineCore* getSingletonPtr(void);

    /**
    * @param strWindowTitle - our application window title
    * @param strIniPath - our path to our .INI file
    * @return result if we succeeded or failed initialization
    */
    bool loadEngine(const String& strWindowTitle,
                    const String& strIniPath);
```

```
/**
 * This method is responsible for unloading
 * @return nothing
 */
void unloadEngine();

/**
 * This method is responsible for launching and running our
 * entire
 * core and application
 * @return int - any error code
 */
int runEngine();
};
```

Deriving itself from the ISingleton object that you saw in Chapter 2, "Design Fundamentals," the EngineCore definition so far is fairly basic and provides you with a simple method to load your engine and allocate some basic system resources (during the initialization phase of your game). It also provides a method to clean up any object memory allocated during the loading phase and/or the lifetime of the engine itself (that is, the destruction phase). Finally, it provides a method to launch the main loop of the engine (that is, the process phase). It is important to introduce and cover this object at this time, as it forms the heart of the Peon engine, along with nearly every game project upon which you will ever embark.

Initializing SDL

When you use the loadEngine method of the EngineCore object that you just defined, you are internally loading and initializing needed components of the SDL. Take a look at the EngineCore.cpp file and notice the use of the SDL_Init function shown in Listing 3.3.

LISTING 3.3   EngineCore::loadEngine

```
bool EngineCore::loadEngine( const String& strWindowTitle,
                             const String& strIniFile)
{
  int retVal = 0;
  char strOutput[512];
```

```
//The SDL_Init method does all the grunt work of initializing
//the subsystems and components of SDL for you.
retVal = SDL_Init( SDL_INIT_EVERYTHING );
if(retVal < 0 )
{
  //there was some kind of error. Make a note of it
  sprintf(strOutput, "Failed to initialize SDL subsystem %s",
  SDL_GetError());

  //output the error message to the debug window of the IDE
  OutputDebugString( strOutput );

  //do the garbage collection
  unloadEngine();

  //return creation failure
  return false;
}

//if the initialization completes successfully, simply
//change the title of the main window to our application
SDL_WM_SetCaption( strWindowTitle.c_str(),
  strWindowTitle.c_str());

return true;
}
```

The SDL/Windows Event Queue

A main driving force behind the design of Windows is that it is an *event-driven* operating system. This means that as you perform an action in your application, either by clicking the mouse or resizing your application window, the corresponding event is being generated and posted to your application's main message queue by the operating system. Figure 3.2 shows an overview of this process.

The SDL follows this same design philosophy, and every SDL application must define and use an event queue to listen for any specific events. Listing 3.4 displays the basic event queue that is contained within the EngineCore::runEngine method.

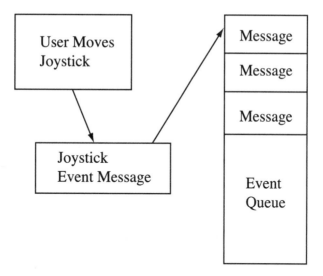

FIGURE 3.2 Event messages generated and passed to the queue.

LISTING 3.4 EngineCore::runEngine

```
int EngineCore::runEngine()
{
  bool bDone = false;  // is main loop finished?
  SDL_Event event;

  // as long as our main loop is not done
  while(!bDone)
  {
    while( SDL_PollEvent(&event) )
    {
      // while we have an event message in the queue,
      // you need to determine what it is
      switch ( event.type )
      {

        case SDL_QUIT : // if user wishes to quit
          bDone = true; // this implies the main loop is done
        break;
```

```
            default: //default is to do nothing
               break;

        } //end switch
     } //end while( SDL_PollEvent )

     //update the game here since the events are done processing
     //ie. the Process Phase

   } //end while( !bDone )
   //the game is finished and is exiting. Do the garbage collection
   unloadEngine();
   //no errors, return 0
   return 0;
}
```

This event queue in Listing 3.4 is a very basic method of structuring the main loop of your application. You are putting the program into a continuous loop, which is only responsible for listening to the SDL event queue. If there was a message received in the queue, test it to see whether it is the quit event. If it is, then signal to the main loop that you are ready to exit. If it is not the quit event, or if there are no messages detected in the event queue, then it is time to process one frame of your game (that is, the process phase). After one frame has been updated and rendered, the loop will start again at the beginning to test whether there is an SDL event message waiting in the queue.

Cleaning Up SDL

When your application has finished or the user has decided to quit your game, it is necessary to perform some cleanup procedures in order to properly free up any memory used by your application. You should never rely on the operating system to do the work for you, as it is not always guaranteed that it will. To clean up any of the underlying SDL constructs and objects, you simply need to use the SDL_Quit function used in the unloadEngine method as shown in Listing 3.5.

LISTING 3.5 EngineCore::unloadEngine

```
void EngineCore::unloadEngine()
{
   //clean up any allocated memory and/or objects
   //be sure to call this last to finish the SDL cleanup
   SDL_Quit();
}
```

Big Endian versus Little Endian

Because SDL is a cross-platform library, you might have aspirations to port your project to other operating systems such as the MacOS or Linux. Even if you stick to the SDL to handle most of the underlying architecture of your game or engine, you occasionally might have to deal with Endian issues depending on whether or not you are working with code targeted for the Intel family of processors used in Windows, or the RISC architecture used on the MacOS platform. Originally named from *Gulliver's Travels*, which takes place in Lilliput, the *Endian* order refers to the order in which the bytes of a 16- or 32-bit word data type are stored in computer memory. Figure 3.3 shows more details.

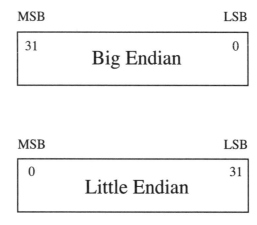

FIGURE 3.3 Big-Endian versus little Endian.

Big-Endian is when the most significant value in the data (that is, the big end) is stored at the lowest storage address (that is, the first); in the little-Endian architecture, the least significant value of the data is stored at the lowest storage address. By default, the version of the SDL library you are linking to for this book is using the little-Endian architecture since you are more than likely working on an Intel/AMD-based processor.

ADDING THE FileLogger

The next step is to allow for some application-level file logging. If and when other subsystems fail to initialize and start up, you need to be made aware of the key reasons for the generated failures. A `FileLogger` object is a valuable tool for any programmer to record any key events or errors generated by your application, which might not always be able to access the console to use a `printf` statement.

Although the Visual Studio environment provides a basic debugging mechanism by allowing your code to throw comments to the debugging window via the `OutputDebugString` API call, which is equivalent to a simple `printf` statement, not all compilers support this function.

You can create your own text output mechanism that logs statements into a flat file. This is useful for outputting any debug information you might want to take a look at, or even for displaying valuable information for support reasons (say to record the player's operating system version, any DirectX/OpenGL version information, video card driver manufacturer, version of the drivers, and so on). Take a quick look at the `FileLogger` object that resides in the code for this chapter on the CD-ROM.

ON THE CD

This object can now be added to the `EngineCore` object, in order to provide a logging mechanism (see Listing 3.6).

LISTING 3.6   `FileLogger` Object Sample Code

```
//create a new instance of the FileLogger and set it to
//filter no messages..ie. log everything
new FileLogger( PEON_LOG_DEBUG );
//open the log file
FileLogger::getSingleton().openLogStream("PeonMain.log");

//log the first statement as a "debug" message
FileLogger::getSingleton().logDebug("EngineCore", "* starting log
  file *");

/* snip */
//log an "error" statement
FileLogger::getSingleton().logError("EngineCore", "renderer failed
  to initialize");
//close the logger
FileLogger::getSingleton().closeLogStream();
```

Now when you compile and run the project, a text file containing the DEBUG level of messages will be created in the same folder as your executable, named `PeonMain.log`. The `FileLogger` object works by implementing a system of logging levels. When you instantiate this object, you must specify what type of logging level you want the instance to capture. There are currently four levels of logging with this object: DEBUG, INFO, ERROR, and FATAL. DEBUG level messages are meant to pinpoint any potential problems that might occur during the testing of the game. For example, an object might not properly initialize, or you might want to verify that a particular code branch is being executed. The INFO level of logging is just meant to inform you of events that might be useful for any application tracing—for example, recording the driver version of OpenGL detected on the system or the amount of system RAM, and so on. The ERROR level is meant to only capture log events that record a failure of some kind. This happens usually when a subsystem or some component fails to properly initialize. If a component registers an ERROR message in the log, it does not necessarily mean that the game must exit. For example, if your game detects that no sound hardware is available, it will fail the initialization of the sound subsystem. However, the game should still function properly; just without any sound feedback to the player. The final FATAL category is used when the application must exit. For example, if the video subsystem fails to initialize then the game should exit immediately.

Using Windows Initialization Files

Prior to the Windows Registry, application configuration information in Windows was loaded and stored from a small file known as an initialization or *INI* file. This file could contain any parameter or other type of application-specific information that could be read during the runtime of the application, thereby being more able to adapt to different system settings of a particular Windows installation. Although it is far more detailed and massive, the current Windows Registry is more or less a giant warehouse of INI information.

For your purposes, though, the System Registry is a bit too "hidden" for your application user, not to mention that you would have to rip out any registry-specific API should you decide to port your game to another platform. The INI family of functions introduced by Microsoft is a lightweight approach capable of loading and storing any type of configuration information that the game could benefit from.

For example, some perfect information to store or load in an INI configuration file is the window size of your game, such as 640 × 480 or 800 × 600. This would allow any client of the game to modify the window size depending upon their machine resources and resolution preference.

Check the source code for this chapter for more details, but you can now throw in the IniConfigReader object into the EngineCore object that already exists. This gives you the ability to read in potential configuration information such as your main window size during the runtime of your game.

First, you add some new variables to the `EngineCore` header file definition, as well as add a `String` parameter to your `loadEngineCore` method for the path of the INI file defined in Listing 3.7.

LISTING 3.7 Code to Add to Your `EngineCore` Header File

```
    int m_dwWidth;
  int m_dwHeight;
  IniConfigReader* m_pConfig;
   /* snip */
  bool loadEngineCore(const String&, const String&);
```

Now you need to modify the `loadEngineCore` method slightly to accommodate the new object, which is shown in Listing 3.8.

LISTING 3.8 Updated Code for Your `EngineCore::loadEngineCore` Method

```
    bool EngineCore::loadApplicationCore(const String& strAppTitle,
      const String& strConfigPath)
  {
    //snip
    m_pConfig = new IniConfigReader( strConfigPath );

    //now read our window size
    //by default, if there's no appropriate value in the INI file
    //called "WindowWidth"
    //or "WindowHeight", then we use a default value of 640x480
    m_dwWidth = (DWORD)m_pConfig->getInt("Application",
     "WindowWidth", 640);
    m_dwHeight = (DWORD)m_pConfig->getInt("Application",
     "WindowHeight", 480);



    //snip
```

So now you can create a new file in your project folder called `System.ini` and edit it as shown in Listing 3.9.

LISTING 3.9 Sample Configuration Information

```
[Application]
WindowWidth=800
WindowHeight=600
```

In the updated `main.cpp` file, you just need to add the path to your `System.ini` file in the method call to `loadEngineCore` noted in Listing 3.10.

LISTING 3.10 Updated `main.cpp` Code

```
#include "PeonMain.h"

using namespace peon;

int main( int argc, char* argv[] )
{
  new EngineCore();

  if(!EngineCore::getSingleton().loadEngineCore(
    "WindowTest", "System.ini")))
  {
    return -1;
  }

  return( EngineCore::getSingleton().runEngine() );
}
```

Take a few minutes to play with the INI file settings. You have no error checking, so it is possible to specify weird window sizes of 310×489 or 1033×21, for example. Internally, the `IniConfigReader` uses the `GetPrivateProfileInt` and `GetPrivateProfileString` function calls, which are native to Windows.

THE COMPONENT OBJECT MODEL

Another aspect of programming in the Windows operating system is to understand the principles behind the *Component Object Model* (COM) technology. Although you do not need to understand the massive inner workings, you should understand a few design aspects of COM architecture that might come in handy.

The Component Object Model was introduced quite a few years ago by Microsoft as a guideline for creating component interfaces. It is essentially an interface for creating *black box* type objects. You have a set of defined inputs and outputs to each object, but you do not care about the logic within the components. You only care that depending upon certain inputs, you expect certain outputs. The basic goal of COM was to create software components that could be interchanged with each other, similar in nature to a stack of Lego blocks. In principle, it is a clean way to organize your software development, as you can isolate (and update) different components of the application without requiring a complete rebuild (or reshipping) of the entire application itself.

For example, you decide to create and ship an application using COM objects to track and display the player's information in a Massively Multiplayer Online Role-Playing Game (MMORG), such as *Everquest* or *World of Warcraft*. After some work with the application, you are able to improve the performance of a COM object the application uses to track in game crafting skills. Since the input and outputs to the COM object have remained the same, you simply need to ship the updated COM object to your customers rather than have them download the entire application again. Do not forget that not everyone is on broadband.

Another benefit to the COM model of component development is that it provides a way to help track resources within the operating system. By deriving your COM object from a known COM interface, you can then keep track of how many times any object is instantiated or destroyed within your application, which is known as *reference counting*. The interface itself uses this internal counter to track how many other interfaces are using it. When an object is created, its internal reference count is incremented. Similarly, when the object is no longer needed, its reference counter is decremented.

If your application then exits with any object having a reference count higher than zero, then you know that there is a memory leak somewhere as you have an instance of an object being created but not destroyed.

IUnknown is the base COM object from which all the components derive and is shown in Listing 3.11.

LISTING 3.11   Sample IUnknown Definition within COM

```
struct IUnknown
{
   //this method is used to access the interface
   virtual HRESULT __stdcall QueryInterface( const IId& iid, (void
   **)ip) = 0;
```

```
//this method is used to increase the interfaces reference count
virtual ULONG __stdcall Addref() = 0;

//this method is used to decrease the interfaces reference count
virtual ULONG __stdcall Release() = 0;
};
```

When the internal reference counter does reach zero, the system's internal garbage collector can remove it from memory.

This is also a reminder to clean up any and every object you have used during the lifetime of your application. This properly decrements the reference counters of some of the internal objects, which the system can then clean up properly. If you leave any objects behind during the garbage collection process, there is no guarantee that Windows will clean it up for you, thereby introducing memory leaks to your host computer as well as your customers.

THE IUNKNOWN OBJECT

You can also create a primitive reference counting mechanism of your own using the IUnknown interface defined in the Peon library. Listing 3.12 defines the object.

LISTING 3.12   /PeonMain/IUnknown.h

```
namespace peon
{
/** This object is used for reference counting to try and help
debug any
 * memory leaks */
class PEONMAIN_API IUnknown
{
protected:
    /** the run-time type identifier
    int      m_RTTI;

    /** the current reference count of this object */
    int      m_refCount;
```

```
        public:
            IUnknown() : m_refCount(1){}
            virtual ~IUnknown(){}

            /** This method just increments our reference count. Ie. we're
making
             * a copy of an existing object */
            void addRefCount() { ++m_refCount; }

            /** This method decrements our internal reference count. Ie.
We're
             * cleaning up a copy of an existing object */
            bool dropRefCount()
            {
                --m_refCount;
                if (!m_refCount)
                {
                    //if this is the final instance of this object, then
clean it
                    //up from the memory heap
                    delete this;
                    return true;
                }

                return false;
            }

        };
    }
```

In practice this takes a bit of getting used to, but it can also help track down potential memory leaks. Whenever you make a copy of an existing object, it is then the appropriate time to increment the object's reference count. When a copy is removed, then you decrement it. Listing 3.13 details this in action.

LISTING 3.13   Using IUnknown

```
    //in this sample, ObjectA is derived from IUnknown
    ObjectA* pObjA = new ObjectA();
```

```
//snip
//we want to use ObjectA as a member variable inside another object
//this means that you now have two copies of pObjA floating around.
ObjectB* pObjB = new ObjectB( pObjA );

//in the constructor of ObjectB
ObjectB::ObjectB( ObjectA* pObjA )
{
  m_pObjA = pObjA;
  m_pObjA->addRefCount();
}

//now in the destructor…do not delete m_pObjA, simply decrement the
//reference Count
ObjectB::~ObjectB()
{
  //do not delete the pointer to ObjectA, as this would then
  //destroy ObjectA which we might not want to do. Just decrement
  //the reference count
  m_pObjB->dropRefCount();
}
```

INTRODUCTION TO DYNAMICALLY LINKED LIBRARIES

Dynamically Linked Libraries (DLLs) are an important and integral aspect of Windows programming, which fits into the COM paradigm. A DLL contains either a library of executable code or resource data that can be loaded and used by any Windows application during execution of the program. Multiple applications can reference a DLL.

The main benefit of using a DLL is that your project need not quit just because an optional feature does not work. Your program can continue as necessary, but simply not allow the user to perform the action requiring the missing DLL.

For example, in Microsoft Word you can edit files and then automatically mail them across the Internet. The Internet module can be contained within a separate DLL so that the main editor can still fully function even if the user has no Internet connection detection.

When working with DLLs in your application, when you compile your program, the machine will only record certain indexes into the DLL. The main work of making the DLL accessible to your program is through the loader mechanism included with Windows. The DLL can be referenced in two ways: loadtime or runtime.

Loadtime linking occurs as you start up and launch your application. The DLL loader will attempt to load the appropriate library referenced from the DLL and add it to your application's memory space.

Runtime linking, also known as delayed loading, is when the DLL loader will only attempt to load the relevant libraries' methods referenced from the DLL when your application needs it.

The Peon engine that you are working with is using loadtime linking for getting the library methods into your program's memory space along with the OpenGL libraries.

The real magic behind the DLL is contained within the /PeonMain/PeonDLL-Header.h file found on the CD-ROM, which is contained in Listing 3.14.

LISTING 3.14   PeonDLLHeader.h

```
#ifdef PEONMAIN_EXPORTS
  #define PEONMAIN_API __declspec(dllexport)
#else
  #define PEONMAIN_API __declspec(dllimport)
#endif
```

This block of compiler preprocessor statements means that if you are building the dynamic linked library itself, every object marked with the PEONMAIN_API tag is exported from the library. Otherwise, your game application using this library will recognize these objects as being imported from a DLL. In practice, this means that you only need to #define the PEONMAIN_EXPORTS statement when you are building the Peon DLL. This is already done for you in the Peon project workspace.

CHAPTER EXERCISES

1. Play around with the IniConfigReader object in the loadEngine method. Add some error checking to only allow "reasonable" window sizes such as 640 × 480, 800 × 600 and 1024 × 768.

2. By using the IniConfigReader object, you are helping to make the application more *data driven*. In other words, some of the game parameters can be modified by the player without needing to recompile the game's source code. Explain how this might be helpful for not only you (the programmer) but also the customer using your application.

3. For further cross-platform functionality, recode the `IniConfigReader` object into one that is capable of working with XML data.

4. Depending upon your logging preferences, add some methods to the `FileLogger` object to record logging messages in HTML format. If you like, have different colors for different severity levels of your logging mechanism. For example, if a critical error is detected and the application needs to exit, log this message using a red color.

SUMMARY

You have taken another step on the road of game programming. In this chapter, you learned only what you need to really know about Windows programming in order to make games using the SDL. You started off by learning how to start up, run, and shut down the SDL. You also learned how to implement a basic log file writer object for recording any helpful debugging information, as well as how to load configuration information from the INI file. You finished this chapter by learning about the design principles behind the Component Object Model and gaining an understanding of the purpose of Dynamically Linked Libraries. In the next chapter, you begin working on the game engine that fuels your *SuperAsteroidArena* project.

4 Introduction to the Peon Engine

Chapter Goals

- Discuss the use and importance of an engine.
- Introduce the Peon engine and some of the objects that will benefit game creation.
- Work on the first timebox of the game: foundation and state management.

After learning some of the SDL basics in the previous chapter, you are probably eager and excited to get more involved in game programming. In this chapter, you will learn about some of the underlying mechanisms contained within the *Peon* engine that you will be working with throughout the remainder of this book.

BASIC ENGINE STRUCTURE

A *game engine* is the core software component of a computer game that typically handles input, sound, networking, AI, and graphics. Although most game engines today focus primarily on graphics techniques, they can also handle collision detection, game object scripting, and dozens of other features.

In other words, not only is a game engine an entity designed to facilitate the creation of games, it becomes the central heart of your game itself. Depending upon the strength and design of your game engine, you should be able to use it in just about any project. An analogy of this is a car's engine. Although there are hundreds of different car models, they all essentially have the same core components such as an internal combustion engine, spark plugs, carburetor, and so on. The benefit of this design is that you should have no trouble driving a Gremlin, and then winning the lottery and stepping into a Porsche 911 Turbo.

Even though you might decide to extend or modify the engine depending upon game requirements, you should still have a useful core system from which to draw. Therein lies the fine line you will walk as a game engine designer: create a system that is too complex and specific, and it loses the capability to be used in different projects. But should you design a system that is too general or ambiguous, then you might find that you have to assign extra man hours to bring the engine up to project requirements.

Some of the large commercial game developers realize the power and cost benefits behind a properly designed game engine. Although a few studios decide to spend man hours on creating inhouse engines from scratch for their games, the majority of teams these days simply purchase a license to an existing engine of some kind to provide the functionality for their games' requirements. The *Quake2/3*, *Unreal*, and *Torque* engines are perfect examples of this. The flexibility of their design and licensing model has allowed for not only the top studios to use them in their titles, but fairly mid-range and independent companies to succeed as well. Project managers are definitely seeing the cost benefits of spending the money on a good engine. The more man hours spent on fixing up or maintaining an old or broken engine takes away precious man hours assigned to designing or developing new game content. Even if you are a lone wolf or small game developer, you can still reap the benefits of a game engine; instead of spending your precious time maintaining a giant library of C/C++ code, you could be creating your next title.

Keep in mind that there are no perfect game engines; it is also crucial to be able to evaluate the limitations of your engine before assigning it to a project. For example, you might have a great 3D game engine that has components that are tested and proven, yet the project requires completely different hardware and/or a different style of scene management than what the engine was optimized for.

The inexperienced developer might try to force the engine to work for the project, which is like a brute force approach to fitting a square peg into a round hole.

The more seasoned veteran might decide that with the engine's known limitations, it would not be a recommended choice to use for the project. Naturally, this might lead to the next step on deciding whether the project could be modified to work with the engine or whether the game concept itself is a good idea.

One has to find the right balance between tailoring the engine around the application and tailoring the application around the engine.

INTRODUCTION TO PEON

Throughout this book you will be adding pieces and components to *Peon*, which is your game engine. You will also learn how to use it within the context of an actual game. You learned about the design of the *SuperAsteroidArena* title back in the design chapter, so this is where you finally start adding some actual code to the game.

The source code to the engine is located on the included CD-ROM in /Peon, so feel free to open it and follow along at your leisure.

The Peon engine/framework is a collection of C/C++ objects that sits on a layer above SDL and Windows. Rrefer to Figure 4.1 for the Peon architecture.

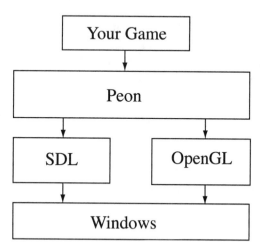

FIGURE 4.1 Peon architecture.

Although the framework is not intended to be the ultimate game engine solution, it does give you a starting point for learning about game creation along with some concepts behind engine design.

The ultimate goal of the engine is to try and keep it as lightweight as possible in order for it to be adaptable to your needs but still useful enough to allow for rapid application development.

This is not meant to be a book on engine programming, but one that focuses on overall game programming.

NOTE

INTRODUCTION TO SOME PEON COMPONENTS

Although the documentation provided with Peon will provide more insight to its use, you wil learn some of the main components in this section as well as their implementation throughout this book.

EngineCore: This is the core component of the engine that you were introduced to in Chapter 3, "Introduction to SDL and Windows." SDL is responsible for registering your application and creating the main window. An additional responsibility is to launch the game into the main loop where it is responsible for processing any events received in the application event queue. It is also responsible for loading and creating the AudioEngine instance, the InputEngine instance, and a SceneRenderer object capable of starting up and shutting down an OpenGL context. Since you want only one instance of this object within your program, by design you are implementing this object using the Singleton design pattern.

AudioEngine: This core component is responsible for handling/processing the sound engine. It is an interface to the audio subsystem, which allows you to load and play audio files using the SDL_Mixer library for any 2D sounds such as midi files. Some 3D positional sound effect playback is handled with OpenAL. Since you want only one instance of this object involved with your application, it is implemented as well within the context of the EngineCore Singleton object. It is covered in further detail for you in Chapter 11, "Working with Sound."

ScriptEngine: This is the small component of the engine which will be able to handle and process scripts that you can read during the launch of a game using the Lua script library (and virtual machine) of script processing. You will learn more about scripting and this object in Chapter 19, "Introduction to Scripting."

SceneRenderer: This is another core component of the Peon engine and is responsible for acting as the interface between your game and the underlying OpenGL commands that are sent to your video hardware. It encapsulates the necessary methods for creating, updating, and destroying an OpenGL surface, and you will learn more about this object along with OpenGL in Chapter 6, "Creating an OpenGL Renderer."

SceneTexture: This is a small component designed to act as a container for texture information used in your game. Accessible through the SceneRenderer, this object is responsible for loading and storing texture data that allows for fast and easy access during the rendering process. You will learn more about this object and texture manipulation in Chapter 6.

SceneFont: One of the primary channels of communication between your game and the player is text to the screen, which updates the player on any situation in the game world. It can display the current players involved in the game along with any other information you need to display to the player. This object is a component of some basic font handling and is discussed in further detail in Chapter 6.

SceneGraphManager: As you learn in Chapter 8, "Scene Geometry Management," one of the fundamental objects or data structures within a useful 3D engine is the concept of a *scene graph*. The scene graph represents every object and/or rendering command within your game. It is a data structure used to increase rendering performance, along with aiding in physics and collision detection calculations.

NetworkEngine: Part of the excitement in multiplayer gaming is actually playing against other human opponents. The NetworkEngine subsystem will be responsible for handling and processing network events that are sent and received to and from other players. Built upon the useful ReplicaNet networking library, this component allows for fast and efficient message communication across the network. You will learn more about networks and ReplicaNet in Chapter 14, "Introduction to Networking," and Chapter 15, "Networking Timebox."

As you can see, the core component objects of the engine are mostly designed to be accessed via the `EngineCore` Singleton object. Remember from Chapter 2, "Design Fundamentals," that the Singleton design pattern specifies that one and only one instance of the object exists. Although perhaps not a perfect design, it does allow for a looser coupling between these core objects and any application using Peon. The key to this approach is ease of use, and you will learn more about the engine as you work through this book.

`ParticleEmitter:`   The purpose of this object is to encapsulate and process a collection of Particle objects for creating a fun and exciting special effect known as a *particle system*. Particle systems can be smoke, fire, air, water, or a host of other special effects.

`Shockwave:`   One of the more interesting special effects for any explosion is the use of the shockwave to depict a radii of energy emitting from a source vector. As an internal timer progresses, the rings of the shockwave are recalculated to appear as though they are growing.

BUILDING UPON THE FOUNDATION

When the underlying core objects are created and instantiated within your application via the `EngineCore` object, the application kernel then puts itself into a process phase, which is responsible for notifying your game of what is happening both within the engine and within the game world itself.

Managing State Information

No matter how large or small your world is, there is always the need to track *state information* within the game. A *state* can be defined as an updated snapshot of the objects contained within your game world.

In other words, think of the responsibilities of a toggle light switch. The switch can only be in one of two states: on or off.

During the updating phase of your game, the computer will make any necessary calculations depending on the current state of the world. In most game projects this entails the use of a `switch` statement as demonstrated in Listing 4.1.

LISTING 4.1 switch Statement for State Processing

```
switch( current_state )
{
 case MAIN_MENU_STATE:
 //do any main menu related tasks such as displaying the main
 //menu,
 //responding to input events generated by the mouse, respond
 //to any button clicks, etc.
 break;

 case PLAYER_ACTIVE_STATE:
 //do any related task for playing the main body of the game.
 //Update the player's position in the world, let him shoot
 //stuff, run around and basically try to save the planet
 break;

 case PLAYER_DEAD_STATE:
 //do anything related to the player's death. Maybe display
 //a dying animation or just a simple "game over" message
 break;

 //snip
}
```

Although this can be effective enough for a game with only a small quantity of possible states, there can be many complications when adding new states to the game. In most cases, these switch blocks also become rather large and increasingly difficult to track or debug.

Within the Peon engine, however, the IApplication and IApplicationState objects are used heavily to define and encapsulate different states that compose your game. To add a new state to your game, you need to derive a new instance of the IApplicationState object and provide definitions for a few overloaded methods.

Working on the First Timebox

It is time to work on the first timebox for the *SuperAsteroidArena* project. Check out your *SuperAsteroidArena* design document from your CVS repository and take a look at the first timebox defined: laying the foundation and basic state management.

You will first need to draft a list of requirements for this timebox. It does not need to be anything complex and could appear as the following:

■ Initialize and start up the application using Peon and SDL.

■ Create some IApplicationState containers that you will fill in as development progresses.

Based on your introduction to SDL in Chapter 3, "Introduction to SDL and Windows," the first requirement should already be in place. You have enough background to load your application with an INI configuration file and present a named main window using SDL.

You should now think of a list of possible states in which the *SuperAsteroid-Arena* project can run. Because you are using a more iterative Agile design approach, this list does not need to be written in stone and can be updated as you progress through the project, depending upon any feedback from yourself or other testers. You might decide the game needs more states, or you might think of a feature in the game that you really want to support. Regardless, a first attempt at the list of states the *SuperAsteroidArena* game can work through is listed here:

LogoState: This state is responsible for loading and presenting your own company logo and perhaps to play a small musical introduction or jingle.

MainMenuState: This state is responsible for loading and presenting any resources needed to have an operational main menu. Since it is the first "real" screen of your game that the player confronts, you should try and create some interesting background effects. You might also decide to simply have a running demo of your game displaying in the background while you present the main menu to the player in the foreground.

RunState: This state is used to contain the game logic, which is where the game will spend the majority of its time. When you are playing the game, it is in this state.

QuitGameState: The purpose of this state is to gracefully exit the application. For most shareware games, you can use this state to present any further information to the player including instructions on how to buy your game, where to view further information, and so on.

When you finish with this current timebox, remember to evaluate what you are working on.

Creating the New Instances of IApplicationState

Now that the basic graphics device is set up and created, you can begin this timebox by creating some new instances of the IApplicationState interface as previously outlined.

As you will learn, when new instances of this object are created, they must be added to the IApplication object, which functions as a *state manager*. The state manager's purpose is to contain the list of every `IApplicationState` instance in the game. It is also responsible for switching between states and cleaning them up when the application is terminated. Listing 4.2 details how to create a new instance of the `IApplicationState` interface.

LISTING 4.2 LogoState Definition

```
/**
* This state is responsible for presenting the developer's Company
* Logo to the player. This can also be a simple animation accompanied
* by some music or even nothing at all.
*/
class LogoState : public peon::IApplicationState
{
  public:
    /** Constructor */
    LogoState();
    /** Destructor */
    ~LogoState();
    /** Overidden method to update this state
    * @param elapsed_time — The time between clock ticks
    */
    void onUpdateState( float elapsed_time );
    /** Overidden method to render this state */
    void onRenderState();
    //snip!
};
```

Taking a view of the design document for *SuperAsteroidArena* again, you can see that within this `LogoState` object you need to display your company logo and play a small midi file. After roughly five to eight seconds, the game will switch itself into the main menu state. In the future, you can replace the `LogoState` with an intro movie, or perhaps some professionally recorded music. Because you have already learned some of the tasks that need to be done with this state in previous chapters, there is more benefit from taking a quick look at the code responsible for updating the `LogoState` object. Listing 4.3 demonstrates this.

LISTING 4.3 LogoState::onUpdateState(float elapsed_time)

```
//snip!
static float current_time = 0.0f;
static bool first_Pass = true;
```

```
if( first_pass )
{
  //It's the first time through this update cycle in this state.
  //Initialize or do any task that needs to happen once per
  //state. For this state, simply begin to play the midi file.
  first_pass = false;
}

current_time += elapsed_time;

if( current_Time > 5.0f )
{
  //out of here...switch to our next state
  EngineCore::getSingleton().getApplication().setState(
MAINMENU_STATE );
}
//snip!
```

Implementing the other states should be just as straightforward during this timebox. Please refer to the project's sourcecode in the /SuperAsteroidArena directory on the CD-ROM. You will be continuously adding to these IApplicationState instances throughout the rest of this book.

ON THE CD

Timebox Evaluation

You are nearing completion of this phase of the design. Take a quick look at the document with any notes you might have created for this timebox. Objectively analyze whether you are satisfied with what you have produced thus far, even if you feel that the implementation done in this timebox has not really accomplished much.

If you would like to add or modify the states that the game can run in, then feel free to inject them into the game along with updating the design document.

Also be sure to start familiarizing yourself with some of the Peon documentation. As you begin to add to the engine, you will become more familiar with its workings and will be able to leverage it in any future application.

CHAPTER EXERCISES

1. Understand the process of adding new state objects into the game world. With your own experience, decide whether this is a better solution than simply processing every state in one block of code using a switch statement.

2. Take a look at the definitions of some of the other game state objects derived from the IApplicationState interface. Feel free to either introduce or subtract methods from the IApplicationState interface that do not help your own design or can possibly do more.

SUMMARY

Throughout this chapter, you discovered the importance of an engine or framework that you can use as a backbone for your game objects. By creating a small layer above the SDL library, you can create some useful middleware that is flexible enough to handle just about any game application you want to make with it. You also were introduced to the Peon engine design basics, which can help do some of the necessary management work for you, as you get on with the content creation of your game.

There is a lot more to learn, but you are making good progress. Now you move on to learning some of the important fundamental mathematics behind most games today. If you already possess a strong background in mathematics, you can probably skip the next chapter. Otherwise, those who require a math refresher should flip through the following chapter.

5 Graphics Programming Mathematics

Chapter Goals

- Discuss the coordinate system used by OpenGL.
- Discuss the Fixed Function Geometry Pipeline.
- Introduce and discuss vectors.
- Introduce and discuss matrices.
- Describe the three coordinate transformations possible: scaling, translation, and rotation.
- Introduce and understand how to manipulate the camera.
- Introduce a discussion on Quaternions.

Before you can dive head-first into some API-specific code, you first need to cover some basic 3D concepts. Most game programmers tend to shy away from the mathematics involved in 3D graphics programming in general, but the majority of the concepts and operations you need to perform are fairly simple to understand despite the hundred years of mathematics behind them.

THE CARTESIAN COORDINATE SYSTEM

No matter which graphics API you use, the objects you will need to manipulate in the scene must have some kind of orientation and position representation. To keep things simple for graphics programmers, you will make heavy use of the Cartesian Coordinate System.

The Cartesian Coordinate System segments space into three seperate axes: the horizontal (x), the vertical (y), and the depth axis (z). The origin (or center) of the world lies at coordinates $(x,y,z):(0, 0, 0)$.

The left-handed coordinate system, which is what Direct3D uses by default, is one in which the positive z-axis points *into* your screen. Conversely, the right-handed coordinate system, used by OpenGL, is one in which the positive z-axis points *out* of the display. This is demonstrated in Figure 5.1.

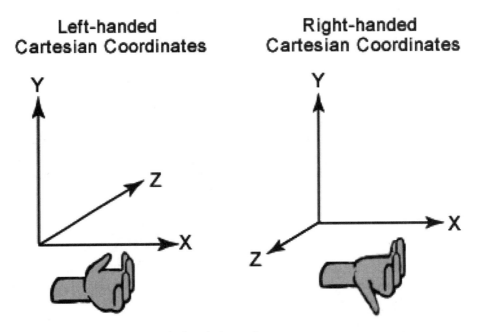

FIGURE 5.1   The left- and right-handed coordinate systems.

For the Peon toolkit, you will stick to a right-handed coordinate system for object positioning which coincides with the one used by OpenGL.

FIXED FUNCTION GEOMETRY PIPELINE

It is not magic that allows you to position and orientate your world objects, but something called a *coordinate transformation*. Every object within the game world is represented on an atomic level by a vertex containing the x,y,z coordinates. The vertex must pass through three types of transformations before you see the final product on the screen. On a higher level, these transformations on the vertex take place in the Fixed Function Geometry Pipeline (FFP) shown in Figure 5.2.

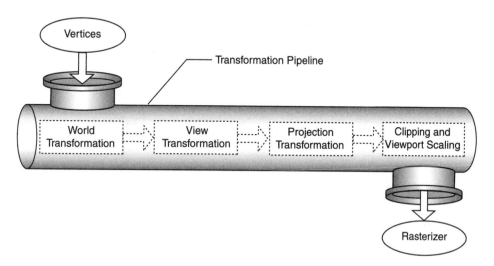

FIGURE 5.2   Fixed Function Geometry Pipeline.

World Transformation: Usually the vertex (or vertices for an object) is defined with a local coordinate system. For example, when you open your favorite modeling tool to create an object, you are manipulating this object within its own local coordinate system. The world transformation stage is where the vertices are converted into the coordinate system of the game world.

View Transformation: When planning each scene, you also need to position your viewpoint (the *camera position*). After the viewpoint is established, the view transformation stage is where every world vertex is oriented with respect to the camera.

Projection Transformation: Now that the world's vertices are organized with respect to the camera viewpoint, you need to scale the vertices to create a feeling of depth between the camera and every object in the scene. At this stage of the graphics pipeline, you have the choice of two projections:

Perspective Projection: Vertices that are positioned close to the camera appear larger than those vertices that are positioned farther away. This is the view projection used by any First Person Shooter game or something in which a feeling of movement through an interactive world is needed.

Orthographic Projection: This type of projection (an *affine projection*) is where the feeling of depth is totally removed. Uses of this projection type are most common in things like CAD tools or for displaying a menu system to the player.

Clipping and Viewport Stage: The final stage of the pipeline finishes off by deciding which vertices are actually visible and which are positioned beyond the confines of your viewing area (the *view frustum*). Vertices that are marked as unviewable are culled from the scene.

INTRODUCTION TO VECTORS

A mathematical entity that describes a direction and magnitude such as a force like acceleration or gravity is known as a *vector*. Vectors are also used to represent a position in a 3D coordinate system. The Peon library has an optimized vector object for you to use called Vector3. Vectors are an important component to graphics programming. For a quick snapshot of the class definition, please browse through the Vector3.h file included with the Peon project shown in Listing 5.1.

LISTING 5.1 Vector3 Definition

```
class PEONMAIN_API Vector3
{
public:

  float x;
  float y;
  float z;

  Vector3(void)
  {
    x = 0.0f;
    y = 0.0f;
    z = 0.0f;
  }
  static Vector3 crossProduct(const Vector3 &v1, const Vector3 &v2);
  static float dotProduct(const Vector3 &v1, const Vector3 &v2 );
  static float distance(const Vector3 &v1, const Vector3 &v2);
}
```

Common Vector Operations

For 3D graphics programming, proper vector manipulation is a crucial aspect with many applications in a Cartesian Coordinate system. To begin with, there will be cases in which you will need to calculate the length of the vector (the *magnitude*). The magnitude of a vector is represented mathematically by a vertical bar on either side of the vector as shown in Equation 5.1.

$$|A| = \sqrt{Ax^2 + Ay^2 + Az^2} \tag{5.1}$$

When you begin manipulating vectors in 3D graphics, it is important that every vector has been reduced to a length of 1.0. This is known as *normalization*, and its usage will become more apparent further on. To normalize the vector, you simply divide the vector *a* by its own magnitude (see Equation 5.2).

$$a = \frac{A}{|A|} \tag{5.2}$$

In many situations in graphics programming you will need to find a perpendicular vector (the *normal vector*), given only two other vectors that lie on the same plane. This is known as the *cross product* of two vectors, and is very useful in lighting, physics, and collision detection calculations, among other things. See Equation 5.3.

$$N = A \times B = (A_y B_z - A_z B_y, A_z B_x - A_x B_z, A_x B_y - A_y B_x) \tag{5.3}$$

Listing 5.2 demonstrates how to perform a cross-product calculation within the Vector3 object.

LISTING 5.2 Vector3::crossProduct

```
Vector3 Vector3::crossProduct(const Vector3 &v1, const Vector3 &v2)
{
  vector3 vCrossProduct;

  vCrossProduct.x = v1.y * v2.z - v1.z * v2.y;
  vCrossProduct.y = v1.z * v2.x - v1.x * v2.z;
  vCrossProduct.z = v1.x * v2.y - v1.y * v2.x;

  return vCrossProduct;
}
```

Another important operation involved in graphics programming is the dot product. There are two possible equations that define the dot product. Equation 5.4 outlines the official algebraic definition of the dot product, which is the sum of the products of each corresponding component to produce a scalar.

$$A \bullet B = A_x B_x + A_y B_y + A_z B_z \qquad (5.4)$$

The other use for the dot product is to calculate the angle between two vectors as defined in Equation 5.5. It becomes the product of the magnitude of the vectors and the cosine of the angle between them.

$$A \bullet B = \|A\|\|B\|\cos\theta \qquad (5.5)$$

In terms of practical code, Listing 5.3 demonstrates how this is done within the Vector3 object.

LISTING 5.3 Vector3::dotProduct

```
float Vector3::dotProduct(const Vector3 &v1, const Vector3 &v2)
{
   return( v1.x * v2.x + v1.y * v2.y + v1.z * v2.z  );
}
```

You will learn more about using the dot product later on, but its primary purpose with respect to graphics programming is to determine the perpendicular vector (known as the "normal vector") from two other vectors.

Another useful method that you can add to your Vector3 object is how to find the distance between two vectors (see Listing 5.4).

LISTING 5.4 Vector3::distance

```
float Vector3::distance(const Vector3 &v1, const Vector3 &v2)
{
   float dx = v1.x - v2.x;
   float dy = v1.y - v2.y;
   float dz = v1.z - v2.z;

   return (float)sqrt( dx * dx + dy * dy + dz * dz );
}
```

As you use more of the Vector3 object in the Peon engine and throughout the rest of this book, you will become more accustomed to how the object works and what it is doing.

INTRODUCTION TO MATRICES

Both the OpenGL and Direct3D API are optimized to use matrices to position the object/point/vertex within the gameworld. A matrix is a two-dimensional array of numbers with a set number of rows and columns. You normally define the dimension of a matrix by the *mxn* notation. For example, if you had a matrix with one row and three columns, you would say that you had a *1 × 3* matrix.

All graphics hardware is optimized for using 4 x 4 matrices.

THE OPENGL MATRIX STACKS

One of the key design principles behind OpenGL is the proper manipulation of the three matrix stacks available to us: the modelview, projection, and texture matrix stacks.

The *modelview matrix* stack can hold up to 32 4 × 4 matrices, with the pipeline using the top matrix on the stack. As with any other stack, you can push and pop various matrices, in order to create complex geometry out of simple, atomic coordinate transformations. Transformations of your modelview matrices are responsible for placing and orientating your objects within the gameworld.

The *projection matrix* stack can hold two 4 × 4 matrices, with the pipeline using the topmost matrix on the stack to perform any projection transformations to the objects in the pipeline. Transformations of the projection matrix are responsible for defining the viewing volume and clipping planes of your scene.

The texture matrix stack can hold two 4 × 4 matrices as well and is responsible for the manipulation of texture coordinates before any texture mapping occurs.

In each case, the OpenGL context uses the `glPushMatrix` and `glPopMatrix` functions for pushing and popping matrices onto any of the matrix stacks, which can be a useful practice to preserve the contents of the matrix stack. This will become clearer in the examples.

The Peon engine contains a matrix object that can be used for some calculations. See Listing 5.5 for an outline to the `Matrix44` object.

LISTING 5.5 `Matrix44` Definition

```
class PEONMAIN_API Matrix44
{
public:
```

```
      float m[16];

   Matrix44()  { identity(); }

   Matrix44( float m0, float m4, float  m8, float m12,
             float m1, float m5, float  m9, float m13,
             float m2, float m6, float m10, float m14,
             float m3, float m7, float m11, float m15 );

   void identity(void);
   void scale(const Vector3 &scale);
   Matrix44 operator + (const Matrix44 &matB);
};
```

Identity Matrix

A useful matrix within graphics programming is the basic identity matrix. Simply put, the values along the main diagonal are 1, while every other value is 0. Identity matrices can be any dimension, but both row and column sizes must be equivalent (see Equation 5.6). For example, an *mxn* where *m = n*.

$$\begin{pmatrix} 1 & 0 & 0 & 0 \\ 0 & 1 & 0 & 0 \\ 0 & 0 & 1 & 0 \\ 0 & 0 & 0 & 1 \end{pmatrix} \tag{5.6}$$

Listing 5.6 demonstrates how the **Matrix44** object is initialized as an identity matrix.

LISTING 5.6   Matrix44::identity

```
void matrix44::identity( void )
{
  m[0]=1.0f; m[4]=0.0f; m[8] =0.0f; m[12]=0.0f;
  m[1]=0.0f; m[5]=1.0f; m[9] =0.0f; m[13]=0.0f;
  m[2]=0.0f; m[6]=0.0f; m[10]=1.0f; m[14]=0.0f;
  m[3]=0.0f; m[7]=0.0f; m[11]=0.0f; m[15]=1.0f;
}
```

Matrix Addition and Subtraction

To perform matrix addition and subtraction, you simply take each element of one matrix and add or subtract it with the same positioned element in the next matrix. See Equations 5.7 and 5.8.

$$\text{Matrix } \mathbf{A} = \begin{pmatrix} 5 & 2 & 1 & 1 \\ 5 & 6 & 7 & 8 \\ 9 & 5 & 4 & 5 \\ 3 & 2 & 2 & 2 \end{pmatrix} \quad \text{Matrix } \mathbf{B} = \begin{pmatrix} 5 & 5 & 5 & 5 \\ 6 & 5 & 6 & 5 \\ 5 & 6 & 5 & 4 \\ 7 & 6 & 5 & 4 \end{pmatrix} \quad (5.7)$$

$$\text{Matrix } \mathbf{A} + \mathbf{B} = \begin{pmatrix} 5+5 & 2+5 & 1+5 & 1+5 \\ 5+6 & 6+5 & 7+6 & 8+5 \\ 9+5 & 5+6 & 4+5 & 5+4 \\ 3+7 & 2+6 & 2+5 & 2+4 \end{pmatrix} \quad (5.8)$$

NOTE

Each matrix involved in addition or subtraction must be the same dimension. Addition and subtraction operations are also associative but not commutative.

For example, $M + (N - O) = (M + N) - O$ *but* $M - N \mathrel{!=} N - M$.

Listing 5.7 shows you how the + operator is overloaded within the Matrix44 object.

LISTING 5.7   matrix44::operator + (const matrix44& operand)

```
matrix44 matrix44::operator + ( const matrix44 &matB )
{
  matrix44 result;
  result.m[0]  = m[0]  + matB.m[0];
  result.m[1]  = m[1]  + matB.m[1];
  result.m[2]  = m[2]  + matB.m[2];
  result.m[3]  = m[3]  + matB.m[3];

  result.m[4]  = m[4]  + matB.m[4];
  result.m[5]  = m[5]  + matB.m[5];
  result.m[6]  = m[6]  + matB.m[6];
  result.m[7]  = m[7]  + matB.m[7];
```

```
result.m[8]  = m[8]  + matB.m[8];
result.m[9]  = m[9]  + matB.m[9];
result.m[10] = m[10] + matB.m[10];
result.m[11] = m[11] + matB.m[11];

result.m[12] = m[12] + matB.m[12];
result.m[13] = m[13] + matB.m[13];
result.m[14] = m[14] + matB.m[14];
result.m[15] = m[15] + matB.m[15];

return result;
}
```

Matrix Multiplication

Although easy to do, matrix multiplication can get confusing if you are not used to it. If your memory is foggy on matrix multiplication, feel free to refer back to this area as often as you want. The only rule about multiplication is that the inner product of the two matrices must be identical. For example, $A_{13} \times B_{35}$ is a legal multiplication, as the number of columns of matrix A is identical to the number of rows of matrix B, whereas $A_{31} \times B_{31}$ is *not* a legal multiplication, as the inner product (the number of columns of matrix A and the number of rows in matrix B) is not identical.

After you have determined that the multiplication can proceed, the dimension of the resulting matrix is the outer product of the two matrices. For example, since $A_{13} \times B_{35}$ is a legal multiplication, the resultant matrix is C_{15}. See Equations 5.9 and 5.10.

$$Matrix\ A = \begin{pmatrix} 1 & 2 \\ 3 & 4 \end{pmatrix} \quad Matrix\ B = \begin{pmatrix} 5 & 6 \\ 7 & 8 \end{pmatrix} \tag{5.9}$$

$$Matrix\ AB = \begin{pmatrix} 1\cdot5+2\cdot7 & 1\cdot6+2\cdot8 \\ 3\cdot5+4\cdot7 & 3\cdot6+4\cdot8 \end{pmatrix} \tag{5.10}$$

Remember that you multiply each element of row A by each element of column B. Also, never forget the basic order of operations, meaning you calculate the multiplication operands before the addition.

NOTE

Coordinate Transformations

Because you can combine transformations by the help of matrix multiplication, you just need to remember that matrices within graphics programming are of a 4×4 dimension. Only three transformations are involved in graphics programming: *scaling, translation,* and *rotation.*

Scaling Transform

This is the act of applying a scalar value to each element in the matrix. This transformation can be useful if you want to grow or shrink your vertices. In 3D graphics, because you normally use the coordinates x,y,z to define a vertex, the scaling factors appear as sx, sy, sz. See Equation 5.11.

$$S = \begin{pmatrix} Sx & 0 & 0 & 0 \\ 0 & Sy & 0 & 0 \\ 0 & 0 & Sz & 0 \\ 0 & 0 & 0 & 1 \end{pmatrix} \quad (5.11)$$

Because you are working with homogenized matrices, the last entry on the main diagonal (S_{44}) is always 1. As you will learn later, this makes it easier to combine several matrices into one final product.

Listing 5.8 demonstrates how to create a scaling matrix with the `Matrix44` object from the Peon library.

LISTING 5.8 `Matrix44::scale(const Vector3 &scale)`

```
void matrix44::scale( const Vector3 &scale )
{
m[0]  = scale.x;
m[5]  = scale.y;
m[10] = scale.z;
}
```

Translation Transform

Translation can be thought of as moving a point from one position in space to another. To perform translation, you simply add the delta values of each axis to the original values of the point being translated. See Equation 5.12.

$$T = \begin{pmatrix} 1 & 0 & 0 & 0 \\ 0 & 1 & 0 & 0 \\ 0 & 0 & 1 & 0 \\ Tx & Ty & Tz & 1 \end{pmatrix} \qquad (5.12)$$

Note that in graphics programming, the point P is always represented in homogenous coordinates. For example, $P(x, y, z, 1)$. This is important, as it allows you to use matrix multiplication to combine several transformation matrices into one final product. If you did not have the point in homogenous coordinates, then many of your transform matrices would violate basic matrix operation rules.

A sample translation matrix can be created by the following Peon code presented in listing 5.9.

LISTING 5.9 Matrix44 Translation Example

```
void Matrix44::translate( const Vector3 &trans )
{
  m[12] = trans.x;
  m[13] = trans.y;
  m[14] = trans.z;
}
```

Rotation Transform

The final transformation type is the most complex transformation among the big three. You can scale a point to any size and can now move this point anywhere in 3D space, so the final operation that you are allowed to perform is to rotate around a given axis.

The following rotation matrix transforms the point (x, y, z) around the x-axis to form the new point (x', y', z'). See Equation 5.13.

$$R_x = \begin{pmatrix} 1 & 0 & 0 & 0 \\ 0 & \cos\theta & \sin\theta & 0 \\ 0 & -\sin\theta & \cos\theta & 0 \\ 0 & 0 & 0 & 1 \end{pmatrix} \qquad (5.13)$$

Listing 5.10 details this rotation in the Matrix44 object.

LISTING 5.10 `void Matrix44::rotate_x(const float &angle)`

```
void Matrix44::rotate_x( const float &angle )
{
  //the given angle is in degrees. You need to convert
  //it to radians.
  float s = sin(PEON_DEGTORAD(angle));
  float c = cos(PEON_DEGTORAD(angle));

  m[5]  =  c;
  m[6]  =  s;
  m[9]  = -s;
  m[10] =  c;
}
```

The following rotation matrix transforms the point (x,y,z) around the y-axis to form the new point (x', y', z'). See Equation 5.14.

$$R_y = \begin{pmatrix} \cos\theta & 0 & -\sin\theta & 0 \\ 0 & 1 & 0 & 0 \\ \sin\theta & 0 & \cos\theta & 0 \\ 0 & 0 & 0 & 1 \end{pmatrix} \qquad (5.14)$$

Listing 5.11 details the rotation around the y-axis using the `Matrix44` object.

LISTING 5.11   `void Matrix44::rotate_y(const Real &angle)`

```
void Matrix44::rotate_y( const float &angle )
{
  float s = sin(PEON_DEGTORAD(angle));
  float c = cos(PEON_DEGTORAD(angle));

  m[0]  =  c;
  m[2]  = -s;
  m[8]  =  s;
  m[10] =  c;

}
```

The last rotation matrix transforms a point (x,y,z) around the z-axis to form the new point (x', y', z'). See Equation 5.15.

$$R_z = \begin{pmatrix} \cos\theta & \sin\theta & 0 & 0 \\ -\sin\theta & \cos\theta & 0 & 0 \\ 0 & 0 & 1 & 0 \\ 0 & 0 & 0 & 1 \end{pmatrix}$$ (5.15)

Note that in these three rotation matrices, the greek letter Theta represents the angle of rotation that you want to perform in radians.

NOTE

In the Peon engine, the matrix rotation around the z-axis is detailed in Listing 5.12.

LISTING 5.12   void Matrix44::rotate_z(const float &angle)

```
void Matrix44::rotate_z( const float &angle )
{
    float s = sin(PEON_DEGTORAD(angle));
    float c = cos(PEON_DEGTORAD(angle));

    m[0] =  c;
    m[1] =  s;
    m[4] =  -s;
    m[5] =  c;

}
```

Matrix Concatenation

It is very important that the matrices involved in your calculations are in the 4×4 dimension (homogenous coordinates), as you can then take several transform matrices and combine them into one matrix, which represents the final transform that you can apply to a vertex in the scene. This can improve some efficiency in any performance critical code, as you can combine several matrix operations into one. This is a process called *matrix concatenation*, which is defined as shown in Equation 5.16.

$$C = M_1 \cdot M_2 \cdot M_{n-1} \cdot M_n$$ (5.16)

In this formula, C represents the final matrix product of the concatenation of the M_1 to M_n matrices.

Remember again that matrix multiplications are not commutative, so care is needed to ensure that the proper order is followed. A rule of thumb that is common in graphics programming practice is to work from the left to the right (also called the *left-to-right* rule). The visible effects of the final composite matrix *C* occur in a left-to-right order.

After all of this introduction to matrices, you should be aware of a little secret: the Peon library does the math for you internally. It still is useful to understand how matrices work, as there are times when performance critical matrix optimizations are needed.

For another quick example on working with the OpenGL matrix stack to demonstrate how to calculate the resultant matrix after a series of operations, assume that you have an object positioned at the world origin (*0.0f, 0.0f, 0.0f*). You want to double the size of the object, rotate it around the x-axis by 30 degrees, and then translate the object to position 10 units in the positive y-axis and 10 units into the screen on the z-axis (*0.0f, 10.0f, –10.0f*). Take a look at listing 5.13 to see how you would compute the final matrix with OpenGL.

LISTING 5.13   A Real-World Example

```
glPushMatrix(); //push the current matrix onto the stack
glLoadIdentity(); //load an identity matrix
glScalef(2.0f, 2.0f, 2.0f); //scale the object by 2.0f in each axis
glRotatef(30.0f, 1.0f, 0.0f, 0.0f ); //apply a rotation around the
x-axis
//by 30 degrees
glTranslatef(0.0f, 10.0f, -10.0f); //translate 10 units into the
screen
//render the object
renderTARDIS();
glPopMatrix(); //restore the matrix from the stack
```

BASIC CAMERA/VIEW ORIENTATION

When learning about Fixed Function Pipeline, you learned the concept of the *view transformation,* which orients each point with respect to the scene camera.

A view transformation matrix contains three vectors: the eye vector, the lookat vector, and the up vector.

Eye vector: This is the vector representing the x,y,z position of your eye in the scene.

Lookat vector: This is the vector representing the x,y,z position of the point in space at which you are looking.

Up vector: This is the vector representing the x,y,z "Up" direction. In most cases, this vector should be always set to (*0.0, 1.0, 0.0*). The positive y-axis represents the upward direction.

Listing 5.14 provides more details.

LISTING 5.14   Creating a View Transformation Matrix with `gluLookAt`

```
Vector3 vecEye( 0.0, 0.0, 1.0 );        //our viewpoint
Vector3 vecLookAt( 0.0, 0.0, -10.0 ); //what we are looking at
Vector3 vecUp( 0.0, 1.0, 0.0);          //the "up" direction
gluLookAt( vecEye.x, vecEye.y, vecEye.z,
           vecLookAt.x, vecLookAt.y, vecLookAt.z,
           vecUp.x, vecUp.y, vecUp.z );
```

Projection Transformations

One of the last stages of the Fixed Function Pipeline is the *Projection Transformation* stage. Remember from the previous section that you have the ability to set the pipeline into two projections: perspective or orthographic.

Perspective

The perspective projection is the one most commonly used for games today, as it provides the depth within the scene, to provide a feeling of reality. But do not assume that only First Person Shooters or Real-Time Strategy games can be made with the perspective projection. Even platformer type titles can be done with a perspective viewpoint. Listing 5.15 documents this process using OpenGL.

LISTING 5.15   Perspective Transformation Matrix with OpenGL

```
//calculate the aspect ratio
float fAspect = (Glfloat)width / (Glfloat) height;
//switch matrix mode to work with the projection stack
glMatrixMode( GL_PROJECTION );
glLoadIdentity();
```

```
//calculate a new perspective matrix using the aspect
//ratio and the near and far clipping planes
gluPerspective( 45.0f, fAspect, 1.0f, 100.0f);
//switch back to the modelview matrix stack
glMatrixMode( GL_MODELVIEW );
glLoadIdentity();
```

Orthographic

The orthographic projection is also very useful, as it allows you to enable the pipeline to remove all feeling of depth from the rendered scene. This can be useful for certain effects you might want to create or for use for the entire game like a plat-former or other 2D type title. One other popular use of the orthographic projection is for displaying the GUI, which is one way for the player to interact with the game. Listing 5.16 shows how this is done with OpenGL.

LISTING 5.16   Creating an Orthographic Projection with OpenGL

```
glMatrixMode( GL_PROJECTION );
glLoadIdentity();
//Calculate an orthographic matrix using the width and height
//of the window
gluOrtho2D( 0, (Glfloat)width, 0, (Glfloat)height );
glMatrixMode( GL_MODELVIEW );
glLoadIdentity();
```

Create a Basic Camera

With this introduction to the world of basic view manipulation, you have learned enough to create your own camera object. Within the Peon library, your default viewpoint manipulator is interfaced through the SceneCamera object which is de-fined in Listing 5.17.

LISTING 5.17   /PeonMain/SceneCamera.h

```
namespace peon
{
  /**
   * This object is our basic camera object for the Peon
   * library. It is only meant to have basic functionality.
   */
```

```
class PEONMAIN_API SceneCamera
{
public:
  SceneCamera();
  ~SceneCamera();
  /**
  * This method just sets our camera/view into a perspective
projection
  */
  void setPerspectiveProj( float fAspect, float z_min,
    float z_max );
  /**
  * This method is responsible for setting the position of the
viewer
  */
  void setViewMatrix( Vector3& vecEye, Vector3& vecLookAt,
    Vector3& vecUp);

};
}
```

As you can see, you are only creating some wrapper utility methods around the projection fundamentals. For nearly every 3D scene in your game, you will need to define your view matrix as a perspective projection. Then you only need to adjust your view transformation matrix of the pipeline with the help of the setViewMatrix method.

Gimbal Lock

Currently, you can store the set of rotation angles which specify the *x*, *y* and *z* rotations around the axii in a Vector3 data structure. For example, Vector3(90.0f, 0.0f, 0.0f) is used for a rotation of *+90* degress in the *x*-axis. In mathematics, this is known as an *Euler* angle. In other words, Eular angles can be represented with a single vector data structure such as a Vector3 object. *Gimbal lock* is a problem associated with Eular angles when you attempt to concatenate multiple transforms into the final product matrix. It is possible for the rotation around one axis to be mapped onto a rotation around another axis, therefore potentially making it impossible to actually rotate around the desired axis.

For example, your object wishes to rotate around the *z*, *y* and *x* axis to produce the final orientation. The rotation around the *z* axis will run smoothly, along with the rotation around the *y* axis. However, after this second rotation, your *x* axis is now mapped onto your *z* axis. Therefore, any rotation in the *x* axis will instead rotate the object around the *z* axis. Worse yet, it is now impossible to rotate your object around the desired *x* axis!

This problem can be solved by using *quaternions.*

Quaternions

Mostly used for either interpolating between two vectors, or manipulating your scene camera, quaternions are a useful mathematical tool to provide a mechanism to rotate any object by any angle around any arbitrary axis. The final rotation is still calculated using matrix operations; however, instead of multiplying the rotation matrices together, quaternions representing the axes of the rotation are multiplied together. This final quaternion product is then converted to the proper rotation matrix.

Within the Peon library, the Quaternion object handles these operations and is defined in the header file Quaternion.h defined in Listing 5.19.

LISTING 5.19   /PeonMain/Quaternion

```
class Quaternion
{
public:
   float m_w, m_x, m_y, m_z;
public:
   Quaternion();
   ~Quaternion();
   //snip
};
```

A quaternion is defined as a four-tuple entity composed of normal and imaginary numbers. There are two equations that can define a quaternion, shown in Equations 5.17 and 5.18.

$$q = w + xi + yj + zk \text{ where } i, j \text{ and } k \text{ are imaginary numbers} \tag{5.17}$$

$$q = \begin{bmatrix} w, v \end{bmatrix} \text{ where } w \text{ represents a scalar value and } v \text{ represents a vector} \tag{5.18}$$

Determining the magnitude of a quaternion is similar to what you have already learned about vectors. You only need to extend the equation to handle the extra component. See Equation 5.19.

$$magnitude = \sqrt{w^2 + x^2 + y^2 + z^2} \tag{5.19}$$

To normalize a quaternion, you apply the same operations that you did for the vector. Namely, you would divide each component by the magnitude of the whole quaternion.

By far the most important operation when using quaternions is multiplication. As you will see, the product of two quaternions does actually help you better position the camera within the game world.

Letting *Q1* and *Q2* be their own respective quaternion, then their multiplication would be similar to Equation 5.20.

$$(Q_1 * Q_2)_w = (w_1 w_2 - x_1 x_2 - y_1 y_2 - z_1 z_2) \tag{5.20}$$

*Similar to matrix multiplication, the product of Q1*Q2 is not equal to Q2*Q1. In other words, quaternion multiplication is not commutative.*

A quaternion not only stores an axis but also a specific amount of rotation around the axis. Once you calculate the final rotation transformation matrices containing quaternions, it is a trivial matter to orient your camera or any other object within the game world to prevent gimbal lock.

Basic Quaternion Algorithm

The basic algorithm to using quaternions for your rotational matrices is straightforward:

1. Use a quaternion to represent your rotation.
2. Generate a temporary quaternion which is the change from the current orientation to the new orientation.
3. Multiply the temporary quaternion created in Step 2 with the original quaternion from Step 1.
4. Convert this product quaternion to a matrix, which will act as the rotational matrix for positioning your vertices in the scene.

When you have finished multiplying the two quaternions together, the final rotation transformation matrix is calculated from the product quaternion. See Equation 5.21.

$$
\begin{bmatrix}
w^2 + x^2 - y^2 - z^2 & 2xy - 2wz & 2xz + 2wy & 0 \\
2xy + 2wz & w^2 - x^2 + y^2 - z^2 & 2yz - 2wz & 0 \\
2xz - 2wy & 2yz - 2wz & w^2 - x^2 - y^2 + z^2 & 0 \\
0 & 0 & 0 & 1
\end{bmatrix} \tag{5.21}
$$

CHAPTER EXERCISES

1. After browsing through both the `Vector3` and `Matrix44` objects in the Peon library, feel free to optimize them in any way possible. Hint: Research the `inline` keyword.
2. Although you learned about gimbal lock and its effect on your objects' final orientation, research some possible solutions for this problem, including how to modify your `SceneCamera` object to use quaternions.
3. You should always maintain your camera position code applied to the `GL_PROJECTION` matrix stack. To understand why, manipulate the camera while in the `GL_MODELVIEW` matrix stack and test the results for yourself.

SUMMARY

Now that you have learned the fixed function geometry system of graphics programming theory, it is much easier to picture and understand just how a point (or vertex) moves through the pipeline and is displayed in the 3D world. You have also learned how to manipulate the key stages of this pipeline to help produce the results needed via various matrix operations. You were introduced to vector and matrix concepts that attempt to make your 3D programming life a little bit easier. By manipulation of the camera's eye and looking at vector components, you can also view the scene from any point in space.

You were also introduced to quaternions, which enable you to calculate object rotations in your game world, without the worry of gimbal lock. Now that you have a mathematics foundation to build upon within graphics programming, in the next chapter you learn about OpenGL, which is a very popular graphics application interface (or API).

6 Creating an OpenGL Renderer

Chapter Goals

- Provide an overview of OpenGL.
- Introduce the basics of creating and using an OpenGL context.
- Introduce the OpenGL internal state machine.
- Introduce rendering primitives and basic texture mapping.
- Provide information on how to use display lists and rendering text.
- Introduce how to add fog effects to your scene.

The *Open Graphics Library* (OpenGL) was architected by Silicon Graphics Incorporated during the late 1980s and quickly became a leading 3D graphics API. It was designed from the beginning to be cross-platform, simple to use, and fast. It was first released and optimized for the high-end workstations, but has gradually migrated to the consumer level thanks to a shared interest among leading graphics developers and video hardware vendors. The OpenGL language specification is not under control by one party but is a collaborative piece of work with contributions by some major hardware manufacturers and other industry leaders. Together, they form the *OpenGL Architecture Review Board* (ARB), and as of this book's writing, have just released the OpenGL 2.0 specification.

Within this chapter, you will start adding and working with components from the Peon engine in order to gain an understanding of the specifics behind manipulating the OpenGL pipeline.

HOW DOES OPENGL OPERATE?

To the uninitiated graphics programmer, it is important to understand what OpenGL is and what it can do for you. OpenGL is a highly procedural graphics API. In other words, rather than relying on the programmer to describe how a scene is structured, you are required to physically define the rendering steps necessary to create the objects and environment for your scene. These rendering steps or methods involve manipulating the API, which includes a few hundred functions. These functions control your graphics device to draw triangles, points, lines, and other complex data in three dimensions. OpenGL also has the capability to add lighting to your scene; use textures for adding more realism; and use blending, shading, animation, and a host of other effects.

OpenGL does not provide any functions for window management on your platform of choice. It also does not provide any custom method for manipulating input or audio devices. It focuses solely on providing a strong graphics architecture. The strength of this approach is that it gives you the freedom to use nearly any programming language or favorite library to manipulate how OpenGL functions with your existing projects.

OPENGL AND INSTALLABLE CLIENT DRIVERS (ICDS)

Starting with the release of Windows 95 SR2, the only implementation of OpenGL provided by Microsoft to Windows developers was through a software-only module using the OpenGL 1.1 specification, which is contained in the opengl32.dll located in your system directory. Because Microsoft began to focus their 3D efforts on the production and promotion of Direct3D, the OpenGL ARB was forced to decide how to enable future OpenGL support on the Windows platform. With a little help from Microsoft, the ARB designed an architecture known as the *Installable Client Driver* (ICD). The ICD would be provided by the video hardware vendors and acted as a proxy between the OpenGL commands in your program and the OpenGL runtime provided by Microsoft. Figure 6.1 provides an overview of this architecture.

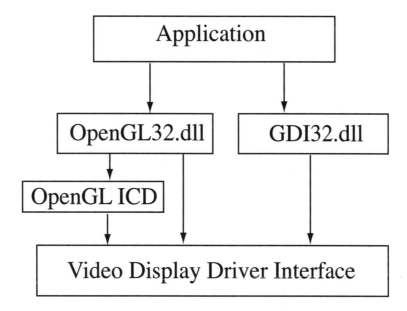

FIGURE 6.1 OpenGL ICD architecture.

UNDERSTANDING THE OPENGL ARCHITECTURE

Since you learned about the Fixed Function Pipeline in Chapter 5, "Graphics Programming Mathematics," you should not have too much trouble understanding the basic OpenGL rendering pipeline shown in Figure 6.2 as a higher level overview.

There are two paths through the pipeline depending on whether the input is an image (that is, pixel data) or vertices representing your game world meshes or objects. The data passes through the pipeline, and the final product is *rendered* (rasterized) onto the video hardware. Although you cannot modify the final surface that is displayed on the video hardware, also known as the *frame buffer*, you do have the ability to manipulate several other buffers, which are combined to compose the final output.

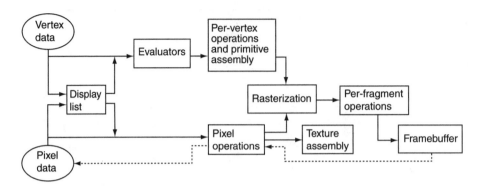

FIGURE 6.2   OpenGL rendering pipeline.

DEFINING THE SCENERENDERER

As you learned in Chapter 4, "Introduction to the Peon Engine," the Peon engine works by providing a SceneRenderer interface that you will use to setup the necessary OpenGL architecture to render your scene data.

ON THE CD

Listing 6.1 provides a shortened outline of the class found in the /Peon/PeonMain/include folder on the CD-ROM.

LISTING 6.1   SceneRenderer Interface

```
namespace peon
{
    /** This object is used to process our rendering commands by acting
    * as a layer or interface above the underlying OpenGL architecture
*/
    class SceneRenderer : public IUnknown
    {
    protected:

      /** width of the context */
      int m_iDeviceWidth;

      /** height of the context */
      int m_iDeviceHeight;
```

```cpp
    /** depth of the context. Usually either 16 or 32 */
    int m_iBitsPerPixel;

    /** are we windowed or fullscreen? */
    bool m_bWindowed;
    /** SDL_Surface to contain the OpenGL commands */
    SDL_Surface* m_pOGLSurface;

    //snip

public:

    /** Constructor */
    SceneRenderer();

    /** Destructor */
    ~SceneRenderer();

    //!
    /** This method is used to load our OpenGL context using params
    * from the INI file. */
    bool loadDevice(IniConfigReader*);

    /** This method is used to unload and destroy our OpenGL
    * context */
    void unloadDevice();

    /** This method is used to clear our back surface in
    * preparation of our next frame of rendering commands */
    bool clearDevice();

    /** This method is used to flip our surface chain. The back
    * surface becomes the front, and the front becomes the back */
    void flipDevice();
    //snip
  };
}
```

LOADING THE OPENGL DEVICE USING SDL

It is within the SceneRenderer::loadDevice method where you get to the nuts and bolts of creating a new SDL_Surface object with OpenGL capabilities. Listing 6.2 details how this is accomplished.

LISTING 6.2 Creating an OpenGL Surface

```
bool SceneRenderer::loadDevice(IniConfigReader* pConfig)
{
  Uint32 iFlags;
  iFlags    = SDL_OPENGL;    // we want an openGL window
  iFlags    |= SDL_HWPALETTE;// access the hardware colour palette
  iFlags    |= SDL_RESIZABLE;// the window should be resizeable


  //use the IniConfigReader object to snag the desired width
  //of the context
  m_iDeviceWidth  = (int)pConfig->getInt("Application",
    "WindowWidth", 640);

  //grab the height
  m_iDeviceHeight = (int)pConfig->getInt("Application",
    "WindowHeight", 480);

  //grab the bit depth 16 or 32
  m_iBitsPerPixel  = (int)pConfig->getInt("Application",
    "WindowDepth", 16);

  //do we want a windowed or fullscreen application
  m_bWindowed      = pConfig->getBool("Application", "Windowed",
    "TRUE");

  //to play nice, you should query SDL for video hardware info
  const SDL_VideoInfo * pVideoInfo = SDL_GetVideoInfo();
  if( NULL == pVideoInfo )
  {
  //failed to grab information
    return false;
  }
```

```
//test if a hardware surface is available
if(pVideoInfo->hw_available)
  iFlags |= SDL_HWSURFACE;
else
  iFlags |= SDL_SWSURFACE;

//test if hardware blitting is available
if(pVideoInfo->blit_hw)
  iFlags |= SDL_HWACCEL;

//to create a fullscreen application, you just need to append
//the proper SDL flag to our list of properties you specify
//when creating the surface.
//
//For debugging, you typically leave it a windowed app in
//order to read any output or trace through the execution
//stack in your debugger. Fullscreen mode is usually reserved
//for the final release of your game.
if(!m_bWindowed)
{
  iFlags |= SDL_FULLSCREEN;
}


// enable double buffering
SDL_GL_SetAttribute( SDL_GL_DOUBLEBUFFER, 1 );

// set the precision of the depth buffer — usually 16 or 32 bits
SDL_GL_SetAttribute( SDL_GL_DEPTH_SIZE, m_iBitsPerPixel);

// disable the stencil buffer
SDL_GL_SetAttribute( SDL_GL_STENCIL_SIZE, 0);

//no accumulation buffer, so disable the accumulation bits
SDL_GL_SetAttribute( SDL_GL_ACCUM_RED_SIZE, 0);
SDL_GL_SetAttribute( SDL_GL_ACCUM_GREEN_SIZE, 0);
SDL_GL_SetAttribute( SDL_GL_ACCUM_BLUE_SIZE, 0);
SDL_GL_SetAttribute( SDL_GL_ACCUM_ALPHA_SIZE, 0);

//we have finished with our parameters: CREATE THE DEVICE!
//m_pOGLSurface is an SDL_Surface which acts as a container
//of sorts for the surface area/buffer that's displayed
//to the main video display. (Because we're using a cross-platform
```

```
                 //library, the SDL_Surface is a very generic data structure).
                 m_pOGLSurface = SDL_SetVideoMode( m_iDeviceWidth,
                   m_iDeviceHeight, m_iBitsPerPixel, iFlags );

                 //if our surface is null then we've got a problem.
                 //quit now
                 if( NULL == m_pOGLDevice) return false;

                 return true;
             }
```

The code shown in Listing 6.1 is responsible for initializing and configuring the OpenGL context with the help of the SDL toolkit. You first begin by specifying what type of pixelformat you want the OpenGL rendering context to have. A *pixelformat* is a way to contain and define the properties of the desired OpenGL context. In Listing 6.2, for example, you are defining a pixelformat to be an OpenGL context created in the video hardware, double-buffered with a depth buffer precision of 16 bits. The final call to SDL_SetVideoMode then attempts to create the OpenGL context given these desired window and pixelformat parameters.

As outlined in the comments of Listing 6.2, you can specify whether or not you want your game running in windowed or full-screen mode. When you are working with an alpha or beta version of your game, it is usually better to keep your application in windowed mode. Depending upon the type of game, you would then specify a full-screen mode when releasing the game to the public. On some of the older video hardware, you also might notice an increase in performance when putting your application in full-screen mode.

WORKING WITH OPENGL SURFACES

After the OpenGL context is created with double buffering enabled, you have two available surfaces of video memory within the graphics hardware with which to work. These two surfaces are known as the *front buffer* (or *primary surface*) and *back buffer* (or *secondary surface*). Managing these two buffers effectively is what creates the illusion of animation and high-speed polygons within your game.

Each surface can be thought of as an array containing color pixels that you display on the monitor. The resolution of the surface defines the precision of these color pixels, so the lower the resolution, the less memory the surface will require within the video hardware.

For example, a common resolution is 800 x 600 x 32, meaning that the surface is 800 pixels wide, 600 pixels high, and using 32-bit color. With 32-bit color, you need 4 bytes per pixel (1 each for red, blue, and green and 1 for the alpha channel). By doing some simple math, you get $800 \times 600 \times 4$ bytes or 1,920,000 bytes (roughly 1.9 MB) of memory allocated for this surface, which is then doubled since you are working with two of them.

CATHODE RAY TUBE MONITORS AND PHOSPHORS

The display surface of a regular CRT monitor is covered by three kinds of phosphors that display a different color, depending upon the monitor's electron gun. A red phosphor emits red light, a green phosphor emits green light, and a blue phosphor emits blue light. This is depicted in Figure 6.3.

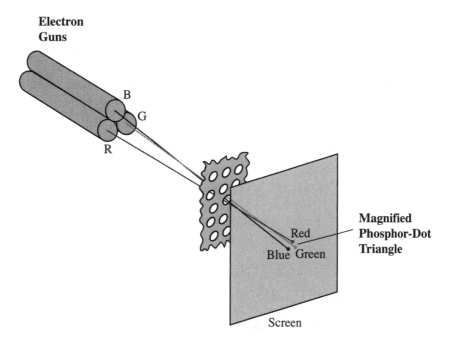

FIGURE 6.3   CRT phosphor depiction.

When the video hardware is presenting an image to the front buffer, the electron gun starts with the upper-left corner of the display. As the electron gun moves from left to right, top to bottom, the video hardware signals the gun how long to keep it on each of the red, green, and blue phosphors before moving to the next pixel. An RGB value of (0,0,0) signals the electron gun to skip over the current pixel since we want the color black. An RGB value of (255,0,0), however, signals the electron gun to remain on the red phosphor as long as possible, but to skip over the green and blue phosphors.

When the electron gun finishes moving pixel by pixel through your display to the bottom-right corner, it moves back to the upper-left corner of your display to start the whole process over again.

This time period when the gun is moving from the bottom-right back to the upper-left corner of the display is known as the vertical retrace period.

The measure of how many times per second the gun is able to update the screen is known as the *refresh rate* and measured in Hertz (Hz). Usually, the video hardware operates within the range of 60 to 85 Hz.

Because the front buffer is the one always presented to the monitor, OpenGL will not allow you to manipulate it directly. Otherwise, there would be an annoying flickering on the monitor since the electron gun is refreshing the current image as it is being displayed. To overcome this flickering, you instead operate on the back buffer surface memory. The back buffer can be thought of as the *next* frame of the scene. When you have finished creating the scene on the back buffer, the surfaces are then flipped so that the back buffer becomes the new frame to be drawn by the electron gun, while the front buffer becomes the new back buffer in which you then proceed to draw the next frame of action.

This is also known as double buffering and has been a common practice for smooth graphics animation for a long time.

Usually, the optimal time to flip the video surfaces is during the vertical retrace period of the monitor; otherwise, you can get *tearing,* which occurs when the top portion of the display is the old front buffer, whereas the bottom portion being drawn is using the new video buffer.

Clearing the Device

Since you are working with a double-buffered mechanism to generate the illusion of smooth animation within the game world, you need to clear the back buffer surface to push the primitive data that composes the next frame. Listing 6.3 demonstrates how to clear the back buffer, taken from the SceneRenderer.h header file.

LISTING 6.3   SceneRenderer::clearDevice()

```
bool SceneRenderer::clearDevice()
{
  //clear the depth and color buffers
  glClear( GL_COLOR_BUFFER_BIT | GL_DEPTH_BUFFER_BIT );
  //reset the current modelview matrix to the identity matrix
  glLoadIdentity();

  return true;
}
```

Flipping the Device

After you finish sending your vertices to the graphics pipeline, you need to signal the hardware to flip the context surfaces—sending the back buffer to the display, while the front buffer becomes your new working surface. Listing 6.4 shows how this is done in the SceneRenderer object.

LISTING 6.4   SceneRenderer::flipDevice()

```
void SceneRenderer::flipDevice()
{
  glFlush(); //flush any commands leftover in the OpenGL pipeline
  SDL_GL_SwapBuffers(); //swap our buffers
}
```

That is all that is needed to create and use an OpenGL context for rendering any desired vertex information.

Unloading the Device

When you are finished with your OpenGL device, you should clean up any memory that you allocated during the lifetime of the object. In the case of the SceneRenderer object, only the memory allocated by the SDL_Surface object, which encapsulates the OpenGL context, needs to be freed. Listing 6.5 demonstrates this.

LISTING 6.5 SceneRenderer::unloadDevice

```
void SceneRenderer::unloadDevice()
{
  //SDL will free the allocated memory for us.
  //Just use the method!
  SDL_FreeSurface( m_pOGLSurface );

}
```

That is all you need to worry about. SDL will take care of the rest for you by managing the proper destruction and cleanup of this surface.

THE OPENGL STATE MACHINE

OpenGL is known as an *immediate mode* API. This means that the current state of the rendering flags within the OpenGL pipeline immediately affect the outcome of your vertex data to the rasterizer. You can control and manipulate these rendering flags (or states) to enable or disable any feature of the pipeline. The two main interfaces that OpenGL provides for state manipulation are the glEnable and glDisable commands. They can be used in conjunction with the glIsEnabled and glIsDisabled functions to query the current state of any rendering flag as shown in Listing 6.6.

LISTING 6.6 glEnable/glDisable

```
glEnable( GL_LIGHTING ); //enable the lighting engine
glDisable( GL_BLEND ); //disable blending

GLboolean current_state;
current_state = glIsEnabled( GL_DEPTH_TEST);
//is our depth testing enabled?
```

Saving and Restoring State Information

You are familiar with the projection and modelview matrix stacks that OpenGL maintains, but there also exists a state stack that is available for the current rendering state of the pipeline. This stack gives you precise control over what you save (that is, push) and what you restore from the stack (that is, pop). The glPushAttrib and glPopAttrib methods are available for this purpose of saving or restoring exact state information such as the current color or point size, and so on. Listing 6.7 demonstrates how they can be used.

LISTING 6.7 glPushAttrib / glPopAttrib

```
//push our current color onto the stack — pretend it's red
glPushAttrib( GL_CURRENT_BIT );

//set our color to white
glColor4f( 1.0f, 1.0f, 1.0f, 1.0f );

//render some primitives
render_primitives();

//restore the saved color state which restores the red color
glPopAttrib();
```

RENDERING PRIMITIVES

The SceneRenderer implementation has been created and is now ready to use. In order to make any object in your game world render to the OpenGL context, you must describe their appearance with the help of *primitives*. These primitives are like the building blocks of the objects in your game world, not unlike forming a DNA sequence to create or clone genetic material. OpenGL allows you to use several different kinds of primitives, which are shown in Table 6.1.

TABLE 6.1 Common OpenGL Primitive Types

Primitive Type	Description
GL_POINTS	Single vertices.
GL_LINES	Vertices are grouped into pairs to render unconnected lines.
GL_TRIANGLES	Vertices are grouped into threes to form unconnected triangles.
GL_TRIANGLE_STRIP	Similar to GL_TRIANGLES, only they are connected.
GL_QUADS	Vertices are grouped into fours to form unconnected quadrilaterals.

For an overview on how these primitives are grouped together, please refer to Figure 6.4.

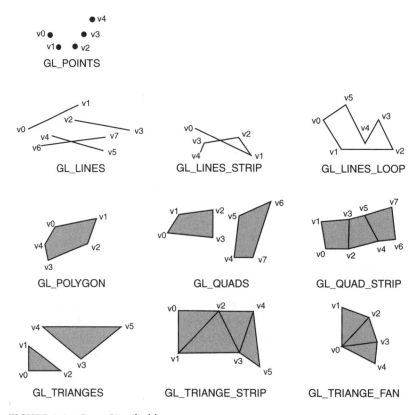

FIGURE 6.4   OpenGL primitives.

To signal OpenGL that you are sending vertices into the graphics pipeline for processing, you must surround any group of vertex definitions with a pair of glBegin and glEnd commands. This prepares the hardware to accept vertex data into the graphics pipeline. Listing 6.8 contains a snippet of OpenGL code demonstrating how to render a basic square.

LISTING 6.8   Basic Square

```
//snip
glClear( GL_COLOR_BUFFER_BIT, GL_DEPTH_BUFFER_BIT );
glLoadIdentity();

//signal to the OpenGL pipeline that you want to start
//rendering individual triangles. Each three vertex
//definitions are grouped into a single triangle,
//therefore you need to specify 6 vertices for one square
glBegin( GL_TRIANGLES );
  glVertex3f( -1.0f, -1.0f, -10.0f ); //bottom-left vertex
  glVertex3f( -1.0f, 1.0f, -10.0f );  //top-left vertex
  glVertex3f( 1.0f, -1.0f, -10.0f );  //bottom-right vertex

  glVertex3f( 1.0f, -1.0f, -10.0f ); //bottom-right vertex
  glVertex3f( -1.0f, 1.0f, -10.0f ); //top-left vertex
  glVertex3f( 1.0f, 1.0f, -10.0f );  //top-right vertex
glEnd();

//finished passing all primitive data to the pipeline
//signal opengl/SDL to flip the buffers for us.
glFlush();
SDL_GL_SwapBuffers();
```

Rendering Vertices with the SceneRenderer

Now that you can render a basic triangle or two with OpenGL, some more functionality needs to be added to the SceneRenderer interface in order to do this within the Peon game engine.

No matter which API you will use to render your primitives, you will still need to define how a primitive is composed and what type of vertex information you want to feed your pipeline. For the triangle data with which you will be working, you only need to create one vertex type (for now): the DiffusePrim. This will simply encapsulate the vertex information that every object using the Peon library needs. Listing 6.9 gives a better picture of the DiffusePrim definition.

LISTING 6.9 DiffusePrim

```
namespace peon
{
  struct PEONMAIN_API DiffusePrim
  {
    float x, y, z; //x,y,z position of the vector
    float r, g, b, a; //diffuse color components (to be discussed)
  };
}
```

At the moment, the only attribute that looks recognizable right now is the x,y,z position of your vertex. The rest will become clearer throughout the rest of this chapter. Listing 6.10 details the new method addition to the SceneRenderer object.

LISTING 6.10 Addition to SceneRenderer.h

```
//snip
//this method is used to pass a group of DiffusePrim
//triangles to the pipeline
void drawPrim( DiffusePrim* pVertices, int count );
```

The final step in implementing this function is to implement the method in the SceneRenderer.cpp file. Listing 6.11 details how this method operates.

LISTING 6.11 drawPrim Implementation

```
void SceneRenderer::drawPrim( DiffusePrim* pVertices, int count )
{
  //push the current modelview matrix onto the matrix stack
  glPushMatrix();

  //push the current color information onto the attribute stack
  glPushAttrib( GL_CURRENT_BIT );
  glLoadIdentity();

  //start pushing triangles through the pipeline
  glBegin( GL_TRIANGLES );
```

```
    for(int i = 0; i < count; i++)
    {
      //specify the diffuse color component of the vertex
      glColor4f( pVertices[i].r, pVertices[i].g,
        pVertices[i].b, pVertices[i].a );

      //specify the position component of the vertex
      glVertex3f( pVertices[i].x, pVertices[i].y, pVertices[i].z );

    }

    //finished
    glEnd();

    //restore the color attribute and the original modelview matrix
    glPopAttrib();
    glPopMatrix();

  }
```

In the /chapter_06/BasicPrims project, there is a method of demonstrating how to pass an array of DiffusePrim objects to the SceneRenderer. Listing 6.12 details how this is done.

LISTING 6.12 MainState.cpp

```
    //define a simple square here using the peon::DiffusePrim type
    DiffusePrim m_oTriPrims[6];

    //snip
    //Put this vertex left 1 unit and down the y-axis 1 unit then move
    //into the screen by 10 units
    m_oTriPrims[0].x = -1.0f;
    m_oTriPrims[0].y = -1.0f;
    m_oTriPrims[0].z = -10.0f;

    //move this vertex up the y-axis by 1 unit, then move into the
screen
    //by 10 units
    m_oTriPrims[1].x = -1.0f;
    m_oTriPrims[1].y = 1.0f;
    m_oTriPrims[1].z = -10.0f;
```

```
        //put this vertex one unit to the right, one unit down and 10 units
in
    m_oTriPrims[2].x = 1.0f;
    m_oTriPrims[2].y = -1.0f;
    m_oTriPrims[2].z = -10.0f;

    //snip - the other 3 vertices are defined similarly

    //Grab the renderer from the EngineCore singleton and pass
    //the triangle data to it
    SceneRenderer* pRenderer =
EngineCore::getSingleton().getRenderer();
    pRenderer->drawPrim( m_oTriPrims, 6 );
```

You will then see in the main window a white triangle on a blue background as shown in Figure 6.5.

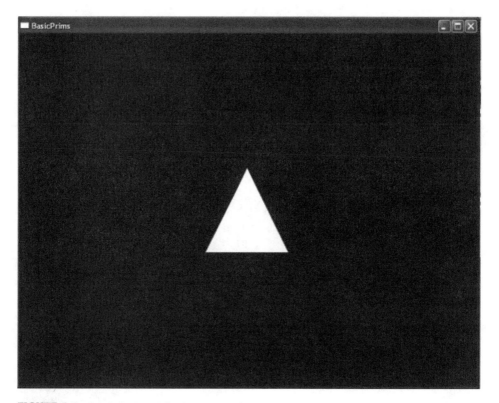

FIGURE 6.5 BasicPrims output.

TEXTURE MAPPING

Giving the scene a real polished look and feel comes from the use of highly detailed textures. The process of texture mapping involves taking an image and attaching it to a polygon or other vertices within the graphics pipeline.

This process can really elevate the quality of the objects within a scene, as well as to help improve the ever important frame rate, since in some cases you might have the option to replace a highly detailed 3D model with that of a texture mapped quadrilateral.

A texture map is broken into a 2D rectangular array of cells, known as *texels*. These texels can then be applied to any object within the game world, rectangular or not.

Although you can use one- or three-dimensional textures for your mapping process, this book focuses only on using two-dimensional textures having just a width and height.

Creating an OpenGL Texture

Before you can use a texture map within the graphics pipeline, you must first load it into OpenGL. OpenGL does have a small image loading library available called *glaux*, but you can take advantage of a helpful SDL library, SDL_Image. It supports a wider variety of image formats than the glaux and minimizes most of your image manipulation needs.

The first step in the process of creating an OpenGL texture is to first load the texture data from the image file. Within the Peon project, this is accomplished by using your SceneRenderer object to load and instantiate the SceneTexture object, which is a handle to the texture information. You can see how this is done in Listing 6.13, which is taken from the SceneTexture object in the Peon engine.

LISTING 6.13 SceneTexture::loadImage()

```
      bool SceneTexture::loadImage( const String& strFilename, bool
bAlpha,
                            bool bMipMaps, bool bRepeat )
    {
       //load the image data to an SDL_Surface structure
       SDL_Surface* pTexSurface = IMG_Load( strFilename.c_str() );
       if( NULL == pTexSurface )
```

```
    {
      //error
      return false;
    }
```

After this is done, you need to allocate and create an array large enough to hold the texture data. You then will loop through the loaded texture information and copy it over to the new array, as shown in Listing 6.14.

LISTING 6.14 Creating the Image Data Array

```
//calculate the total size of the image data. If you are needing
//the alpha channel then account for that
int dim = pTexSurface->w * pTexSurface->h * ((bAlpha) ? 4: 3);
GLubyte *pData = new GLubyte[ dim ];

//loop through our SDL_Surface and copy it into the array
//if the image has an extra alpha channel of information then
//be sure to append that
int pos = 0;
for( int y = (pTexSurface->h – 1); y > -1; y–)
{
  for(int x = 0; x < pTexSurface->w; x++)
  {
    Uint8 r, g, b, a;

    //getPixel is defined in the SDL documentation. It just
    //grabs the pixel data from a given SDL_Surface at
    //coordinates x,y
    Uint32 color = getPixel(pTexSurface, x, y);

    //Next, just pull the r,g,b diffuse color component
    //values from the pixel we just pulled from the SDL_Surface
    if(!bAlpha)
      SDL_GetRGB( color, pTexSurface->format, &r, &g, &b);
    else
      SDL_GetRGBA( color, pTexSurface->format, &r, &g, &b, &a);

    pData[pos] = r; pos++;
    pData[pos] = g; pos++;
    pData[pos] = b; pos++;
    if( bAlpha )
    {
```

```
            //if we need the alpha channel information then copy it over
            pData[pos] = a; pos++;
        }
      }
    }
  }
```

After you have finished this step, you now have the image data copied into the allocated array in memory. Also take note that you will need to allocate extra bytes should the image contain an alpha channel. The *alpha channel* stores extra information for the texture, which is most commonly used to calculate transparency or blending effects. More use of the alpha channel is described later in this chapter.

Now it is time to create a texture handle within OpenGL. This is necessary, as OpenGL will then be able to optimize where this texture data will reside in memory. The glGenTextures function is used to create a new texture handle. You are then going to be working with this texture handle within the OpenGL pipeline, so you must use the glBindTexture to bind (or glue) the desired texture handle to the current working texture stack within OpenGL as shown in Listing 6.15.

LISTING 6.15   Generating and Loading an OpenGL Texture Handle with glTexImage2D

```
    //m_tex is a GLuint value which acts as a handle and contains an
    //automatically generated value from OpenGL

    //if the alpha channel information is needed, set as GL_RGBA,
otherwise
    //use GL_RGB
    int type = (bAlpha) ? GL_RGBA : GL_RGB;
    glGenTextures(1, &m_tex);          // Generate texture ID
    glBindTexture(GL_TEXTURE_2D, m_tex);
```

Now that the texture handle has been created within OpenGL memory, you can decide whether you want to have OpenGL automatically generate mipmapped textures for you of the same image. *Mipmapping* is a process by which textures are generated based upon the distance of the viewer to the texture. Having mipmapped textures can increase the visual effect of a texture, which is meant to preserve the resolution of the image no matter how far or close the camera is to the textured object. For example, in any virtual world or FPS, the player tends to move through levels and will hide behind objects if they are being attacked. Without mipmapping, a simple wall texture that appears as some regular bricks will appear normal from a distance. As the player moves closer, however, the brick texture will appear distorted and pixilated. Mipmapping preserves the original texture image by making the brick appear the same no matter how close or far away the camera is. Listing 6.16 proceeds to generate mipmaps of the texture if you so desire.

LISTING 6.16 Enabling Mipmapping

```
    int filter_min, filter_mag;

filter_min = (bMipMaps) ? GL_NEAREST_MIPMAP_NEAREST : GL_NEAREST;
filter_mag = GL_NEAREST;

  glTexParameteri(GL_TEXTURE_2D, GL_TEXTURE_MIN_FILTER,
                  filter_min);

  glTexParameteri(GL_TEXTURE_2D, GL_TEXTURE_MAG_FILTER,
                  filter_mag);

  glTexParameteri(GL_TEXTURE_2D, GL_TEXTURE_WRAP_S,
                  (bRepeat) ? GL_REPEAT : GL_CLAMP);

  glTexParameteri(GL_TEXTURE_2D, GL_TEXTURE_WRAP_T,
                  (bRepeat) ? GL_REPEAT : GL_CLAMP);

  if(bMipMaps)
  {
    gluBuild2DMipmaps(GL_TEXTURE_2D, type, pTexSurface->w,
      pTexSurface->h, type, GL_UNSIGNED_BYTE, pData);
  }else
  {
      glTexImage2D(GL_TEXTURE_2D, 0, type, pTexSurface->w,
        pTexSurface->h, 0, type, GL_UNSIGNED_BYTE, pData);
  }


  //now that we are finished, do some garbage collection
  //clean up our array and destroy the surface you loaded
  delete [] pData;
  SDL_FreeSurface( pTexSurface );

  //return the texture handle
  return true;
}
```

Using the Texture Map

Now that your texture information is loaded into the OpenGL context, you can then apply it to any primitive data you want to pass through the pipeline. To let the pipeline know which texel to apply to which primitive, you need to understand basic texture coordinates.

2D texture coordinates are usually defined as (s,t) or (u,v) pairs, and range from 0.0f to 1.0f inclusive. The upper-left corner of the texture map is referenced as (0.0f, 1.0f), and the lower-right corner is referenced as (1.0f, 0.0f).

Before OpenGL can apply the texture data to any vertices, the individual texture coordinates must be defined using the `glTexCoord2f` function within the `glBegin`/`glEnd` block. Listing 6.17 takes the simple square you created earlier and applies the necessary texture map information.

LISTING 6.17   A Simple Textured Square

```
glClear( GL_COLOR_BUFFER_BIT | GL_DEPTH_BUFFER_BIT );
glLoadIdentity();

//signal to the hardware you want to start rendering
//triangles
//The texture data has been loaded into the triangle_texture variable
glBindTexture(GL_TEXTURE_2D, triangle_texture );
glBegin( GL_TRIANGLES );

  //first triangle vertices
  glTexCoord2f( 0.0f, 0.0f); glVertex3f( -1.0f, -1.0f, -10.0f );
  glTexCoord2f( 0.0f, 1.0f); glVertex3f( -1.0f, 1.0f, -10.0f );
  glTexCoord2f( 1.0f, 0.0f); glVertex3f( 1.0f, -1.0f, -10.0f );

  //second triangle vertices
  glTexCoord2f( 1.0f, 0.0f); glVertex3f( 1.0f, -1.0f, -10.0f );
  glTexCoord2f( 0.0f, 1.0f); glVertex3f( -1.0f, 1.0f, -10.0f );
  glTexCoord2f( 1.0f, 1.0f); glVertex3f( 1.0f, 1.0f, -10.0f );
glEnd();

glFlush();
SDL_GL_SwapBuffers();
```

Using the SceneTexture

ON THE CD

When everything is compiled within the project, a demonstration of how to use the SceneTexture interface can help you understand how everything will fit together. In the /chapter_source/chapter_06/BasicTexture project on the CD-ROM, you can see how the texture data is loaded and displayed onto the square you created in the BasicPrims project. Listing 6.18 details the pertinent function methods for texture manipulation.

LISTING 6.18 BasicTexture

```
SceneTexture* pTex = NULL;

//load our texture accepting our default texture parameters
pTex = pRenderer->loadImage("data\\textures\\sdl_logo.bmp");

//now set it before rendering the square.
glBindTexture(GL_TEXTURE_2D, pTex->getTex() );
pRenderer->drawPrim( m_oVerts, 6);
```

When the project is compiled and run, you should see a window come up with the SDL logo being displayed on the square as shown in Figure 6.6.

FIGURE 6.6 BasicTexture output.

With the power of encapsulation, you have now made working with texture data a simple task for your project. Well done!

RENDERING TEXT

A critical component of any game is to provide effective feedback to the player for him to understand what is expected during the game—not to mention the player's general progress or status. From displaying the player's current score, to providing instructions to the player on what he must do next, rendering text is a critical component of games. For handling text on your OpenGL context, you have two real options: system fonts or texture bitmapped fonts.

Although SDL has some external libraries to help with creating True Type font strings, most game programmers use texture bitmapped fonts to render their text to the player. It can give the game a more professional feel, and there is no reliance on any specific underlying system fonts on the machine. The only magic behind using texture mapped fonts is that the font texture must contain the alphabet in *ASCII* order, which is then cached into a *display list*.

OPENGL DISPLAY LISTS

OpenGL can use several methods and algorithms to cache rendering instructions in order to improve the performance of the data in your scene. Using display lists allows the OpenGL context to store commands in an optimal memory location most often directly within the video memory itself. When you signal the context to process the display list, OpenGL will then execute the entries in the same order they were stored.

The general procedure for using display lists is to first have OpenGL generate a display list handle using glGenLists(). You then will compile a new list of commands that you want to have cached within the display list using glNewList(). To signal the context that you want to use the display list, you will need to work with the glCallList() function. Finally, the glDeleteLists() function is used to free this stored memory. Listing 6.19 outlines a small sample of using display lists, which is taken from the /chapter_06/BasicDisplayList sample on the CD-ROM.

ON THE CD

LISTING 6.19 Small Display List Sample

```
//similar to texture handle creation, create a display list handle
GLuint tri_display_list = glGenLists(1);
```

```
//compile a basic triangle within this new list
glNewList( tri_display_list, GL_COMPILE );

glBegin( GL_TRIANGLES );
glVertex3f( -1.0f, 0.0f, -10.0f );
glVertex3f( 0.0f, 1.0f, -10.0f);
glVertex3f(1.0f, 0.0f, -10.0);

glEnd();

//you are finished with the display list. Close it off
glEndList();

//snip
//now let's render it.
glClear(GL_COLOR_BUFFER_BIT | GL_DEPTH_BUFFER_BIT);
glLoadIdentity();

glCallList( tri_display_list );

glFlush();
SDL_GL_SwapBuffers();

//snip
//now let's free the memory allocated to the display list
glDeleteLists(tri_display_list, 1);
```

Storing the Font Characters

The first step in rendering some bitmapped font text is to first create and load a display list that contains the texture coordinates of each character of the font. Listing 6.20 documents a way to take the number of rows and columns of your font texture and loop through each character storing the texture coordinates to use later. This is taken from the SceneFont object in the /Peon/PeonMain/include folder on the CD-ROM.

ON THE CD

LISTING 6.20 Storing Texture Coordinates of Each Character

```
bool SceneFont::loadFont(int char_width, int char_height,
                         int char_spacing)
{
  int     loop;
```

```
float   cx;
                    // Holds Our X Character Coord
  floatcy;
                    // Holds Our Y Character Coord
  float   cwx;
                // CharWidth in texture units
  float    cwy;

m_char_width = char_width;
m_char_height = char_height;
m_char_spacing = char_spacing;

cwx         = (1.0f / 256.0f) * m_char_width;
cwy         = (1.0f / 256.0f) * m_char_height;

//Calculate the number of display lists we need
//by taking the product of the rows and columns
m_display_list = glGenLists(m_fxCount * m_fyCount);

for (loop=0; loop<(m_fxCount * m_fyCount); loop++)
{
  // X position of current character
  cx = float(loop%m_fxCount) * cwx;
  // Y position of current character
  cy = float(loop/m_fyCount) * cwy;

  // Signal a new list
  glNewList(m_display_list + loop,GL_COMPILE);

  // Use A Quad For Each character in the ASCII table
  glBegin(GL_QUADS);

    glTexCoord2f(cx,1-cy-cwy); glVertex2i(0,m_char_height);
    glTexCoord2f(cx+cwx,1-cy-cwy);
      glVertex2i(m_char_width, m_char_height);

    glTexCoord2f(cx+cwx,1-cy); glVertex2i( m_char_width, 0);

    glTexCoord2f(cx,1-cy); glVertex2i(0, 0);

  glEnd();
```

```
      //move to the right to work with the next character
      glTranslated(m_char_spacing,0,0);
      //the list is finished. Close it off
      glEndList();

    }
    //finished. Return no problems.
    return true;
  }
```

When that is finished, this font display list is then used whenever you want to render any text. An example of using the SceneFont object to render some text is detailed in Listing 6.21.

LISTING 6.21   SceneFont::drawText()

```
      void SceneFont::drawText(float xpos, float ypos, const String&
  strText)
    {
    //snip!
    //put the matrix mode to the modelview
    glMatrixMode(GL_MODELVIEW);
    glPushMatrix();
    glLoadIdentity();
    //translate to the coordinates passed into this function
    glTranslatef(xpos,ypos,0.0f);
    glColor4f(1.0f, 1.0f, 1.0f,1.0f);

    //set the list base to the beginning of our ASCII alphabet
    glListBase( m_display_list - 32 );
    //call each display list associated with the appropriate
    //letter in the ASCII table
    glCallLists((int)strText.length(), GL_BYTE, strText.c_str());

    //snip!
    }
```

The SceneFont in Action

Now that you have created and implemented a way to present text data to the OpenGL context, you can run through a sample demonstrating how to use it. The BasicFont project demonstrates one way of using the SceneFont object. In the

ON THE CD /chapter_06/BasicFont/Main.cpp implementation file on the CD-ROM, Listing 6.22 demonstrates how to load a new SceneFont.

LISTING 6.22 Loading a New SceneFont

```
//m_pFontTexture is defined as a SceneTexture object
m_pFontTexture = EngineCore::getSingleton().getRenderer()
   ->loadTexture("data\\textures\\font.png");

//the characters in the font texture are 16 pixels wide,
//16 pixels high and 14 pixels apart from each other
m_pFont = EngineCore::getSingleton().getRenderer()
   ->loadFont(16, 16, 14);
```

Printing Text

Now that the SceneFont is loaded into the program, you can use it to display any text you want. For this sample, you are simply displaying the words "Hello World" in the upper-left corner of the context, which is detailed in Listing 6.23.

Within the SceneFont *object you are switching into an orthographic projection to position and render your text without any appearance of depth. As such, the coordinates 0,0 represent the top left corner of your context.*

NOTE

LISTING 6.23 Printing Text

```
//snip
//grab a handle to the current SceneRenderer
SceneRenderer* pRenderer =
EngineCore::getSingleton().getRenderer();

//set the texture for the font image
pRenderer->setTexture( m_pFontTexture );

//print "Hello World" to coordinates 10,10 from the upper-left corner
m_pFont->drawText( 10, 10, "Hello World");
```

Cleaning Up

There is not much more involved in displaying characters from a given font bitmap. Now you need to properly clean up the allocated memory used during your sample; Listing 6.24 details how to dispose of the used resources.

LISTING 6.24 Garbage Disposal

```
//unload the font object in memory
EngineCore::getSingleton().getRenderer()->
  unloadFont( m_pFont );

//unload the font texture data in memory
EngineCore::getSingleton().getRenderer()->
  unloadTexture( m_pFontTexture );
```

After you launch the /chapter_source/bin/BasicFont.exe binary, you will see a window displayed with your text as shown in Figure 6.7.

FIGURE 6.7 BasicFont output.

Although displaying information to the player is of a critical importance, you can see how easy it is to make this happen with OpenGL. Feel free to experiment with different font bitmaps of different sizes to get used to using the SceneFont object.

RENDERING A SIMPLE CUBE

You have learned enough information on rendering OpenGL primitives to tackle something more interesting than a square or rectangle. A basic geometric object that beginner graphics programmers often render is a cube. Cubes are an excellent way to learn how vertices interact with each other, along with learning how to properly position the object and apply texture coordinate information. Working from the /chapter_06/BasicCube project, you can create a display list to store your geometric vertices. Listing 6.25 demonstrates how this is done.

LISTING 6.25   Creating a Display List for the Cube

```
//m_uTriDisplayList is defined as a GLuint variable type
//Generate a display list handle with OpenGL
m_uTriDisplayList = glGenLists(1);
 //open the new list for vertex compilation
glNewList( m_uTriDisplayList, GL_COMPILE );
//Until now you've been working with the GL_TRIANGLES primitive
//which is more than capable of handling a cube. For brevity
//purposes in this listing, using the GL_QUAD type is an option
glBegin(GL_QUADS);
 //the front
glTexCoord2f(0.0f, 0.0f); glVertex3f(-1.0f, -1.0f,  1.0f);
glTexCoord2f(1.0f, 0.0f); glVertex3f( 1.0f, -1.0f,  1.0f);
glTexCoord2f(1.0f, 1.0f); glVertex3f( 1.0f,  1.0f,  1.0f);
glTexCoord2f(0.0f, 1.0f); glVertex3f(-1.0f,  1.0f,  1.0f);
 //the back
glTexCoord2f(1.0f, 0.0f); glVertex3f(-1.0f, -1.0f, -1.0f);
glTexCoord2f(1.0f, 1.0f); glVertex3f(-1.0f,  1.0f, -1.0f);
glTexCoord2f(0.0f, 1.0f); glVertex3f( 1.0f,  1.0f, -1.0f);
glTexCoord2f(0.0f, 0.0f); glVertex3f( 1.0f, -1.0f, -1.0f);
 //the top
glTexCoord2f(0.0f, 1.0f); glVertex3f(-1.0f,  1.0f, -1.0f);
glTexCoord2f(0.0f, 0.0f); glVertex3f(-1.0f,  1.0f,  1.0f);
glTexCoord2f(1.0f, 0.0f); glVertex3f( 1.0f,  1.0f,  1.0f);
glTexCoord2f(1.0f, 1.0f); glVertex3f( 1.0f,  1.0f, -1.0f);
 //the bottom
glTexCoord2f(1.0f, 1.0f); glVertex3f(-1.0f, -1.0f, -1.0f);
glTexCoord2f(0.0f, 1.0f); glVertex3f( 1.0f, -1.0f, -1.0f);
glTexCoord2f(0.0f, 0.0f); glVertex3f( 1.0f, -1.0f,  1.0f);
glTexCoord2f(1.0f, 0.0f); glVertex3f(-1.0f, -1.0f,  1.0f);
 //the right
glTexCoord2f(1.0f, 0.0f); glVertex3f( 1.0f, -1.0f, -1.0f);
glTexCoord2f(1.0f, 1.0f); glVertex3f( 1.0f,  1.0f, -1.0f);
glTexCoord2f(0.0f, 1.0f); glVertex3f( 1.0f,  1.0f,  1.0f);
glTexCoord2f(0.0f, 0.0f); glVertex3f( 1.0f, -1.0f,  1.0f);
 //the left
```

```
glTexCoord2f(0.0f, 0.0f); glVertex3f(-1.0f, -1.0f, -1.0f);
glTexCoord2f(1.0f, 0.0f); glVertex3f(-1.0f, -1.0f,  1.0f);
glTexCoord2f(1.0f, 1.0f); glVertex3f(-1.0f,  1.0f,  1.0f);
glTexCoord2f(0.0f, 1.0f); glVertex3f(-1.0f,  1.0f, -1.0f);
//Finished sending primitives
glEnd();
//you are finished with the display list. Close it off
glEndList();
```

Moving the Cube

Although you learned about object translation, rotation, and scaling in Chapter 5, "Graphics Programming Mathematics," you can now directly manipulate your new cube object to experiment with the effects of these graphics transformations.

Rendering the Cube

The cube has been positioned within the game world and is awaiting presentation to the screen. You have already learned how to render an object using a display list, so the following code snippet of Listing 6.26 should not come as a surprise.

LISTING 6.26 Render the Cube

```
//store the current matrix onto the stack, giving you a new one
glPushMatrix();
//reset the matrix to the identity
glLoadIdentity();
//apply a transformation to orient the object 5 units into the scene
glTranslatef(0.0f, 0.0f, -5.0f);
//rotate the object on the y-axis by m_fYRotation degrees
glRotatef(m_fYRotation, 0.0f, 1.0f, 0.0f);
//rotate the object on the z-axis by m_fZRotation degrees
glRotatef(m_fZRotation, 0.0f, 0.0f, 1.0f );
//call and execute the cube's display list
glCallList( m_uTriDisplayList );
//restore our matrix
glPopMatrix();
```

WORKING WITH FOG

In most early 3D games, you might have remembered the heavy use of fog effects to hide any limitations of the hardware back at that time. Games such as *Turok: The Dinosaur Hunter* from Acclaim used this effect extensively through each level and seamlessly incorporated fog into the scene. The final effect was two-fold: not only did the fog add a mysterious element to the whole *Turok* jungle environment experience, but it enabled the game to obscure objects that were farther away, thus improving scene performance. Within OpenGL, fog calculations are a simple matter for the state machine, and everything is done in hardware for you.

OpenGL fog is calculated by blending the color of the fog with each pixel in the affected area. The blending calculation uses a factor that is dependent upon the distance of the viewer from the fog, how dense the fog is supposed to be, and which fog mode is enabled.

To enable the fog calculations in OpenGL, you only need to enable its state, after which you specify any additional parameters.

ON THE CD

/chapter_06/BasicFog is a small demo project that demonstrates how fog is used. Listing 6.27 details the pertinent sections of code performed during the setup of the scene.

LISTING 6.27   A Sample of Fog

```
GLuint fog_modes = GL_EXP;

GLfloat fog_color[4] = {0.5f, 0.5f, 0.5f, 1.0f}; //use a basic grey
glFogi( GL_FOG_MODE, fog_mode); //set the mode to GL_EXP
glFogfv( GL_FOG_COLOR, fog_color ); //apply the grey fog color
glFogf( GL_FOG_DENSITY, 0.35f); //set the density of the fog
glHint(GL_FOG_HINT, GL_NICEST); //apply fog calculations per pixel
glFogf( GL_FOG_START, 5.0f ); //set the front fog "plane"
glFogf( GL_FOG_END, 15.0f ); //set the rear fog "plane"
glEnable( GL_FOG ); //enable the fog calculations
```

There are three basic fog modes that you can use in OpenGL: *exp, exp2,* and *linear.*

GL_EXP: A basic fog effect that pretty much applies the fog color to the entire scene. The final fog effect of this type is not very realistic and meant for much older hardware.

GL_EXP2:　This is the successor to the GL_EXP fog type. It will apply the fog color to the entire scene, but will also apply some depth information to each fogged pixel.

GL_LINEAR:　This is the overall best fog rendering mode available. You can specify a fog band, and OpenGL will properly calculate how much of the fog color to apply to pixels moving in and out of this band area.

BasicFog Demo

After you launch the BasicFog compiled binary, you will be able to see how fog calculations are performed by OpenGL. Figure 6.8 shows a sample output.

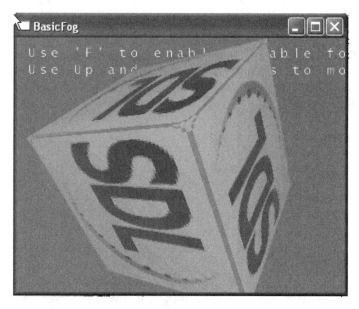

FIGURE 6.8　BasicFog output.

CHAPTER EXERCISES

1. Taking the SceneFont object that you used to render text with, find a way to further optimize the class. *Hint: The less state changes the OpenGL context needs to make, the faster the scene.*

2. Open the BasicFog project and experiment with different fog colors and density levels. It is interesting to adjust the color to see the final scene produced by OpenGL.
3. Just for fun, do a small comparison of OpenGL and Direct3D. Keep a small list handy of what you like and dislike about each API. This will help you on any future gaming projects.

SUMMARY

Although this was a whirlwind introductory tour of OpenGL, you learned quite a lot about creating and using an OpenGL context. The concepts behind the Fixed Function Pipeline and the architecture of OpenGL itself should be much clearer now as you begin to develop some experience with the API. You learned what texture mapping is and how to do it. You also learned about using display lists to cache certain OpenGL commands to optimize rendering, as well as how to load and use your own font texture, and you were given an introduction to the use of fog within a scene. With these basics covered in OpenGL, in the next chapter you will focus more on some of the advanced capabilities of the popular graphics API.

7 More OpenGL Techniques

Chapter Goals

- Introduce and describe the OpenGL lighting system.
- Discuss blending techniques to create transparent polygons.
- Introduce and discuss the OpenGL extension mechanism.

By now, you have a basic footing in OpenGL programming, but you have much more to learn about how to create a proper lighting level to increase the realism of your game, along with many other effects/tricks that can be done. This chapter focuses both on increasing your knowledge of OpenGL as well as adding these new techniques to the SceneRenderer interface in the Peon engine.

LIGHTING AND MATERIALS

You have learned how to create vertices and position them within your game world using the DiffusePrim object. To add another feeling of realism, you need to learn an important aspect of 3D programming— adding proper lighting to the scene.

To approximate the look and feel of light within the real world, OpenGL uses several calculations (and approximations) to create the red, blue, and green components of light as well as how these light rays interact with objects within the scene.

One of the aids that OpenGL uses to compute the color components of a scene object or mesh is through the use of a *material*. A material defines the basic lighting properties such as how an object absorbs or reflects light. The three important characteristics of materials used in lighting calculations are *ambient*, *diffuse*, and *specular*.

Ambient: *Ambient light* does not seem to come from any particular source within the game world, and so surfaces containing these light properties reflect the light in all directions. It creates a general level of light throughout the scene.

Diffuse: Unlike ambient lighting, *diffuse light* comes from a particular direction and usually is reflected evenly across your object. This kind of lighting is what gives every object its color in your scene, from the color of your monsters to how the player appears.. Think of it as the way light is reflected off of everything you encounter in your world.

Specular: *Specular lighting* is another kind of directional lighting; however, it is reflected in a particular direction and creates a bright spot on the surface of reflection. This bright spot, also known as a *specular highlight,* can be used in your scenes to create effects such as shiny objects or spotlights.

The OpenGL pipeline has been optimized for lighting calculations so all you need to do is enable a few of the internal states. You also will need to properly select and position all of your light sources within the scene, after which you will need to select the material you want to use for your objects in order to properly define how they will reflect light.

LISTING 7.1   Using OpenGL Lighting

```
//snip
//the ambient light..it is a 4-tuple property
float ambient_light[] = { 0.5f, 0.5f, 0.5f, 1.0f };

//the diffuse light..another 4-tuple property
float diffuse_light[] = { 0.25f, 0.25f, 0.25f, 1.0f };

//the position of the light — the 1.0f at the end means the first
//three values are the x,y,z position of the light in your world
float position_light[] = { 0.0f, 0.0f, 0.0f, 1.0f };
```

```
//a definition of a generic ambient material
float material_ambient[] = { 1.0f, 1.0f, 1.0f, 1.0f };
//provide a default diffuse material
float material_diffuse[] = { 1.0f, 1.0f, 1.0f, 1.0f };

//now you set up your FFP states
//enable the lighting state machine in OpenGL
glEnable( GL_LIGHTING );

//setup the materials for the 1st light, refrenced as LIGHT0
glMaterialfv( GL_FRONT, GL_AMBIENT, material_ambient );
glMaterialfv( GL_FRONT, GL_DIFFUSE, material_diffuse );

//setup light 0
glLightfv( GL_LIGHT0, GL_AMBIENT, ambient_light );
glLightfv( GL_LIGHT0, GL_DIFFUSE, diffuse_light );
glLightfv( GL_LIGHT0, GL_POSITION, position_light );

//finally enable the light
glEnable( GL_LIGHT0 );
```

In OpenGL, you can use up to eight lights at a time per scene or more depending upon the available hardware. As you might imagine, this gets incredibly computationally expensive and can really cause performance problems. Be sure to find the optimal number of lights for your scene to achieve the desired effect but use as few as necessary.

Defining Surface Normals

Recall from Chapter 5, "Graphics Programming Mathematics," that the normal vector is perpendicular to a plane or surface. Normal vectors are critical components of the lighting pipeline as they help OpenGL calculate the orientation of the object to the light source.

Do not forget that taking the cross product of any two vectors on the same plane is one method of obtaining the surface normal. Refer back to Chapter 5 on how to calculate the cross product.

Using the glNormal family of functions, you embed the primitive's normal direction in the rendering code as you pass in the vertices for the object. Listing 7.2 should help clear this up.

LISTING 7.2 Rendering a Flat Square

```
glClear( GL_COLOR_BUFFER_BIT | GL_DEPTH_BUFFER_BIT );
glPushMatrix();
glLoadIdentity();

//the goal is to render a quad which is just a flat square
//the vector normal to the surface of this quad is just straight
//up, so you'll define it as 0.0f, 1.0f, 0.0f.
glBegin( GL_QUADS );
  glNormal3f( 0.0f, 1.0f, 0.0f );
  glVertex3f( -1.0f, 1.0f, 1.0f );
  glVertex3f( -1.0f, 1.0f, -1.0f);
  glVertex3f( 1.0f, 1.0f, -1.0f);
  glVertex3f( 1.0f, 1.0f, 1.0f);
glEnd();

glPopMatrix();
glFlush();
SDL_GL_SwapBuffers();
```

Adding Light Support to the SceneRenderer

You can add this lighting capability to the Peon engine. The goal is to add some basic but useful lighting support into the SceneRenderer interface.

You need to define a simple light object that you can create and use for manipulating the lighting levels in your scene. In the /Peon/PeonMain/include folder, there is the SceneLight.h file, which is shown in Listing 7.3.

LISTING 7.3 SceneLight.h

```
namespace peon
{
/**
* \brief This object handles any light settings we want
*/
class PEONMAIN_API SceneLight
{
public:
        //! Handles the diffuse component
    Vector4 m_vecDiffuse;
```

```
            //! Handles the ambient component
        Vector4 m_vecAmbient;

            //! Handles the position/direction of the light
        Vector4 m_vecPosition;


    public:
        /**
        * Constructor
        */
        SceneLight(){};
        /**
        * Destructor
        */
        virtual ~SceneLight(){};
        //snip!
    };
}
```

Next, you will need a way to set a light within the SceneRenderer interface in order to apply whatever lighting modifications you want. In the /Peon/PeonMain/ SceneRenderer.h file, you can add this support. Listing 7.4 details what you are adding.

ON THE CD

LISTING 7.4 Adding to SceneRenderer.h

```
class PEONMAIN_API SceneRenderer
{
  //snip

  //only provide support for 8 lights.
  //Anything less would be uncivilized.
  SceneLight m_oLights[7];
  //snip

  //now add a method to set a light
  void setLight( int light_slot, SceneLight& oLight ) = 0;

  //snip
};
```

As you can see, the SceneRenderer interface now provides you with an accessor method for linking a particular SceneLight object into the scene.

Implementing Light Support in SceneRenderer

The bulk of the work that needs to be done is within the SceneRenderer.cpp file where you take the SceneLight object that you defined earlier and work it into the available OpenGL commands. Listing 7.5 details what it is you are modifying.

LISTING 7.5 Modifications to SceneRenderer.cpp

```cpp
void SceneRenderer::setLight( int light_slot, SceneLight& oLight)
{
  m_oLights[light_slot] = oLight;
  GLenum eLight = GL_LIGHT0;
  switch( light_slot )
  {
    case 1:
      eLight = GL_LIGHT1;
    break;

    case 2:
      eLight = GL_LIGHT2;
    break;

    case 3:
      eLight = GL_LIGHT3;
    break;

    case 4:
      eLight = GL_LIGHT4;
    break;

    case 5:
      eLight = GL_LIGHT5;
    break;

    case 6:
      eLight = GL_LIGHT6;
    break;
```

```
    case 7:
      eLight = GL_LIGHT7;
    break;
  }

  float ambient[4];
  float diffuse[4];
  float position[4];

  ambient[0] = oLight.m_vecAmbient.x;
  ambient[1] = oLight.m_vecAmbient.y;
  ambient[2] = oLight.m_vecAmbient.z;
  ambient[3] = oLight.m_vecAmbient.w;

  diffuse[0] = oLight.m_vecDiffuse.x;
  diffuse[1] = oLight.m_vecDiffuse.y;
  diffuse[2] = oLight.m_vecDiffuse.z;
  diffuse[3] = oLight.m_vecDiffuse.w;

  position[0] = oLight.m_vecPosition.x;
  position[1] = oLight.m_vecPosition.y;
  position[2] = oLight.m_vecPosition.z;
  position[3] = oLight.m_vecPosition.w;

  glLightfv( eLight, GL_AMBIENT,  ambient );
  // Set our ambience values (Default color without direct light)

  glLightfv( eLight, GL_DIFFUSE,  diffuse );
  // Set our diffuse color (The light color)

  glLightfv( eLight, GL_POSITION, position );
  // This sets our light position

  glEnable( eLight );
  // Turn this light on

  //if we're setting a light, then at least we should
  //enable lighting
  glEnable( GL_LIGHTING );
  glEnable( GL_COLOR_MATERIAL );
}
```

Sample Demonstration

Included in the source code for this chapter is the BasicLight demonstration project. It is an example of how to create a new SceneLight object and adjust some basic lighting properties for use in your rendering pipeline.

ALPHA-BLENDING AND TRANSPARENCIES

Blending operations within OpenGL enables you to create effects using transparency in your scenes. Blending allows you to create or simulate water, windows, glass, and just about any object that you want to be able to see through.

Blending is also most often used for rendering textured sprites and backgrounds, as you can then use the help of the alpha channel information stored in your texture data to seamlessly display your sprite in your scene. Normally when you create a texture or other image that you want to use within your game, the image data is stored in a format containing the three common Red-Blue-Green channels. Some additional image formats, such as the popular Targa (or TGA), enable you to access additional information stored in the Alpha channel, which has the added benefit of helping OpenGL calculate which sections to draw and which should be blended with the background scenery.

When you enable any blending operations in the pipeline, it is a signal for OpenGL to combine the color information of the incoming primitive with the color data that already exists within the frame buffer. The result is then stored back into the frame buffer. Color values are typically represented within OpenGL in the RGBA format. This means the RGB values represent the red, green, and blue colors, with the alpha component representing the opacity of the object. The lower the opacity of an object, the more transparent it is.

In this case, the alpha channel acts as a mask for determining how opaque or transparent a texel is. A texel containing the actual sprite data has an opaque alpha channel value (1.0f), but a texel outside of the sprite should contain a fully transparent alpha channel value (0.0f).

The blending equation used by OpenGL is shown in Equation 7.1.

$$(RsSr + RdDr, GsSg + GdDg, BsSb + BdDb, AsSa + AdDa) \tag{7.1}$$

The S and D components are the source and destination blend factors that you specify with the glBlendFunc method. The incoming primitive is labeled the *source*, and the currently stored pixel within the frame buffer is referred to as the *destination*.

Listing 7.6 provides a sample of using some blending within the scene, as you will be placing two textured objects within the scene.

LISTING 7.6   Sample Blending

```
glClear( GL_COLOR_BUFFER_BIT | GL_DEPTH_BUFFER_BIT );
glLoadIdentity();

//snip

//enable blending states
glEnable( GL_BLEND );
glBlendFunc( GL_SRC_ALPHA, GL_ONE_MINUS_SRC_ALPHA );

//snip

//render a simple object..this could be a window, etc
//specify an alpha channel of 0.5 in order to allow
//us to see through this object
glBegin(GL_TRIANGLES);
glColor4f( 1.0f, 1.0f, 1.0f, 0.5f );
//vertex 1, 2, 3, 4, 5, 6
glEnd();

glFlush();
SDL_GL_SwapBuffers();
```

The `glBlendFunc` method is the one responsible for letting the OpenGL context know which blending operation to perform on the source and destination pixel colors.

For the majority of the transparency effects used in your game, you will only need to use the `GL_ONE_MINUS_SRC_ALPHA` blending calculation to properly render transparent artifacts to the screen.

NOTE

Sample Demonstration

ON THE CD

Now that you have been given an introduction to using and enabling blending calculations within OpenGL, you can see how this works in the `BasicBlending` sample included on the CD-ROM. You need to indicate only which states to switch the graphics pipeline to, and the underlying OpenGL layer will handle the rest.

VERTEX ARRAYS

Until now you have been defining and rendering simple objects for use in rendering with OpenGL. There will come a time, however, when you need to work with various models composed of hundreds or thousands of vertices in your game world. Declaring each of these models within your code is just not a practical solution.

Vertex arrays give you a way to store large batches of vertices within different types of arrays. For example, you could store the vertices containing position information in one array, the vertex texture information in another, and so on. This design is open enough to let you decide how you want to store and batch your scene data, while allowing OpenGL to optimize the location in memory where your vertices are stored. Depending upon the available memory on your graphics card, OpenGL can either store your vertex data in video memory or system memory.

To use vertex arrays, you must enable/disable them using a slightly different function pair of `glEnableClientState`/`glDisableClientState`. The parameters you use in each method define the type of array you want to enable or disable.

The type of array you can enable or disable is shown in Table 7.1

TABLE 7.1 Vertex Array Types

Flag	Description
GL_COLOR_ARRAY	Contains color info for each vertex
GL_EDGE_FLAG_ARRAY	Contains edge flags for each vertex
GL_INDEX_ARRAY	Contains indices to the color palette for each vertex
GL_NORMAL_ARRAY	Contains normal information for each vertex
GL_TEXTURE_COORD_ARRAY	Contains texture coordinate data for each vertex
GL_VERTEX_ARRAY	Contains position of each vertex

ON THE CD

Listing 7.7 demonstrates a way to set up vertex arrays, contained in the `BasicVertexArray` sample project on the CD-ROM.

LISTING 7.7 BasicVertexArray

```
// Array of all vertex data. It is just a plain unit square
sVertex SquarePoints[4] =
```

```
{
    { 1.0f, -1.0f, 0.0f },
    { -1.0f, -1.0f, 0.0f },
    { -1.0f, 1.0f, 0.0f },
    { 1.0f, 1.0f, 0.0f }
};

// Stucture to hold all texture coordinate information
struct sTexCoords
{
    float t, u;
};

// Array of all texture coords for each point.
sTexCoords SquareTexCoords[4] =
{
    { 1.0f, 0.0f },
    { 0.0f, 0.0f },
    { 0.0f, 1.0f },
    { 1.0f, 1.0f }
};

// Structure to hold all colors for each point.
struct sColor
{
    float r, g, b, a;
};

// Array of all colors for each point. Every side is a different
//color for a more interesting demo
sColor SquarePointColors[4] =
{
    { 1.0f, 0.0f, 1.0f, 1.0f },
    { 1.0f, 0.0f, 1.0f, 1.0f },
    { 1.0f, 0.5f, 1.0f, 1.0f },
    { 0.5f, 1.0f, 1.0f, 1.0f }
};


glClear(GL_COLOR_BUFFER_BIT | GL_DEPTH_BUFFER_BIT);
glLoadIdentity();
```

```
// Translate and rotate the object.
glTranslatef(0.0f, 0.0f, -6.0f);
glRotatef(-50.0f, 1.0f, 0.0f, 0.0f);
glRotatef(-15.0f, 0.0f, 1.0f, 0.0f);

// Bind the texture.
glBindTexture(GL_TEXTURE_2D, square_tex);

// Enable all client states we are using.
glEnableClientState(GL_VERTEX_ARRAY);
glEnableClientState(GL_COLOR_ARRAY);
glEnableClientState(GL_TEXTURE_COORD_ARRAY);

// Load the data to each pointer type we need.
glVertexPointer(3, GL_FLOAT, 0, SquarePoints);
glColorPointer(4, GL_FLOAT, 0, SquarePointColors);
glTexCoordPointer(2, GL_FLOAT, 0, SquareTexCoords);

    // Draw the entire object.
    glDrawArrays(GL_QUADS, 0, 4);

    // Disable all the client states we enabled.
    glDisableClientState(GL_VERTEX_ARRAY);
    glDisableClientState(GL_COLOR_ARRAY);
    glDisableClientState(GL_TEXTURE_COORD_ARRAY);

    SDL_GL_SwapBuffers();
```

Vertex arrays help to speed up the rendering process through OpenGL, as they offload more vertex processing to the video hardware rather than have the CPU spend precious cycles feeding the pipeline one vertex at a time.

THE OPENGL EXTENSION MECHANISM

An important design aspect of the OpenGL API is the concept of the *extension mechanism*. Because graphics hardware capabilities often advance more rapidly than the core specification can keep up with, vendors have the ability to add new rendering features to expose any new functionality in the graphics hardware.

When you want to take advantage or query the extensions supported by the current OpenGL context, you need to parse through a character array return by the glGetExtensions function.

ARB:	An extension approved by the OpenGL ARB
EXT:	An extension agreed upon by multiple vendors
NV:	A proprietary extension of NVIDIA Corporation
ATI:	A proprietary extension of ATI Technologies Inc.
APPLE:	A proprietary extension of Apple Computer Inc.

The simplest method of extension querying is to search for the name of the extension within the space delimited list of extensions supported on the hardware returned by the `glGetExtensions` function. Listing 7.8 demonstrates one way of handling this mechanism, which is defined within the `SceneRenderer`.

LISTING 7.8 Simple Method to Query Extensions

```
bool SceneRenderer::isExtensionSupported( const String& ext )
{
  int pos = 0;
  bool supported = false;
  int n = (int)ext.length();

  String extensions ((char *)glGetString(GL_EXTENSIONS));
  while( !supported )
  {
    //if the extension defined in string 'ext' is within 'extensions'
    if ( extensions.compare(pos, n, ext) >= 0 )
    {
      return true;
    }
    pos = extensions.find(' ' , pos) + 1;
    if( pos <= 0 )
      return false;
  }
  return false;
}
```

After you have determined whether your video hardware can support the desired extension, simply use the `SDL_GL_GetProcAddress` method to grab the necessary function pointer from the OpenGL ICD provided by the video hardware vendor. You learn more about this as you go through some extensions throughout this chapter.

Be careful when using extensions in your game. It is important to verify that the desired extension is supported, along with a backup procedure in case it is not available.

MULTITEXTURING

A common use of the extension mechanism is to query the video hardware for *multitexturing* support. Multitexturing is the practice of combining the data of two or more textures to the same set of vertices.

For example, one common use of multitexturing in a game might be to display scorch marks on a building wall. The data from the scorch texture can be applied to the texture information of the building exterior and presented in one pass through the pipeline.

The OpenGL Architecture Review Board defines multitexturing specification as a set of *texture units* that form a chain. Each texture unit passes its output to the inputs of the next texture unit in the chain until the final product is rasterized to the OpenGL framebuffer. Listing 7.9 details how to query the hardware for multitexturing support.

LISTING 7.9   Querying Extensions for Multitexturing Support

```
//Somewhere in the file, include a definition for the function.
//This can be directly cut and pasted from the glext.h header
//file.
PFNGLMULTITEXCOORD2FARBPROC glMultiTexCoord2fARB = NULL;

//pRenderer is a valid SceneRenderer pointer
if( pRenderer->isExtensionSupported( "GL_ARB_Multitexture" ) )
{
  //the hardware supports this extension, so load the handle to the
  //relevant function using SDL_GL_GetProcAddress
  pglMultiTexCoord2fARB = (PFNGLMULTITEXCOORD2FARBPROC)
  SDL_GL_GetProcAddress("glMultiTexCoord2fARB");

}
```

A possible backup procedure you might want to try if the multitexturing extension is not supported is multipass rendering in which you would set your bottom layer texture, render the quad, set the bottom layer texture again with the overlay, and then re-render the quad again using the same vertices.

Working with the Texture Units

A single texture unit is composed of the texture image, a texture matrix stack, and some filtering parameters, among other useful properties.

Using the `glActiveTextureARB` function, you need to specify the current texture unit that you are assigning any texture parameters. After this, all of the `glTexImage*()`, `glTexParameter*()`, `glTexEnv*()`, `glTexGen*()`, and the `glBindTexture` functions will affect the chosen texture unit.

Since you are applying more than one texture for the surface you are working with, you need a way to define multiple sets of texture coordinates. The `glMultiTexCoord2fARB` function allows you to do this within the current texture unit. You must use this method before you specify the vertex position within the `glBegin`/`glEnd` pair. Listing 7.10 demonstrates one way to accomplish multitexturing taken from the /chapter_07/BasicMultitexturing sample on the CD-ROM.

ON THE CD

LISTING 7.10   Multitexturing

```
//some multitexturing function pointers
PFNGLMULTITEXCOORD2FARBPROC glMultiTexCoord2fARB = NULL;
PFNGLACTIVETEXTUREARBPROC glActiveTextureARB = NULL;
PFNGLCLIENTACTIVETEXTUREARBPROC glClientActiveTextureARB = NULL;
if( peon::EngineCore::getSingleton().getRenderer()-
>isExtensionSupported(
    "GL_ARB_multitexture" ) )
{
    glMultiTexCoord2fARB = (PFNGLMULTITEXCOORD2FARBPROC)
    SDL_GL_GetProcAddress("glMultiTexCoord2fARB");

    glActiveTextureARB = (PFNGLACTIVETEXTUREARBPROC)
    SDL_GL_GetProcAddress("glActiveTextureARB");

    glClientActiveTextureARB = (PFNGLCLIENTACTIVETEXTUREARBPROC)
    SDL_GL_GetProcAddress("glClientActiveTextureARB");

}

//load your textures into OpenGL
SceneRenderer* pRenderer =
EngineCore::getSingleton().getRenderer();
SceneTexture* pTex1 = pRenderer->
    loadImage("data\\textures\\brick.bmp");
```

```
SceneTexture* pTex2 = pRenderer->
  loadImage("data\\textures\\scorch.bmp");


//activate the first texture in the pipeline
glActiveTextureARB(GL_TEXTURE0_ARB);
glEnable(GL_TEXTURE_2D);
glBindTexture( GL_TEXTURE_2D, pTex1->getTex());

//activate the second texture in the pipeline
glActiveTextureARB( GL_TEXTURE1_ARB );
glEnable(GL_TEXTURE_2D);
glBindTexture( GL_TEXTURE_2D, pTex2->getTex());
//add other texture manipulation states here

//render your quad here with multitexturing support!
glBegin(GL_QUADS);
  glNormal3f( 0.0f, 0.0f, 1.0f); //normal coming out of the screen

  glMultiTexCoord2fARB( GL_TEXTURE0_ARB, 1.0f, 1.0f);
  glMultiTexCoord2fARB( GL_TEXTURE1_ARB, 1.0f, 1.0f);
  glVertex3f( 1.0f, 1.0f, 1.0f );

  glMultiTexCoord2fARB( GL_TEXTURE0_ARB, 0.0f, 1.0f);
  glMultiTexCoord2fARB( GL_TEXTURE1_ARB, 0.0f, 1.0f);
  glVertex3f( -1.0f, 1.0f, 1.0f );

  glMultiTexCoord2fARB( GL_TEXTURE0_ARB, 0.0f, 0.0f);
  glMultiTexCoord2fARB( GL_TEXTURE1_ARB, 0.0f, 0.0f);
  glVertex3f( -1.0f, -1.0f, 1.0f );

  glMultiTexCoord2fARB( GL_TEXTURE0_ARB, 1.0f, 0.0f);
  glMultiTexCoord2fARB( GL_TEXTURE1_ARB, 1.0f, 0.0f);
  glVertex3f( 1.0f, -1.0f, 1.0f );
glEnd();
```

CHAPTER EXERCISES

1. Inspect further OpenGL documentation for other uses and properties available in the lighting engine of the API. Experiment with spotlights, ambient effects, and attenuation to create the lighting effect you want and add them to the SceneLight object in the Peon engine.

2. Although you learned only the basics about blending, experiment with different colors, alpha buffer values, and even blending operations to see how they affect the output to your final scene.

3. Be sure to inspect the OpenGL specification for the additional extensions that are available to you. A large number of useful ones available can help to streamline your scene.

SUMMARY

Although you still have not learned every aspect of OpenGL programming, you have quickly been introduced to a lot of topics. It is important to understand the basics first, before you can jump ahead to some more advanced effects that you will learn later in this book. The approach of this chapter was to build upon your basic OpenGL knowledge. You learned about how OpenGL processes commands to light your scene, along with how to use blending operations to create the transparency effect you can use in your games. Vertex arrays are methods that you can use to speed up the vertex rendering within your scene, as they have the capability to cache large batches of vertices that you can specify in the scene or load from a model. You were also introduced to how to query the OpenGL extension mechanism to add multitexturing capabilities to your repertoire. You can now use OpenGL within your game projects. In the next chapter you will learn how to use the OpenGL objects you created in the Peon engine, which will help you understand some basic concepts around scene management and how to improve the rendering performance of your game world.

8 Scene Geometry Management

Chapter Goals

- Introduce the OpenGL depth buffer.
- Introduce view frustum culling.
- Introduce and discuss scene graphs.
- Create a simple scene graph within the Peon engine.

As more objects and state changes in the graphics pipeline start to accumulate in your game world, you will notice scene performance begin to drastically degrade. With the Fixed Function Pipeline model that you have been working with so far, pixel visibility is not determined until the final transformation stage of the pipeline. As your game world data increases, relying on the hardware to process the information is simply not enough, as you are potentially sending thousands of primitives to the pipeline that are not even relevant to the scene. Removing objects and primitives before they reach the pipeline is labeled in a broad sense as "*culling techniques*," which you will learn more of in this chapter.

THE DEPTH BUFFER

The bulk of scene geometry management techniques involves the attempt to organize your scene such that unnecessary pixel information is not sent through the graphics pipeline. Another concept involved in this discussion on geometry management is the theory behind *hidden surface removal*. In a more concrete implementation of hidden surface removal, the OpenGL pipeline provides an additional buffer known as the *depth buffer*. As the pipeline processes the pixel data for the scene to be presented to the video display, the depth information (*z* coordinate) is stored in this buffer which is usually represented as a two dimensional array. As pixel information is added to the array, the hardware determines if another pixel already occupies the same position. If this *z*-coordinate collision is detected, then the hardware will overwrite the location in memory with whichever pixel is closest to the camera. The depth buffer preserves the illusion of depth within a scene by overlapping objects which are further away by objects that are closer to the camera.

Although you will gain much more experience with the depth buffer in OpenGL, you will only ever really need to worry about when to enable or disable it. Using the familiar `glEnable`/`glDisable` commands with the `GL_DEPTH_TEST` parameter, you can enable or disable OpenGL from using the depth information when rendering the scene. Normally you would keep the usage of the depth buffer enabled to maintain proper object depth positioning. A situation where you might think of disabling the depth buffer is when you wish to achieve a transparency effect. For example, an object passing behind a window would require the disabling of the depth buffer in order to ensure the object viewable from the window is not removed from the scene.

VIEW FRUSTUM CULLING

A common method of filtering down the amount of vertices sent through the graphics pipeline is a technique known as *View Frustum culling*. This technique involves taking your view and projection matrices and calculating a bounding box for the entire view volume. If a vertex (or mesh) is marked as being outside of this bounding box, it is not visible by the currently active camera, so you do not need to send it through the pipeline.

In Figure 8.1, the area cone projected by the scene's camera is segmented into six planes.

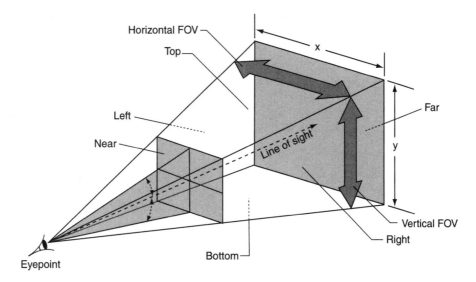

FIGURE 8.1 The camera's View Frustum.

As you can see from Figure 8.1, you need to extract the plane information for the six clipping planes formed by the View Frustum and then use it to test whether or not your vertex lies somewhere within, on, or outside these boundaries (that is, *clipping spaces*).

The SceneCamera object of the Peon engine that was introduced in Chapter 5, "Graphics Programming Mathematics," contains the necessary code for using a View Frustum culler agent with your applications. Please inspect Listing 8.1 for using this culler object.

LISTING 8.1 Calculating the Six Planes of the View Volume

```
void SceneCamera::generateViewFrustum()
{
  float matProj[16];    // projection matrix
  float matView[16];    // model-view matrix
  float mat_mvp[16];    // model-view-projection matrix

  //glGetFloatv with the GL_PROJECTION_MATRIX flag will
  //pull the projection matrix from the FFP.
  glGetFloatv( GL_PROJECTION_MATRIX, matProj );
```

```
              //glGetFloatv with the GL_MODELVIEW_MATRIX flag will pull
              //the view matrix from the FFP.
              glGetFloatv( GL_MODELVIEW_MATRIX, matView );

              // The product of the projection matrix and the model-view matrix
              // produces the concatenated model-view-projection matrix. Note
              //that the Matrix44 object could be used here, but the longhand
              //demonstrates and reinforces the calculations.
              mat_mvp[ 0] = matView[ 0] * matProj[ 0] + matView[ 1] * matProj[
          4] + matView[ 2] *
                  matProj[ 8] + matView[ 3] * matProj[12];

      mat_mvp[ 1] = matView[ 0] * matProj[ 1] + matView[ 1] * matProj[ 5] +
      matView[ 2] * matProj[ 9] + matView[ 3] * matProj[13];
      mat_mvp[ 2] = matView[ 0] * matProj[ 2] + matView[ 1] * matProj[ 6] +
      matView[ 2] * matProj[10] + matView[ 3] * matProj[14];
      mat_mvp[ 3] = matView[ 0] * matProj[ 3] + matView[ 1] * matProj[ 7] +
      matView[ 2] * matProj[11] + matView[ 3] * matProj[15];

      mat_mvp[ 4] = matView[ 4] * matProj[ 0] + matView[ 5] * matProj[ 4] +
      matView[ 6] * matProj[ 8] + matView[ 7] * matProj[12];
      mat_mvp[ 5] = matView[ 4] * matProj[ 1] + matView[ 5] * matProj[ 5] +
      matView[ 6] * matProj[ 9] + matView[ 7] * matProj[13];
      mat_mvp[ 6] = matView[ 4] * matProj[ 2] + matView[ 5] * matProj[ 6] +
      matView[ 6] * matProj[10] + matView[ 7] * matProj[14];
      mat_mvp[ 7] = matView[ 4] * matProj[ 3] + matView[ 5] * matProj[ 7] +
      matView[ 6] * matProj[11] + matView[ 7] * matProj[15];

      mat_mvp[ 8] = matView[ 8] * matProj[ 0] + matView[ 9] * matProj[ 4] +
      matView[10] * matProj[ 8] + matView[11] * matProj[12];
      mat_mvp[ 9] = matView[ 8] * matProj[ 1] + matView[ 9] * matProj[ 5] +
      matView[10] * matProj[ 9] + matView[11] * matProj[13];
      mat_mvp[10] = matView[ 8] * matProj[ 2] + matView[ 9] * matProj[ 6] +
      matView[10] * matProj[10] + matView[11] * matProj[14];
      mat_mvp[11] = matView[ 8] * matProj[ 3] + matView[ 9] * matProj[ 7] +
      matView[10] * matProj[11] + matView[11] * matProj[15];

      mat_mvp[12] = matView[12] * matProj[ 0] + matView[13] * matProj[ 4] +
      matView[14] * matProj[ 8] + matView[15] * matProj[12];
      mat_mvp[13] = matView[12] * matProj[ 1] + matView[13] * matProj[ 5] +
      matView[14] * matProj[ 9] + matView[15] * matProj[13];
      mat_mvp[14] = matView[12] * matProj[ 2] + matView[13] * matProj[ 6] +
      matView[14] * matProj[10] + matView[15] * matProj[14];
```

```
mat_mvp[15] = matView[12] * matProj[ 3] + matView[13] * matProj[ 7] +
matView[14] * matProj[11] + matView[15] * matProj[15];

    // This will extract the RIGHT side of the frustum
    m_oFrustum[RIGHT].normal.x = mat_mvp[ 3] - mat_mvp[ 0];
    m_oFrustum[RIGHT].normal.y = mat_mvp[ 7] - mat_mvp[ 4];
    m_oFrustum[RIGHT].normal.z = mat_mvp[11] - mat_mvp[ 8];
    m_oFrustum[RIGHT].d = mat_mvp[15] - mat_mvp[12];

    // normalize the RIGHT Plane using the a,b,c and d components
    m_oFrustum[RIGHT].normalise();

    // This will extract the LEFT Plane of the frustum
    m_oFrustum[LEFT].normal.x = mat_mvp[ 3] + mat_mvp[ 0];
    m_oFrustum[LEFT].normal.y = mat_mvp[ 7] + mat_mvp[ 4];
    m_oFrustum[LEFT].normal.z = mat_mvp[11] + mat_mvp[ 8];
    m_oFrustum[LEFT].d = mat_mvp[15] + mat_mvp[12];

    // normalize the LEFT Plane
    m_oFrustum[LEFT].normalise();

    // This will extract the BOTTOM Plane of the frustum
    m_oFrustum[BOTTOM].normal.x = mat_mvp[ 3] + mat_mvp[ 1];
    m_oFrustum[BOTTOM].normal.y = mat_mvp[ 7] + mat_mvp[ 5];
    m_oFrustum[BOTTOM].normal.z = mat_mvp[11] + mat_mvp[ 9];
    m_oFrustum[BOTTOM].d = mat_mvp[15] + mat_mvp[13];

    // Normalize the BOTTOM Plane
    m_oFrustum[BOTTOM].normalise();

    // This will extract the TOP Plane of the frustum
    m_oFrustum[TOP].normal.x = mat_mvp[ 3] - mat_mvp[ 1];
    m_oFrustum[TOP].normal.y = mat_mvp[ 7] - mat_mvp[ 5];
    m_oFrustum[TOP].normal.z = mat_mvp[11] - mat_mvp[ 9];
    m_oFrustum[TOP].d = mat_mvp[15] - mat_mvp[13];

    // Normalize the TOP Plane
    m_oFrustum[TOP].normalise();

    // This will extract the BACK Plane of the frustum
    m_oFrustum[BACK].normal.x = mat_mvp[ 3] - mat_mvp[ 2];
    m_oFrustum[BACK].normal.y = mat_mvp[ 7] - mat_mvp[ 6];
    m_oFrustum[BACK].normal.z = mat_mvp[11] - mat_mvp[10];
    m_oFrustum[BACK].d = mat_mvp[15] - mat_mvp[14];
```

```
// Normalize the BACK Plane
m_oFrustum[BACK].normalise();

// This will extract the FRONT Plane of the frustum
m_oFrustum[FRONT].normal.x = mat_mvp[ 3] + mat_mvp[ 2];
m_oFrustum[FRONT].normal.y = mat_mvp[ 7] + mat_mvp[ 6];
m_oFrustum[FRONT].normal.z = mat_mvp[11] + mat_mvp[10];
m_oFrustum[FRONT].d = mat_mvp[15] + mat_mvp[14];

// Normalize the FRONT Plane
m_oFrustum[FRONT].normalise();
}
```

After you have obtained your six View Frustum planes, you can begin testing where the bounding sphere around each mesh is in relation to the clipping planes. Listing 8.2 demonstrates one way to accomplish this using the math you will learn about in Chapter 13, "Collision Detection and Physics Techniques."

LISTING 8.2 Testing Bounding Sphere with the Plane

```
bool SceneCamera::isSphereInFrustum( float x, float y, float z,
  float fRadius )
{
  for( int i = 0; i < 6; ++i )
  {
    if( m_oFrustum[i].normal.x * x +
        m_oFrustum [i].normal.y * y +
        m_oFrustum [i].normal.z * z +
        m_oFrustum [i].d <= -fRadius )
        return false;
  }
  return true;
}
```

ON THE CD
Check the /chapter_08/BasicViewFrustum sample contained on the CD-ROM. You will be able to enable or disable the View Frustum testing to see for yourself how performance is affected.

BASIC SCENE HIERARCHY MANAGEMENT

While the View Frustum culling technique is an important addition to your graphics repertoire, there is still room for improvement, as you are always processing every mesh within the game world through the View Frustum calculations no matter where the relative positions are from the player.

In order to improve this process, most 3D engines create and use a hierarchy structure to organize and model mesh and primitive data within the game world. These hierarchy approaches are known as *scene graphs,* and they can offer a tremendous performance boost to your application.

Most scene graphs are modeled as a tree structure also known as *directed acyclic graphs* (DAGs) since scene graphs cannot contain cycles. DAG structures are formed such that a single parent node can have up to *n* child nodes, which can themselves be parents to other children. Child nodes lower down in the hierarchy are forbidden from then attempting to become parents to nodes higher up on the graph, which would form a *cycle* (or a loop). Each child node can contain the objects you want to draw along with other information that you are about to learn. Figure 8.2 details a simple DAG structure.

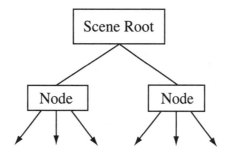

FIGURE 8.2   Simple DAG structure.

The immediate benefit to this approach of scene construction can be seen when you want to add large structures such as office buildings to your game world. Each building could itself contain *n* number of nodes that represent each room. Each room could then contain many child nodes, which describe any object in the room such as a table, desk, chair, cactus, and so forth. If the entire building is marked as invisible to the player, then there is no need to process any child nodes within the structure. Figure 8.3 presents this simple graph.

An additional benefit to using scene graphs is also realized when you attempt to move or manipulate the parent node object. Each child node will then move to follow the parent, which saves you from having to recompute any transform operations should you be forced to move objects within the game world.

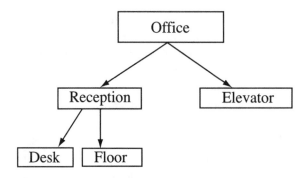

FIGURE 8.3 Simple office scene graph.

For example, in the office building scene, if you move your desk you tend to also keep your lamp, monitor, and other desk accessories.

Sorting Rendering States

Using a scene graph approach to contain your world objects not only can increase rendering performance of your scene, but it can also serve to minimize any unnecessary state changes within the graphics pipeline itself. Usually any change of state within the graphics pipeline such as setting a texture, or adjusting lighting or fog calculations, has an associated cost of performance on your 3D hardware. Even on the newest hardware available, it is always a benefit to your game to minimize as many state changes as possible.

For a real-world example, imagine that you are rendering a large collection of similar objects such as a fleet of jet fighters. Each jet fighter will have a multitude of m state changes in order to properly render its craft texture, rubber tires, metallic landing gears, and so on. Without any sorting, the pipeline might need to make $m \times n$ state changes (m states multiplied by n fighter jets). Compare this to a state sorting algorithm approach in which you could instead keep the current state to render each appropriate section of the n fighter jets (that is, render all the rubber tires and then all the landing gears, and so on). This would then reduce your necessary rendering state changes to an $m \times 1$ algorithm.

Animation Rendering

Using a scene graph approach can also aid with rendering or manipulating any animated meshes. The animation can be constructed in the hierarchy to allow easy calculation of any transforms that need to be applied to various nodes in the graph.

For example, your player mesh within the game world probably will contain two arms and two legs connected by a torso. Several animations can be rendered, depending upon the associative state in which the player is currently. There might be walking, running, death animations, and so forth. After you have calculated which state the player is in, you can then transform each child node of your player mesh to perform the desired animation.

INTRODUCTION TO THE PEON SCENE GRAPH

You should now be able to create your own rudimentary node hierarchy to process your scene objects.

You begin with the SceneRoot and ISceneNode base object definitions within the Peon game engine. The basic algorithm the scene manager follows is to traverse each ISceneNode object in the hierarchy and adjust the rendering pipeline accordingly. At a high level your game objects should all fit somewhere within the hierarchy to allow for smooth rendering and collision detection. Listing 8.3 details the base element of the graph, the ISceneNode.

LISTING 8.3 ISceneNode.h

```
namespace peon
{
  /**
   * This object is used as our base root interface for anything
   * that needs to be added to the scene hierarchy */
  class PEONMAIN_API ISceneNode : public IUnknown
  {
    protected:
      /** Is this node visible? */
      bool              m_bIsVisible;

      /** The parent node */
      ISceneNode*       m_pParentNode;

      /** Linked list of our child nodes */
      std::list<ISceneNode*>  m_oChildrenNodes;

      /** This method is used to prepare the node for rendering.
       * Last minute state changes, etc. should be done here */
      virtual void onPreRender();
```

```
      /** This method is used to render the node. */
      virtual void onRender();

      /** Add a child node to our list */
      virtual void addChildNode(ISceneNode* pChild);

      /** Drop a child node from this current node */
      virtual void dropNode(ISceneNode* pChild);

       /** snip! */
   };
 }
```

The ISceneNode is an abstract base class entity that contains the common set of methods and variables that all nodes within the scene graph will share. Any ISceneNode object can be a parent to a hierarchy of child nodes, while also being a child node itself within the scene graph. One of the strengths of a hierarchy approach to object management such as this is that if you should mark one node in the tree as invisible, then the scene graph manager should skip the processing of all the child nodes.

The SceneRoot object within the Peon engine contains not only the top-most node of the graph, known as the *root node*, but also a host of useful objects for processing and rendering the graph. Listing 8.4 details the SceneRoot object.

LISTING 8.4 SceneRoot.h

```
namespace peon
{
  /** This object represents the topmost (or bottom-most) node
  * of the scene hierarchy tree.
  */
  class PEONMAIN_API SceneRoot : public ISingleton<SceneRoot>,
    public ISceneNode
  {
  public:
    /** Constructor */
    SceneRoot( SceneRenderer* pRenderer );
    /** Destructor */
    ~SceneRoot();
    /** return a reference to this object */
    static SceneRoot& getSingleton(void);
```

```
        /** return a pointer to this object */
        static SceneRoot* getSingletonPtr(void);
        /** snip! */
    };
}
```

As you can see, this object implements the Singleton design pattern. You want only one scene graph within your game at a time, and this is an easy way to implement this. During the first instantiation of this object, you will need to pass a handle to the SceneRenderer interface, which will be used to render the nodes in the graph as they are traversed.

Scene Graph States

As you learn more about what a scene graph is and what it can provide for your application, an important consideration is any rendering state information. Conceptually, the scene graph contains not only the objects within your scene, but also any necessary transformations and rendering state information to render those objects. In other words, it is not enough to store the object you want to insert into the hierarchy; you also need to specify exactly how this object will appear.

Scene Graph Passes

To maximize the efficiency of the rendering process behind the scene graph, you will need some way of sorting the nodes of the graph by either the type of node or the requested rendering operation for the node. This is important, as you could potentially have a real mix of techniques and meshes within the same scene at one time. For example, for a scene involving many objects of a similar type, you can optimize the processing by generally sorting the scene objects by the texture, then by any buffered vertex information. Keeping in mind your introduction to the OpenGL pipeline, you should attempt to minimize state switching as much as possible.

In other words, by sorting the scene by texture, you can achieve something like:

- Select Alien Ship texture handle
- For each Alien Ship, render vertices

Instead of a situation that is largely unoptimized and problematic:

- For each Alien Ship: select Alien Ship texture and then render the vertices

Optimizing the scene graph is beyond the scope of this material, however the preceding should be kept in mind when attempting to find any performance critical areas.

Scene Graph Traversal

For processing the nodes in the scene graph, either during rendering passes or for animation and collision, you will need a somewhat efficient method to traverse the data structure. You were just introduced to the concepts on minimizing state changes within the graphics pipeline, and so this must be kept in mind when performing any scene traversal. You must also remember to flag nodes, which are not visible as there is no point in traversing the tree to any child nodes, when the parent object cannot be seen by the player. The algorithm that you will use for the scene graph traversal is meant to be quite simple.

For each node in the hierarchy, the tree first determines whether it is visible or not to the player.

If it is visible, then check which node type it is. If the node is a render state, then process the render state commands. Otherwise, if it is an opaque (solid) object, add it to the solid objects display list. If the object is transparent, then add it to the transparent display list.

To render the scene graph you would then process each list, first applying the necessary OpenGL render state commands. Next you would then process each opaque object. Finally, you would then render the transparent objects in the scene.

BINARY SPACE PARTITIONING TREES

Binary Space Partitioning trees (BSP trees) were first made popular as a graphics data structure with the release of *Wolf3D* and *Doom* by Id Software. Although they might not make an appearance in every 3D graphics application, they can still have their place in the majority of engines made today depending upon your game world layout.

Typically when using a BSP for your level or scene, you would create a separate BSP compiler responsible for taking the map data and compiling it into a binary format (known as a *WAD* for the Id games), which the engine can then use for the traversal/rendering process. In the case of *Wolf3D* and *Doom*, these two components were separated so that the level builders could build and test their levels without the reliance of the engine.

OCTREE DATA STRUCTURE

You can also create a hierarchy that subdivides the scene into eight smaller segments, which is referred to as an *octree*. The purpose of this structure is to allow for an increase of complexity to your scene, while at the same time reducing the overhead for object visibility calculations. See Figure 8.4, which presents the theoretical view of your octree.

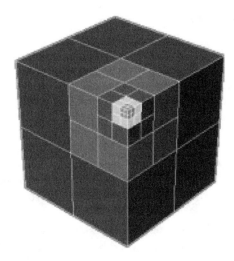

FIGURE 8.4   Octree visualization.

Building Your Octree

Although somewhat intensive, the algorithm first cycles through every vertex in the scene adding the x, y, and z components together. When this is done, the center point of the world is calculated by dividing each component by the total number of vertices in the scene. This information becomes used as the overall encompassing cube, which you then subdivide in your data structure.

The Occluder Query

Although you have touched upon a large number of algorithms used for culling objects before they are passed into the graphics pipeline, there is still definite room for improvement. Most geometry management techniques either want to cull too many objects, or too few of them, still leaving a large amount of meshes to be sent through the pipeline.

One facet that you have not yet heard about is the concept of *occluders*. Occluders are objects within the scene which partially or fully block the camera from seeing other objects. Usually an occluder is a large block or building that hides other smaller buildings behind it.

This is important. Although these small objects pass the View Frustum test, they will not be seen by the player, even though the pipeline must process them.

To this extent, the OpenGL ARB has released a small handy occluder extension, the `GL_ARB_occlusion_query`. Listing 8.5 defines the function pointer prototypes that you will need to use when querying for the extension.

LISTING 8.5 Occluder Extension Basics

```
PFNGLGENQUERIESARBPROC       glGenQueriesARB        = NULL;
PFNGLDELETEQUERIESARBPROC    glDeleteQueriesARB     = NULL;
PFNGLISQUERYARBPROC          glIsQueryARB           = NULL;
PFNGLBEGINQUERYARBPROC       glBeginQueryARB        = NULL;
PFNGLENDQUERYARBPROC         glEndQueryARB          = NULL;
PFNGLGETQUERYIVARBPROC       glGetQueryivARB        = NULL;
PFNGLGETQUERYOBJECTIVARBPROC glGetQueryObjectivARB  = NULL;
PFNGLGETQUERYOBJECTUIVARBPROC glGetQueryObjectuivARB = NULL;
```

The first task is to query which extensions are available to you. Listing 8.6 documents this, although you should be familiar with the code now.

LISTING 8.6 Querying for Occlusion Query Support

```
//pRenderer is a pre-defined SceneRenderer
if( !pRenderer->isExtensionSupported( "GL_ARB_occlusion_query") )
{
  //you just do not have the necessary updated drivers.
  //return nicely...
  return false;
}

//initialize the function pointers to grab the needed extension
//methods from the vendor provided OpenGL dll..
glGenQueriesARB = (PFNGLGENQUERIESARBPROC)
  SDL_GL_GetProcAddress ("glGenQueriesARB");

glDeleteQueriesARB = (PFNGLDELETEQUERIESARBPROC)
  SDL_GL_GetProcAddress ("glDeleteQueriesARB");

glIsQueryARB        = (PFNGLISQUERYARBPROC)
  SDL_GL_GetProcAddress ("glIsQueryARB");

glBeginQueryARB     = (PFNGLBEGINQUERYARBPROC)
  SDL_GL_GetProcAddress ("glBeginQueryARB");
```

```
glEndQueryARB          = (PFNGLENDQUERYARBPROC)
  SDL_GL_GetProcAddress ("glEndQueryARB");

glGetQueryivARB        = (PFNGLGETQUERYIVARBPROC)
  SDL_GL_GetProcAddress ("glGetQueryivARB");

glGetQueryObjectivARB  = (PFNGLGETQUERYOBJECTIVARBPROC)
  SDL_GL_GetProcAddress ("glGetQueryObjectivARB");

glGetQueryObjectuivARB = (PFNGLGETQUERYOBJECTUIVARBPROC)
  SDL_GL_GetProcAddress ("glGetQueryObjectuivARB");
```

The next step is to generate some occlusion query handles that will store the occlusion calculations. Listing 8.7 shows how this is accomplished.

LISTING 8.7   Generate Occlusion Query Handles

```
GLuint planeQuery = -1;
GLuint boxQuery   = -1;

//generate the query objects for the plane and the box
//looks similar to generating texture handles..
glGenQueriesARB( 1, &boxQuery );
glGenQueriesARB( 1, &planeQuery );
```

Occlusion Query Algorithm

The Occlusion Query algorithm is fairly straightforward but can sound a little awkward at first. You first render every object in the scene in order to capture their z positions in the depth buffer. Next, you render every object in the scene again so that the occlusion query can determine the object's visibility status. If the resultant query finds zero pixels are visible for an object, then it is culled from the scene. Listing 8.8 demonstrates how this is done with the box and plane objects you have in the scene.

LISTING 8.8   Rendering Process using Occlusion Culling

```
glClear( GL_COLOR_BUFFER_BIT | GL_DEPTH_BUFFER_BIT );

glMatrixMode( GL_MODELVIEW );
glLoadIdentity();
glTranslatef( 0.0f, 0.0f, -1.5f );
```

```
//first render your objects to capture their z-buffer information

//render the plane

//render the box

//now render the objects again but wrap them inside the occluder
//objects
glBeginQueryARB( GL_SAMPLES_PASSED_ARB, planeQuery );
{
  //render the plane
}
glEndQueryARB( GL_SAMPLES_PASSED_ARB );

//render the box
glBeginQueryARB( GL_SAMPLES_PASSED_ARB, boxQuery );
{
  //render the box
}
glEndQueryARB( GL_SAMPLES_PASSED_ARB );

SDL_GL_SwapBuffers();
```

Cleanup

Do not forget to clean up and deallocate the occluder queries you used in this sample. Listing 8.9 demonstrates it.

LISTING 8.9   Occlusion Cleanup

```
glDeleteQueriesARB( 1, &boxQuery );
glDeleteQueriesARB( 1, &planeQuery );
```

CHAPTER EXERCISES

1. The scene graph algorithms outlined in this chapter are a basic approach to scene graph uses. Feel free to investigate how to optimize the necessary objects to increase the scene performance.
2. Another technique known as portal rendering exists to help out with a level containing both indoor and outdoor geometry. Is the portal rendering technique efficient for every type of scene or level? Why, or why not?

3. After working with the `GL_ARB_occlusion_query` extension, list some advantages and disadvantages you think the algorithm might have. Do you have any suggestions on how to improve it?
4. Create a small program that will use the occlusion query extension. Create a way to enable and disable the occlusion query to verify how it affects the scene's performance.

SUMMARY

Properly organizing and constructing the geometry involved in your scene can be a critical factor in determining how fast you are able to render the game world. Simply relying on the video hardware to do the work for you is not good enough, and often one or more software organizations are necessary. You have learned about the OpenGL depth buffer, binary space partition trees, and the octree model of scene organization. Although there are many other techniques out there for geometry management, the ones you learned about here are a good selection and starting point for any graphics programmer.

You also learned some more useful objects from the Peon engine, which allow you to construct a hierarchical scene graph of your game world that makes it easier to both perform View Frustum calculations and render the objects in the scene. One of the primary aspects of a game is the quick feedback you receive when you use an input device to control your player in the game world. In the next chapter, you focus on adding most of the graphics components involved in the *SuperAsteroidArena* project.

9 Graphics Timebox

Chapter Goals

- Add some basic objects to *SuperAsteroidArena*.
- Implement some textured font rendering to display text.

It is finally time to add some graphics to your *SuperAsteroidArena* project. If you recall, in Chapter 5, "Graphics Programming Mathematics," you started to create a basic skeleton for the game. At this point, you should have a basic application window along with some stub IApplicationState instances for managing the state of the game.

TIMEBOX REQUIREMENTS

Before you can begin work implementing new features in the *SuperAsteroidArena* project, you will now create some requirements for this timebox. After you checkout the design document from the CVS repository, the approach of this timebox is to implement some basic graphics support for the game. A list of requirements you might consider in a first draft approach is as follows:

- Display some text to the player.
- Display the asteroids to the player.
- Display the player's ship.
- Present the starfield background.
- Create some buttons on the main menu for the player.

This is a good requirement list so far and will keep you busy for the majority of this timebox.

THE LOGOSTATE

Referring to the design document, the purpose of the LogoState is to display your company logo (or personal name) before the main title screen. This state is optional and is purely left to your own discretion. This state is currently composed of the following items, which are presented to the player:

- A starfield background
- Black "letterbox" bars on the top and bottom strips of the screen
- A company logo

THE MAINMENUSTATE

From the design document, the basic purpose of the main menu screen is to provide the player with an entry point for your game. In the previous timebox covered in Chapter 3, "Introduction to SDL and Windows," you initially created some stub state objects, which are acting as placeholders within your game application. In this timebox, you will now add some meat to these stubs.

The first state you will focus on is the MainMenuState object. This encapsulates the main menu of your game, which is the first state of the game that accepts player input. Upon entering this state, the player will be presented with the following:

- A starfield background
- Some slowly moving asteroids
- The main title of the game
- A menu of buttons for the player

Loading Common Data

For each application state that you have been presented with thus far, there are quite a few common objects that are shared among each state. For example, it seems pointless for each state to create its own Skybox object, when you can create it once and share it among each state. To centralize and simplify working with some of these common graphics elements, you can create a new object for the game; the GraphicsResourceManager.

This object will be responsible for acting as a common hub or datastore for your texture data and other common graphics artifacts. Listing 9.1 details an outline of the manager for you.

LISTING 9.1 GraphicsResourceManager.h

```
namespace arena
{
  /**
  * This object is a "wrapper" object around the graphics
  * objects that we'll need for the game. This way we can
  * try to provide some abstraction layer in case we want to alter
  * how our graphics are rendering.
  */
  class GraphicsResourceManager : public peon::IUnknown
  {
  protected:
    peon::SceneRenderer*    m_pRenderer;
    peon::SceneTexture      m_oTextures[ARENA_MAX_TEXTURES];
    peon::SceneFont*        m_pConsoleFont;
  public:
    GraphicsResourceManager();
    ~GraphicsResourceManager();

    bool loadManager();
    void unloadManager();

    peon::Renderer* getRenderer(){ return m_pRenderer; }
    peon::Texture*  getTexture(int tex){ return &m_oTextures[tex];
}
    peon::TextureFont* getConsoleFont(){ return m_pConsoleFont; }
  };
}
```

For every object that you want to render to the screen, you will need to load the respective texture information. In the `onLoadWorld` method of this application, you will load every texture needed for the background, title screen, and the asteroids themselves. Listing 9.2 demonstrates how this is done within the `MainApp::onLoad-World` method.

LISTING 9.2   bool `MainApp::onLoadWorld`

```
bool MainApp::onLoadWorld()
{
//load textures, display lists and font stuff here
//Everything should be done in the GraphicsResourceManager
m_pGraphicsResourceManager = new GraphicsResourceManager();
if(!m_pGraphicsResourceManager->loadManager())
{
  //there was an error
  return false;
}

return true;
}
```

Rendering the Starfield

One of the first steps you will make in this timebox is to render the background starfield to the game player. Although this is an easy task, it is a good thing to get out of the way as soon as possible in order to provide you with some feedback that the game is starting to take shape. The texture information was loaded during the `onLoadWorld` method of the `MainApp`, and the display list for the background was loaded and compiled as well during this initialization. Listing 9.3 demonstrates how to render the starfield.

LISTING 9.3   onRender()

```
void MainMenuState::onRender()
{
  //render the skybox
  m_pSkybox->onRender();
}
```

Rendering Text to the Player

Adding text support to your game is an important asset and can help provide some feedback of the game's current state along with displaying any helpful messages to the player. You were introduced to the SceneFont object of the Peon library in Chapter 6, "Creating an OpenGL Renderer."

Listing 9.4 demonstrates one way to do this within the GraphicsResourceManager.

LISTING 9.4   Loading the SceneFont

```
//snip
m_pFontTexture = peon::EngineCore::getSingleton().getRenderer()->
    loadTexture("data\\textures\\font.png");
m_pFont = peon::EngineCore::getSingleton().getRenderer()->loadFont();
//snip
```

Creating the Graphical User Interface

Although it is sometimes tackled fairly late in the project schedule, the presentation of an interface to your player for manipulating game data is an important and often critical component of any entertainment product. Reflect on any game you have excitedly purchased in the store, only to install it at home and proceed to fight with the controls in order to enjoy the game to its fullest. The *Graphical User Interface* (GUI, pronounced as "Goo-ey") defines the layout and presentation style of any components that are used by the player to interface with the game.

Although it is certainly possible to create your own set of GUI tools, it can be an arduous process for the beginner to tackle. Luckily for you there is a clean library of GUI objects that allow you to quickly create a mechanism for your player to interact with the game. In most beginner projects, the GUI system is reduced to a collection of buttons that allow the player to change the state of the game in a primitive way. This can even be as simple as providing a main menu that displays a Quit button to exit the game. Depending upon the requirements of the game itself, this simple system can be sufficient. The *Crazy Eddie GUI* toolkit (CEGUI) was created for this very purpose: to allow you to get back to working on your game content, as opposed to spending time on fiddling with GUI controls. The cross-platform CEGUI toolkit contains more than enough quality GUI widgets which allow you to present buttons, text boxes, and list boxes along with a host of other useful objects.

Initializing the CEGUI Library

The CEGUI system is meant to be a fast and simple toolkit to incorporate in any project. As such, there is not much that you need to set up or configure when using the library. The first step of using the toolkit is to create a renderer object with which you can present the CEGUI widgets. Listing 9.5 details how this is done.

LISTING 9.5   Initializing CEGUI

```
//first create a renderer to use. Although the toolkit also supports
//Direct3D, you will need the OpenGL interface.
int width = EngineCore::getSingleton().getRenderer()->getWidth();
int height = EngineCore::getSingleton().getRenderer()->getHeight();
CEGUI::OpenGLRenderer* renderer = new
CEGUI::OpenGLRenderer(0,width,height);

//you next initialize the CEGUI::System singleton object by using this
//created renderer.
new CEGUI::System(renderer);
```

This is all that is needed to set up the CEGUI subsystem. Please inspect more of the source code of the *SuperAsteroidArena* project for further details.

THE ACTIVESTATE

After you have finished adding the necessary components for displaying your objects in the MainMenuState, the game will switch to the ActiveState if the player decides to either start a new single-player game or join an existing multiplayer session. Most of the objects that you need to render have already been created.

TIMEBOX EVALUATION

With the addition of most of the preliminary graphics assets into your game, you should sit down with your original design documentation and evaluate this timebox. Make some observations as to whether or not your requirements for this phase were met. Are you satisfied with the workings of the GUI system so far? Is it legible and easy to use? Even though a game like *SuperAsteroidArena* requires only a few buttons, are they properly arranged (with necessary spacing, padding, positioning, and so on)? Are you satisfied with the art assets you are using so far, such as the background or the player/asteroid textures?

If anything needs to be changed or altered, update the documentation and create a new timebox to reflect the decision.

CHAPTER EXERCISES

1. Experiment with some different textures for your game thus far. Add a favorite background or even alter the asteroid texture to either increase or decrease the level of realism.
2. Work with the different states defined in your game so far to have different instructions provided for the player depending on the state.
3. Experiment with different font textures to find one that fits your design.
4. Experiment with your GUI design. Is it intuitive? In other words, can the player simply sit down and "live" your game world without the need of a readme file or instruction manual?

SUMMARY

You have built an even stronger OpenGL foundation from which to work and have added some very useful objects to your Peon repertoire. Although the game is still in its infancy, you were able to add some basic display objects to the *SuperAsteroidArena* project. You were also able to add some basic font support to the engine, allowing you to load and display text using any character font texture. Although you need much more added to the game, it is exciting to see some results happening before your eyes!

With the graphics foundation already covered, the next chapter focuses on working with the input devices that are used by the player to interact with your game.

10 ∷ Working with Input Devices

Chapter Goals

- Introduce acquiring basic input using SDL.
- Introduce and explain how to process keyboard, mouse, and joystick events.

As you move forward with the creation and evolution of the game engine, you will eventually need to provide a way for the player to interact with the game world. Whether this is through the keyboard, mouse, or joystick input devices, your game must respond to the player in a timely fashion.

INTRODUCTION TO INPUT USING SDL

Since the SDL is a cross-platform game programming library, you do not need to concern yourself with working with any underlying hardware device layer. The SDL does the grunt work of creating and initializing your input devices, using some platform-specific code that you do need to worry about.

What is important, however, is how you access the input devices within your game. Besides being able to view objects within your game world, the next critical component of your game to the player is how well it responds to input. Months of hard work on the game can evaporate in seconds if the control response is sluggish or completely unusable. When the player presses a key or moves the joystick, the resulting action should feel near-instantaneous.

As with a lot of the components of the SDL, you need to respond to specific event messages that are sent to the event queue when the player performs an input action. In other words, every time you press a key on the keyboard, a key event message is generated within SDL, and it is sent to your main event queue for processing.

Using the Keyboard

When the input subsystem is initialized by the SDL, you need to worry about processing keyboard event messages generated by the player. When the player triggers an event by pressing or releasing a key, an SDL_Event structure is generated and dumped into the event queue of the main loop. Listing 10.1 provides you with an idea of what this structure looks like.

LISTING 10.1 SDL_KeyboardEvent Structure

```
typedef struct
{
  Uint8 type;        //SDL_KEYDOWN or SDL_KEYUP
  Uint8 state;       //SDL_PRESSED or SDL_RELEASED
  SDL_keysym keysym; //the data containing the scan code and name
} SDL_KeyboardEvent;
```

To discover which key was pressed or released, you can dig through the event message, as done in Listing 10.2.

LISTING 10.2 Digging through the Keyboard SDL_Event

```
SDL_Event event;
while( SDL_PollEvent( &event ) )
{
  // We are only looking for the SDL_KEYDOWN and SDL_KEYUP events
  switch( event.type )
  {
    case SDL_KEYDOWN:
    case SDL_KEYUP:
      DisplayKeyInfo( &event.key );
    break;
```

```
          default:
          break;
      }
  }
```

As you can see, the event queue is waiting to receive the SDL_KEYDOWN or SDL_KEYUP event messages, which are generated when the player presses or releases a key. With closer examination of the SDL_EVENT reference passed to the DisplayKeyInfo function in Listing 10.2, you can easily test which key was pressed or released. Listing 10.3 has an example of this.

LISTING 10.3 DisplayKeyInfo

```
void DisplayKeyInfo( SDL_KeyboardEvent *key )
{
  // Is it a release or a press?
  if( key->type == SDL_KEYUP )
    OutputDebugString( "Release:- " );
  else
    OutputDebugString( "Press:- " );

  // Print the hardware scancode
  OutputDebugString( "Scancode: 0x%02X", key->keysym.scancode );

  // Print the name of the key
  OutputDebugString( ", Name: %s\n",
    SDL_GetKeyName( key->keysym.sym ) );

}
```

The *scancode* of the key event message refers to the hexadecimal value of the key pressed, which is what you need to use for determining what action the player intends to perform.

Using the Mouse

Similar to the method you use to process and detect keyboard events, an SDL_Event structure is also generated for every mouse action. Since you need to respond not only to mouse movements, but the different mouse buttons as well, processing the mouse event message is slightly more complicated than the keyboard.

Listing 10.4 and Listing 10.5 document the two SDL_Event structures you need to handle in the event queue: the SDL_MouseMotionEvent and the SDL_MouseButtonEvent.

LISTING 10.4   `SDL_MouseMotionEvent` **Structure**

```
typedef struct
{
  Uint8 type;        //SDL_MOUSEMOTION
  Uint8 state;       //the current button state of the mouse
  Uint16 x, y;       //the current x and y coordinates of the mouse
  Sint16 xrel, yrel; //the relative motion in x and y direction
} SDL_MouseMotionEvent;
```

After you have an idea of what kind of data this structure is grabbing from the mouse, you can query the main event queue for the `SDL_MouseButtonEvent` message as well, as shown in Listing 10.5.

LISTING 10.5   `SDL_MouseButtonEvent` **Structure**

```
typedef struct
{
  Uint8 type; //SDL_MOUSEBUTTONUP or SDL_MOUSEBUTTONDOWN
  Uint8 button; //the button index (left, middle or right button)
  Uint8 state; //SDL_PRESSED or SDL_RELEASED
  Uint16 x, y; //the coordinates at the time the button was pressed
} SDL_MouseButtonEvent;
```

The new event queue could appear somewhat similar to Listing 10.2, only you can now process any events generated by the mouse. An example is shown for you in Listing 10.6.

LISTING 10.6   Event Queue with `SDL_Mouse` Support

```
SDL_Event event;
while( SDL_PollEvent( &event ) )
{
  int x, y;
Uint8 button;
  switch( event.type )
  {
    //The SDL_MOUSEBUTTON message is sent to the queue when SDL
detects
    //that you've pressed a mouse button.
    case SDL_MOUSEBUTTON:
      //do some button action
      if(event.button & SDL_BUTTON(1))
      {
```

```
              strcat( m_strMouseInfo, "  LMB");
          }else if(button & SDL_BUTTON(3))
          {
              strcat( m_strMouseInfo, "  RMB");
          }

          break;

          //The SDL_MOUSEMOTION message is sent to the queue when SDL
    detects
          //mouse movement
          case SDL_MOUSEMOTION:
            //do some motion action
            // Get the mouse's current X,Y position
            SDL_GetMouseState(&x, &y);
          sprintf(m_strMouseInfo, "Mouse Position (x,y): ( %d, %d )", x,
    y);

          break;

          default:
          break;
      }
    }
```

Using the Joystick

Listing 10.6 demonstrates how to initialize the joystick subsystem contained with the SDL. This performs any low-level operating system-specific methods to set up a way to reference one or more joysticks attached to the computer.

LISTING 10.6   Joystick Subsystem Initialization

```
    if( SDL_Init( SDL_INIT_JOYSTICK ) < 0)
    {
     //return error code
    }
```

Joystick Enumeration

Before you can use the joystick within your application, it is necessary to allow the joystick subsystem to enumerate (or discover) the available joysticks connected to the computer.

A useful function available to you is the SDL_NumJoysticks method that queries the machine for the number of connected joysticks. This is a quick filter you can use before you bother with any more joystick initialization functions, as shown in Listing 10.7.

LISTING 10.7 Using SDL_NumJoysticks

```
bool joystick_found = true;
int joystick_count = 0;

joystick_count = SDL_NumJoysticks();
if(joystick_count <= 0)
{
  joystick_found = false;
  return false;
}
```

Opening a Joystick

Before you can capture any data from the joystick, you first need to properly initialize it within SDL. A joystick is encapsulated by the SDL_Joystick object and acts as a container of sorts for the polled joystick data. You use the SDL_JoystickOpen method as demonstrated in Listing 10.8.

LISTING 10.8 Obtaining a Valid SDL_Joystick

```
SDL_Joystick* pJoy = NULL;
if( joystick_found)
{
  pJoy = SDL_JoystickOpen( 0 );
  if(pJoy != NULL)
  {
    printf("Name: %s\n", SDL_JoystickName(0));
    printf("Number of Axes: %d\n", SDL_JoystickNumAxes(joy));
    printf("Number of Buttons: %d\n", SDL_JoystickNumButtons(joy));
  }
}
```

Processing Joystick Events

Working with joystick data is somewhat different from working with input data received from the keyboard or mouse. Under the SDL, there are two choices for obtaining joystick data: the event queue or polling the joystick directly. To remain within the event queue paradigm, you will learn how to process joystick events through the main queue.

To signal to SDL that you want to use the event queue to handle the joystick event messages, you need to use the SDL_JoystickEventState method with a parameter of SDL_ENABLE. If you were to launch the program now as is, your main event queue would get flooded with quite a bit of garbage joystick data. You need to set a minimum threshold that the joystick will respond to. This is known as the joystick device's *deadzone*. See Listing 10.9 for further clarification.

LISTING 10.9   Responding to Joystick Events in the Main Event Queue

```
//enable the event queue to listen for joystick states generated
//by SDL.
SDL_JoystickEventState(SDL_ENABLE);

SDL_Event event;
while( SDL_PollEvent( &event ) )
{
  switch( event.type ){

  case SDL_JOYSTICKAXISMOTION:
    //define some dead-zone for the joystick
    if((event.jaxis.value < -3200)||(event.jaxis.value > 3200))
    {
      if( event.jaxis.axis == 0)
      {
        // Left-right movement code goes here
      }

      if( event.jaxis.axis == 1)
      {
        // Up-Down movement code goes here
      }
    }

  break;
  //Handle Joystick Button Presses
  case SDL_JOYBUTTONDOWN:
    if ( event.jbutton.button == 0 )
    {
      // code goes here. Zap that alien or activate shields.
    }
```

```
      break;

    default:
      break;
    }
  }
```

Cleaning up the Joystick

After you have finished with the game and are in the process of freeing up any allocated resources, do not forget to free the memory used by the SDL_Joystick object. This can be done with a call to the SDL_JoystickClose method as shown in Listing 10.10.

LISTING 10.10 Using SDL_JoystickClose

```
//Cleanup memory for the first joystick only. If more are in
//the system, then loop through them to clean them all up.

if(SDL_JoystickOpened(0))
  SDL_JoystickClose(pJoy);
```

ADDING INPUT SUPPORT TO PEON

Now that you are familiar with working with SDL_Event messages sent with any input device event, you can add this capability into the Peon engine. For a simpler approach to processing input, you will modify the IApplicationState object that you have been using in order to add input notification functions. This provides the most flexibility for users of the engine. Listing 10.11 details the modifications of the IApplicationState object.

LISTING 10.11 /PeonMain/include/IApplicationState.h

```
namespace peon
{
  class PEONMAIN_API IApplicationState
  {
  //snip
```

```
//provide a mechanism to handle key down and key up messages
//note that these methods are not defined as pure-virtual. This
//is to allow the implementation of this state object to only use
//what they need….they may not even need input at all, etc.
virtual void onKeyEvent( SDL_KeyboardEvent *pEvent){};

//the following methods will handle mouse events
virtual void onMouseButton( SDL_MouseEvent* pEvent){};
virtual void onMouseMotion( SDL_MouseEvent* pEvent){};
//snip
};
}
```

Then from within the main event loop of the EngineCore object, it is just a matter of passing the right input event message to the current IApplicationState object. These modifications are here for you in Listing 10.12.

LISTING 10.12 Modifications to EngineCore::runEngine()

```
int EngineCore::runEngine()
{
  //snip
  while(! done)
  {
    while( SDL_PollEvent(&event) )
    {
      switch ( event.type )
      {

        case SDL_KEYDOWN:
        case SDL_KEYUP:
          if(m_pApplication)
            m_pApplication->getCurrentState()->onKeyEvent(event);
        break;
        //snip!
    }
    }
  }
  //snip!
}
```

You will learn more about implementing these input event messages during the next timebox of the *SuperAsteroidArena* project, covered in Chapter 12, "Input and Sound Timebox."

CHAPTER EXERCISES

1. Some games allow the player to provide a customized input file for remapping the keyboard. Incorporate the IniConfigReader object into your input system to allow it to pull desired key mappings from an .INI configuration file.
2. Centralize the input events into a common structure that you will update with each input event message. For example, if the player should press the left arrow on the keyboard, move the mouse left, or move the joystick left, then your input structure should just signal that a left motion was detected. This allows the player to use the device of his preference.
3. Instead of responding to events in the SDL message queue, compare your application performance and/or feedback with polling the input devices directly every update cycle of your game. Are there situations in which one method is preferred over the other?

SUMMARY

Using the features of the SDL, you were shown how to create and access the standard input devices found on most PCs today: the keyboard, mouse, and joystick. You were also given more experience in using the SDL event queue to process event messages generated from these input devices. Input handling within a game is an important facet to incorporating the player into your game world. If your input response is slow or sluggish, especially in an action game, then it can almost ruin the game experience for any player.

One of the other core components of a video game is the audio feedback generated for the player depending upon the action in the game. In the next chapter, you will learn how to use and manipulate your sound hardware to add more meat to your game.

11 Working With Sound

Chapter Goals

- Discuss sound properties.
- Introduce the layers of sound involved in a game.
- Introduce the SDL_Mixer library.
- Introduce 3D positional sound using OpenAL.
- Introduce how to play both WAV and Ogg-Vorbis files.

Although mostly overlooked until the later stages of a project, the audio environment for a game is one of the most critical aspects involved in presenting the overall package to the player. The right balance of audio cues within your game can create an incredible experience that can really draw the player into the game world.

SOUND MECHANICS

Sound is a wave emitted from a source that travels through some kind of medium, which is usually air or water. You can hear sound in your everyday environments here on Earth, as the medium the sound waves travel through involves air molecules. However, contrary to most science fiction movies, explosions or laser fire cannot be heard in space as there are no air molecules for the sound waves to travel through, hence no sound *effect*.

For sound programming purposes, there are two characteristics to describe sound waves:

Amplitude: If you were to look at your sound wave figure, the amplitude is the measure of the height of the sound wave from the base to the crest.

Frequency: This attribute defines the number of cycles per second that the sound wave pulses. This is also known as the pitch of a sound and is measured in Hz (hertz).

DIGITIZED SOUND

When you record or store an audio effect into a digitized form, you are telling the computer to record the amplitude of the sound. How often the amplitude is recorded is known as the *sampling rate.*

For example, CD-quality audio has a sampling frequency rate of 44,000 Hz, which means that the computer makes 44,000 measurements per second of the sound source. Taking fewer measurements per second will shrink the size of the resulting data file but will diminish the quality of the sample since the computer is taking less measurements of the sound effect.

SOUND LAYERS

Within a high-performance game situation you can have multiple layers of sound that help draw the player into the game world. For most games you work with approximately four layers: background, environment, effects, and speech. The background layer is simply the music that conveys an overall atmosphere of the game to the player. For instance, in a haunted house environment the background layer might simply contain some ghostly, haunting music to help chill the player.

The environment layer mostly describes audio effects that contribute to the locale of the game. In the same haunted house, for example, environment effects can be things like creaking floors, mysterious doors opening and closing, chains dragging on the floor, and perhaps an occasional ghostly wail.

Effects is another sound layer that most games use; these sounds are from the character or surrounding environment itself. This is mostly sound effects heard from player actions, such as using an item from the player's inventory, direct manipulation of objects within the game world, and so on. For example, as the player moves through the haunted house, he is breathing quickly with each freaky sound. Every footstep produces creaks and groans in the floorboards of the old house. With each old door, we hear squeaks and squeals of the door handle turning and then opening on its rusty hinges.

A final sound layer that most developers use in their games is speech. Most often speech is delivered during plot advancing moments of the game such as a cut scene of some kind, or is used to flesh out the characters around the player. To continue the haunted mansion example, the speech layer could be the voiceover of the player himself who is reading a will from his long lost uncle, which has a decree that the player must stay in his house for one night to inherit the extensive family fortune.

There are probably many more sound layers you could define on your own, but for the most part these are the most common.

INTRODUCTION TO SDL_MIXER

As you discovered in Chapter 10, "Working with Input Devices," on using the SDL for input device management, the benefit of using the library is felt immediately since you do not need to concern yourself with any low-level input device manipulation. For audio purposes, there exists a helpful SDL component called SDL_Mixer, which encapsulates any low-level system specific audio device tasks. With SDL_Mixer you can play two broad types of audio datafiles: music data and digitized sound effects data.

WORKING WITH AUDIO MUSIC DATA

Although the SDL_Mixer library supports a wide variety of music data that you can load into your programs, here you focus only on probably the two most popular formats for game music: MIDI and Ogg-Vorbis.

Musical Instrument Device Interface (*MIDI*) is a format/language that describes musical compositions as a function of time. Instead of working with digital samples, a MIDI composition is described as a collection of instruments, keys, and some special codes. Each channel in the MIDI specification is also responsible for a different instrument. For example, you might have 16 channels available, each one representing a different instrument, such as a piano, drums, guitar, flute, trumpet, saxophone, and so on. The actual playback of a MIDI composition is left to the hardware, which means that depending upon the kind of audio hardware installed, the tune might sound different on one machine than the other. Although the MIDI format can contain only synthesized music, the actual file size for this format is very small, which is why it was so popular for a time.

Ogg Vorbis is an audio compression scheme comparable to other formats such as MPEG-3, with the exception that Ogg Vorbis is completely open source, unpatented, and license-free. For a lot of commercial and independent game projects, it is replacing the MPEG-3 format, which requires rather expensive royalty fees. For proof of this, you can find a lot of the recent AAA titles have some of their audio data stored in Ogg-Vorbis format, such as *Unreal Tournament 2004*, *Jedi Knight II*, and a host of others. For working with music data, Listing 11.1 demonstrates how to initialize the SDL_Mixer library taken from the /chapter_11/BasicMidi sample project.

LISTING 11.1 Initializing SDL_Mixer Subsystem

```
int audio_rate     = 22050;     //a 22050 Hz frequency rate
Uint16 audio_format = AUDIO_S16; // 16-bit stereo
int audio_channels = 2; //specify 2 audio channels
int audio_buffers  = 4096; //desired buffer size for output

//Initialize the SDL subsystem
SDL_Init( SDL_INIT_EVERYTHING );

//This is where we create a handle to the audio device.
//Mix_OpenAudio takes as its parameters the desired audio format
if(Mix_OpenAudio(audio_rate, //frequency
  audio_format, //audio format
  audio_channels, //2 for stereo, 1 for mono
  audio_buffers)) //bytes used per output sample
{
  OutputDebugString("Unable to open audio!\n");
  return false;
}

//query the audio layer to see what we really ended up with.
//We can throw these values into a log file to help debugging.
Mix_QuerySpec(&audio_rate, &audio_format, &audio_channels);
```

From Listing 11.1, you can immediately see what kind of information you will need in order to initialize the SDL_Mixer audio subsystem.

First, you need to decide on an audio format you want to provide for your game. As you can see, you are using an audio rate of 22,050 kHz, 16-bit stereo with two channels.

In the sample, you are using the `Mix_OpenAudio` function to initialize and create your main audio format.

Proceeding with Listing 11.2, you learn how to load some music data and then play it.

LISTING 11.2   Using `Mix_Music`

```
Mix_Music *pMusic = NULL;

// Actually loads up the music
pMusic = Mix_LoadMUS("data\\media\\archive.mid");

//snip
//further on in our event queue we can enable or disable the sound
//when you hit the 'm' key
while(!done)
{
  while(SDL_PollEvent(&event))
  {
    switch(event.type)
    {
      case SDL_QUIT:
    done = 1;
  break;

      case SDL_KEYDOWN:
      case SDL_KEYUP:
    switch(event.key.keysym.sym)
      {
        case SDLK_m:
        //if the 'm' key is detected being pushed down
        if(key.state == SDL_PRESSED)
        {
          Mix_PlayMusic(pMusic, //our Mix_Music structure
          0);      //0 to play once, -1 for infinite loop
        }
        break;
      }
  }
}
```

You need to use the `Mix_Music` data structure to store the audio data loaded during the `Mix_LoadMUS` function. For the purposes of demonstration, the music data is only started by the '*m*' key and simply plays a single time. Should you want to use this audio data for your background music in a game you will probably want it to infinitely loop.

Cleaning Up

After you are finished with your music data, to avoid any memory leaks, you need to properly clean everything up. Listing 11.3 details the necessary steps to clean up the `Mix_Music` structure and the underlying `SDL_Mixer` interfaces.

LISTING 11.3 Cleaning up `Mix_Music`

```
Mix_HaltMusic();

// Unload the music from memory
Mix_FreeMusic(pMusic);
pMusic = NULL;
//close and destroy the SDL_Mixer interfaces
Mix_CloseAudio();
```

You have now learned how to load, play, and clean up audio music data and can confidently use it in any SDL application.

Working with Audio Sound Effects Data

The other kind of audio data most often used during gameplay is sound effects data.

After the audio hardware is created and initialized, you then need to create and load the sound effects data as shown in Listing 11.5, which is taken from the /chapter_11/BasicWAV project.

ON THE CD

LISTING 11.5 Loading Sound Effects

```
//Mix_Chunk is used like Mix_Music only for short sound effects
Mix_Chunk *pExplosion = NULL;
//Every sound that gets played is assigned to a channel. This
assignment
//is the specific information about a sample that is playing. It is
//not the same as the number of channels specified during audio
device
```

```
//creation. (ie. 2 for stereo, 1 for mono, etc)
int sound_channel = -1;
pExplosion = Mix_LoadWAV("explosion.wav");
if(!pExplosion)
{
  //the sound data failed to load properly
  return false;
}
```

Sound Effect Playback

Now that you have loaded your sound effects, you need to learn how to use SDL_Mixer to play them back. You will take advantage of the Mix_PlayChannel function to send the sound effect data to the audio hardware. An SDL_Mixer *channel* is used to store information about a sound sample that is playing and should not be confused with the number of channels you requested when you originally created the audio subsystem with the Mix_OpenAudio function. Listing 11.6 demonstrates how you can do this.

LISTING 11.6 Using Mix_PlayChannel

```
while(!done)
{
  while(SDL_PollEvent(&event))
  {
    switch(event.type)
    {
      case SDL_QUIT:
      done = 1;
    break;

      case SDL_KEYDOWN:
      case SDL_KEYUP:
    switch(event.key.keysym.sym)
      {
        case SDLK_s:
          if(key.state == SDL_PRESSED)
          {
            sound_channel = Mix_PlayChannel(
              -1, //the channel we should play on. -1 for don't care
              pExplosion, //the Mix_Chunk data
              -1); //the number of times sound should be looped.
          }
```

```
        break;
          }
        }
      }
```

Cleaning Up

As with the music audio data, you need to free up any memory resources allocated for the `Mix_Chunk` sound effect data structure. This is done with the help of the `Mix_HaltChannel` method, which takes the sample channel as the only argument, shown in Listing 11.7.

LISTING 11.7 `Mix_Chunk` Cleanup

```
Mix_HaltChannel(sound_channel);
Mix_FreeChunk( pExplosion );
sound_channel = -1;
```

INTRODUCTION TO OPENAL

You have learned much about creating and playing some background music and sound effects for your game. However, at the beginning of this chapter it was mentioned that a possible sound layer within a game is that of environmental sound. Normally, most games will play a looping music track in the background, which provides some ambient environment or atmosphere. Other times, you might want to play sound effects from different locations in your game world. To accomplish this, you need to be introduced to a high-quality audio API called Open Audio Library (*OpenAL*), which makes it simple to position and play a sound within 3D space. This gives you the chance to play a sound more loudly as the player approaches it, and to make it quieter as the player moves farther away. OpenAL was created and designed to be a cross-platform, high-performance audio library and purposefully meant to seamlessly integrate with OpenGL with the design of its function format and usage.

There are four important components to work with in OpenAL:

■ The *Audio Library Context* is a high-level object that represents the sound device capable of functioning across multiple platforms such as Windows, Linux, or MacOS.

■ The *source object* represents some properties around the position in space from which the sound emits.

- The *listener object* represents the audio properties of the position in space from which you want to hear the sound. In most cases, this is the player's position in your game world.
- The *audio buffer* represents some properties on how to play the sound, along with the actual sound data itself.

Intializing the OpenAL Device Context

Before you can begin to play any sounds, you must first initialize your OpenAL context. This simply creates a link between your application and the local audio hardware installed on your machine. Listing 11.8 demonstrates how this is done and is taken from the /chapter_11/BasicSoundOpenAL project on the CD-ROM.

LISTING 11.8 OpenAL initialization

```
ALCcontext *pContext;
ALCdevice *pDevice;

//open a link to the audio hardware using the DirectSound3D
//underlay
pDevice = alcOpenDevice((ALubyte*)"DirectSound3D");
if(pDevice == NULL)
{
  return false;
}

//Create a valid context
pContext=alcCreateContext(pDevice,NULL);

//make it the current active context
alcMakeContextCurrent(pContext);
```

Loading Sound Effects

The next step in using the OpenAL device is to load up any sound effect or musical data you want to use in your scene. You need to create an OpenAL buffer, which is responsible for containing your audio data that you then attach to either a source or listener object within the game world. The only data format a buffer object will support is *Pulse Code Modulation* (PCM) data stored in the WAV format, which is a native audio format on Windows. Listing 11.9 demonstrates how to load some audio data into an OpenAL buffer.

LISTING 11.9 Loading WAV Data into a Buffer

```
char* alWAVBuffer; //data for the buffer
ALenum alFormatBuffer; //for the buffer format
ALsizei alFreqBuffer; //for the frequency of the buffer
long alBufferLen; //the bit depth
ALboolean alLoop; //looped

unsigned int alBuffer;

//load the wave file
alutLoadWAVFile(strWaveFile.c_str(),//WAV filename
&alFormatBuffer,                    //OpenAL format specifier
(void **) &alWAVBuffer,             //size of the WAV file in bytes
(unsigned int *)&alBufferLen,       //bit depth of WAV..16 or 32
&alFreqBuffer,                      //frequency of the WAV file
&loop);                             //looping indicator for data

//create a buffer..similar to glGenTexture
alGenBuffers(1, &alBuffer);

//fill the buffer with the audio data loaded
alBufferData(alBuffer,     //buffer handle
   alFormatBuffer,         //format type of the data
   alWAVBuffer,            //handle to audio data
   alBufferLen,            //size of audio data in bytes
   alFreqBuffer);          //frequency of audio data

positionBuffer( alBuffer );

//release the data
alutUnloadWAV(alFormatBuffer, alWAVBuffer, alBufferLen,
   alFreqBuffer);
```

Similarly to the process of texture image loading under OpenGL, after you have finished working with the raw data and have loaded it into your context, you must free the associated data loaded into memory.

Working with the Source Object

One of the fundamental aspects of working with OpenAL in your game world is the use of positional sound. When you have a valid buffer loaded with data, you will need to attach it to a source object within your scene. The advantage of using OpenAL is that you can have the sound move in conjunction with the associative object itself, giving you a very realistic scene. Perhaps you have a monster moving through your level or maybe some water dripping from the walls of your dungeon. Positioning these sounds can really create some fantastic environments that your player will remember.

Since OpenAL is designed for smooth integration with OpenGL, when you work with the location coordinates of your source or listener objects, you are using a right-handed coordinate system.

Listing 11.10 demonstrates how to set up and configure an OpenAL source object.

LISTING 11.10   Positioning the Source

```
unsigned int alSource; //source object handle

// Bind buffer with a source.
alGenSources(1, &alSource);

//if there's an error caught by the system, then exit
if( alGetError() != AL_NO_ERROR)
  return AL_FALSE;

//some default coordinate positions. Initialize to the origin
//of the world for now
float vecPos[] = { 0.0f, 0.0f, 0.0f };
float vecVel[] = { 0.0f, 0.0f, 0.0f );

//attach the source object with the WAV data in the buffer
alSourcei (alSource, AL_BUFFER,   alBuffer );

//control the pitch of the data
alSourcef (alSource, AL_PITCH,    1.0f    );

//Gain helps you define a scalar amplitude multiplier
alSourcef (alSource, AL_GAIN,     1.0f    );

//specify the source position
alSourcefv(alSource, AL_POSITION, vecPos);
```

```
//specify the source velocity
alSourcefv(alSource, AL_VELOCITY, vecVel);

//loop the data once you hit the end? Default is false
alSourcei(alSource, AL_LOOPING,  AL_FALSE );
```

As you can see, there are tweak several properties that you can tweak to properly position your sound source. With the AL_BUFFER flag you are specifying which OpenAL buffer you want to attach to this source. There are two positional flags, AL_VELOCITY and AL_POSITION, that you should understand the difference between. The AL_POSITION specifies the position of the sound in world coordinates. The AL_VELOCTIY parameter, on the other hand, specifies the current speed and velocity of the sound source. The velocity does not affect your source position, and OpenAL will not update a new velocity position based upon an updated position. The OpenAL driver will use the velocity information when calculating the Doppler effect on your audio source.

Positioning the Listener Object

Similarly to the source object, the listener object encapsulates and represents an object capable of hearing the sound in the game world. With OpenAL you only have one listener, which takes advantage of most of the same properties as the source object.

Listing 11.11 provides an example of configuring your listener.

LISTING 11.11   Positioning Your Listener

```
float listenerx, listenery, listenerz;
float vecOrient[6];

//pick an arbitrary listener location. Normally this might
//represent the location of your player in the game world as
//he or she runs through the forests or the Deadmines.
listenerx=10.0f;
listenery=0.0f;
listenerz=5.0f;

vecOrient[0] = fvecx; //forward vector x value
vecOrient[1] = fvecy; //forward vector y value
vecOrient[2] = fvecz; //forward vector z value
vecOrient[3] = uvecx; //up vector x value
vecOrient[4] = uvecy; //up vector y value
vecOrient[5] = uvecz; //up vector z value
```

```
//set current listener position
alListener3f(AL_POSITION, listenerx, listenery, listenerz);

//set current listener orientation, which represents the forward and
//up vectors of your view matrix
alListenerfv(AL_ORIENTATION, vecOrient);
```

As you can see, the AL_ORIENTATION can represent the up and forward vectors taken from your scene's view matrix.

Playing the Sound

The buffer has been loaded, the source and listener objects have been positioned, and so the OpenAL context is ready to play the sound. Using the AL_LOOPING parameter of your source object you can also specify the context if you want the sound to loop after it has finished playing. Listing 11.12 shows how to play the sound.

```
//tell the sound to loop continuously
//AL_TRUE for yes, AL_FALSE for no
alSourcei(alSource,AL_LOOPING,AL_TRUE);

//play the sound
alSourcePlay(alSource);
```

Stopping the Sound

Listing 11.13 demonstrates how to stop a sound source that is currently playing.

LISTING 11.13   Stop the Sound

```
//To stop the sound:
alSourceStop(alSource);
```

Shutting Down the OpenAL Context

All things must come to an end, and OpenAL is no exception. During the unloading of your game you will need to clean up any audio buffers, source objects, and your OpenAL context and device link. Listing 11.14 provides an example for performing this garbage collection of your OpenAL environment.

LISTING 11.14 OpenAL Cleanup

```
//delete our source
alDeleteSources(1,&alSource);

//delete our buffer
alDeleteBuffers(1,&alBuffer);

//Get active context
pContext=alcGetCurrentContext();

//Get device for active context
pDevice=alcGetContextsDevice(pContext);

//Disable context
alcMakeContextCurrent(NULL);

//Release context(s)
alcDestroyContext(pContext);

//Close device
alcCloseDevice(pDevice);

alutExit();
```

PLAYING OGG-VORBIS DATA WITH OPENAL

ON THE CD

Although the default WAV format supported by OpenAL provides a lot of flexibility in terms of working with simple sound effects to fully fledged musical scores, there may be cases in which the overall size of your game is under a very tight control. Although you learned how to load and use Ogg-Vorbis files with SDL_Mixer, there might eventually be a need to use OpenAL to play your Ogg-Vorbis data. Listing 11.15 demonstrates how to load your data into an OpenAL buffer and is taken from the /chapter_11/BasicOggOpenAL sample.

LISTING 11.15 Loading Ogg-Vorbis Data into a Buffer

```
#include <ogg/ogg.h>
#include <vorbis/codec.h>
#include <vorbis/vorbisenc.h>
```

```c
#include <vorbis/vorbisfile.h>
#define BUFFER_SIZE 32768 //32 KB buffer
//snip

FILE*            oggFile;       // file handle
OggVorbis_File   oggStream;     // stream handle
vorbis_info*     vorbisInfo;    // some formatting data
vorbis_comment*  vorbisComment; // user comments
int result;
char vorbis_data[BUFFER_SIZE];

//physically open the file
if(!(oggFile = fopen(path.c_str(), "rb")))
  return false;
//Open the OggVorbis_File using the existing FILE pointer
if((result = ov_open(oggFile, &oggStream, NULL, 0)) < 0)
{
  fclose(oggFile);
  return false;
}

vorbisInfo = ov_info(&oggStream, -1);
vorbisComment = ov_comment(&oggStream, -1);
//if you only want one channel, then make sure we're working in MONO
//format
if(vorbisInfo->channels == 1)
  format = AL_FORMAT_MONO16;
else
 format = AL_FORMAT_STEREO16;

// The frequency of the sampling rate
freq = vorbisInfo->rate;

long bytes = 0;
int endian = 0;  // 0 for Little-Endian, 1 for Big-Endian
if(SDL_BYTEORDER == SDL_BIG_ENDIAN)
{
  endian = 1;
}

do
{
```

```
// Read up to a buffer's worth of decoded sound data
bytes = ov_read(&oggFile, vorbis_data, BUFFER_SIZE, endian,
                2, 1, &oggStream);
// Append to end of buffer
buffer.insert(buffer.end(), array, array + bytes);
} while (bytes > 0);

ov_clear(&oggFile);
```

There is a little more work involved to load Ogg-Vorbis data, but thankfully the Ogg-Vorbis objects and methods take care of most of the work for you. After opening the audio data file, the application determines the underlying Endian format to use. OpenAL will then proceed to load the audio data into the Ogg buffer.

Playing the Ogg Buffer

Now that the sound is loaded into an OpenAL buffer, you can manipulate and play it back in the same way that you are accustomed to with the WAV file. Listing 11.16 demonstrates how to do this.

LISTING 11.16 Playing the Ogg Buffer

```
//tell the sound to loop continuously
//AL_TRUE for yes, AL_FALSE for no
alSourcei(alSource,AL_LOOPING,AL_TRUE);

//play the sound
alSourcePlay(alSource);
```

The cleanup and garbage collection of the buffer is identical to how you removed the OpenAL buffer in Listing 11.14.

CHAPTER EXERCISES

1. Check the OpenAL documentation to learn more parameters that you can use for your source and listener objects.
2. Manipulate your listener to move around the world in response to the keyboard. Provided you set the parameters properly, you should be able to move around the sound and hear it change depending upon where you are in relation to it and your distance from the sound.

3. You have the option of playing sound effect WAV data in either OpenAL or SDL_Mixer. Take some time to experiment with each one to determine whether there is a situation in which one API is better than the other.

SUMMARY

This chapter accomplished the task of introducing you to the SDL_Mixer library that enables you to play and enjoy audio resources within your game, without worrying about any low-level code to manipulate the audio hardware. You learned how to load and play both MIDI and Ogg-Vorbis audio data, as well as learning how to load and play sound effect files stored in the WAV format. You also learned about using the OpenAL API, which allows you to position and play sound effects in 3D space. With the stengths of both libraries at your fingertips, playing background music while adding explosion and laser sound effects is no problem and will only add more depth and fun to any game you create! In the next chapter, you focus on adding both input and sound to the *SuperAsteroidArena* game.

12 Input and Sound Timebox

Chapter Goals

- Incorporate the input objects into your game engine.
- Incorporate the audio objects into your game engine.
- Add input and sound support to *SuperAsteroidArena*.

Now that you have had an introduction to using SDL to detect which input message was received, you can combine the SDL_Mixer and OpenAL libraries to handle your audio feedback.

TIMEBOX REQUIREMENTS

Once again, it is time to checkout your design document for the *SuperAsteroidArena* project to work with a list of requirements for this timebox. The goal of this timebox is to update the player to respond to keyboard input. This entails moving the player in the game world, along with playing any additional audio feedback to accompany the player's actions. You can create a list of requirements similar to the following:

- Add the ability to process input into the game.
- Add the ability to load and play audio resources in the game.
- Add audio resources to most of the game states that exist already.
- When the player moves the input device, the player's ship should respond accordingly.

As you can see, these requirements will add a whole new depth and feel to the game so far. Hopefully, it is becoming easier to see why the Agile method is used often, as it provides you with quick results and continuous feedback to maintain your excitement level in the project.

If you are not actually seeing anything for the first few days or weeks of a game project, then the game itself unfortunately has a higher chance of not being completed. Although it can be healthy to sometimes take a few days off from the project to provide you with a mental break, do not take too long.

NOTE

REQUIRED INPUT EVENTS

Before implementing any code for processing input events received from the event queue, you should work with a preliminary list of actions that the player will want/need to perform during the execution of the game.

In the case of the *SuperAsteroidArena* game, you can create a list of actions affected by the player's input:

- Rotate the ship (left or right).
- Enable/disable the ship's main engines (that is, thrust).
- Enable/disable the sound effects.
- Enable/disable the background music.

To make this happen in the game project, you need to override the events generated by the IApplicationState interface. By responding to the different input controls, you can best manipulate the player's ship around the game world.

Listing 12.1 provides some more details on adding support for these keys in the game.

LISTING 12.1 Adding Key Event Support

```
//Within the ActiveState.h definition
class ActiveState : public IApplicationState
{
  //snip
  //override the onKeyEvent message to help process incoming
  //input commands
  void onKeyEvent( SDL_KeyboardEvent* pEvent);
};
```

Now that you have provided definitions for the input methods that you are able
to override, you can implement them within the ActiveState.cpp module. The
basic algorithm used is to detect which key was pressed and then invoke the appropriate response in your code.

Rotating the Player's Ship

One of the input actions you have in the design document is to rotate the player's
ship left or right, depending upon which direction key/input is received. To properly rotate the player's ship, you will need to manipulate the object's rotation
around the z-axis. Listing 12.2 describes how to add some code to help rotate the
player's orientation.

LISTING 12.2 Player Rotation

```
void ActiveState::onKeyEvent(SDL_KeyboardEvent* pEvent)
{

  switch( pEvent->keysym.sym )
  {
  case SDL_LEFT:
  //rotate the ship to the left
  m_oOurPlayer.vecRot.z += (m_oOurPlayer.fTurningRate *
  -1.0f * fTimeKey);
break;
case SDL_RIGHT:
  //rotate the ship to the right
  m_oOurPlayer.vecRot.z += (m_oOurPlayer.fTurningRate *
  1.0f * fTimeKey);
```

```
break;
};

}
```

After you compile and run the game, you should now have the ability to rotate the ship left and right using the arrow keys on your keyboard.

Activating the Player's Engines

According to the design document, the player must also be able to activate some thrust engines in order to move forward. Listing 12.3 details how to add some forward motion to your player's ship in the game world.

LISTING 12.3 Adding Forward Movement

```
void ActiveState::onKeyDown( SDL_KeyboardEvent* pEvent)
{

switch( pEvent->keysym.sym)
{
case SDK_LEFT:
//snip
break;
case SDK_RIGHT:
//snip
break;
case SDK_UP:
//apply forward movement to the player
float velocity = 0.05f * fTimeKey;
//first grab our rotation, and convert it from
//degrees into radians
float fX = PEON_DEGTORAD(m_oOurPlayer.vecRot.z);

//now update the player's position based upon the
//sin and cos values of the rotation (in radians)
m_oOurPlayer.vecVel.x += velocity * cosf(fX);
m_oOurPlayer.vecVel.y += velocity * sinf(fX);

break;
};
}
```

USING THE AUDIOENGINE

Another important component of the Peon library created during the EngineCore
initialization process is the AudioEngine subsystem. This object attempts to encapsulate both the SDL_Mixer and OpenAL toolkits you learned about in the preceding chapter. Listing 12.4 provides a detailed look at the AudioEngine component.

LISTING 12.4   AudioEngine

```
namespace peon
{
/**
* This structure is responsible for encapsulating a 3D sound
* within our game world. It should be fairly generic enough
* to handle most situations
*/
struct PEONMAIN_API AudioNode
{
/** the source buffer */
ALuint sound_source;
/** the actual sound buffer */
int sound_buffer;
/** loop the sound? */
bool sound_loop;
/** sound's position in 3D space */
ALfloat sound_position[3];
/** sound's velocity within the game world */
ALfloat sound_velocity[3];
};


/**
* This object is our interface to the audio device detected
* on the machine. This should give us an easy mechanism to
* load and playback audio data.
*/
class PEONMAIN_API AudioEngine : public ISingleton<AudioEngine>
{
public:
/** Constructor */
AudioEngine();
/** Destructor */
```

```
~AudioEngine();
/** snip. Standard ISingleton overrides. snip. */
/**
* This method makes the necessary calls to load up a
* Mix_Music instance which is used for playback of
* MIDI files
* @param strFilename - path to the MIDI file
* @return Mix_Music* - pointer to our Mix_Music object
*/
Mix_Music* loadMIDI( const String& strFilename );

/**
* This method makes the necessary calls to load up a
* Mix_Chunk instance which is used for playback of
* MIDI files
* @param strFilename - path to the WAV file
* @return Mix_Music* - pointer to our Mix_Chunk object
*/
Mix_Chunk* loadWAVChunk( const String& strFilename );

/**
* This method internally loads the audio resource
* into some OpenAL compatible buffers. When you wish
* to work with a resource, you need to reference it by
* the slot you stored it in.
* @param strFilename - path to WAV file
* @param slot - slot to store resource
* @return bool - true if sound loaded properly
*/
bool loadAudioNode( const String& strWAVFile, AudioNode* pNode );

};
}
```

Loading Sounds

To demonstrate how easy and flexible the AudioEngine component is, you can now load and play some sound and music files within your project. Listing 12.5 details the sound data you are going to load for some sound effects within *SuperAsteroidArena*.

LISTING 12.5 Loading Sounds

```
bool MainApp::onLoadWorld()
{
//snip the other code
//defined as peon::AudioNode m_oAudioNodes[MAX_AUDIO_SAMPLES]
peon::AudioEngine::getSingleton().loadAudioNode(
"data\\media\\laser.wav",
&m_oAudioNodes[0] );

//load the rest of the audio data the same way
return true;
}
```

Playing Sounds

Now that the audio data is available to use in memory, you can play it at your leisure within any state of the game. Listing 12.6 details how this is done.

LISTING 12.6 Playing Audio

```
//if the laser sound is loaded into AudioNode slot 0, you need
//to "set" the sound within the AudioEngine
peon::AudioEngine::getSingleton().setAudioNode( &m_oAudioNodes[0] );

//Now it is okay to play the audio node!
peon::AudioEngine::getSingleton().playAudioNode( &m_oAudioNodes[0] );
```

Unloading Sounds

As with the other objects created during the runtime of the game, you will need to ensure that the AudioNode objects are cleaned up. Listing 12.7 details how to properly unload the AudioNode objects created during this application.

LISTING 12.7 Unloading Sounds

```
void MainApp::onUnloadWorld()
{
//clean up the audio node objects
for(int i = 0; i < AUDIO_MAX_SOUNDS; i++)
{
```

```
        //just use the AudioEngine object of the peon library to unload any
        //audio data
        peon::AudioEngine::getSingleton().unloadAudioNode( &m_oAudioNodes[i]
    );
    }
    }
```

TIMEBOX EVALUATION

Now that you have added some input and audio mechanisms to your game in this timebox, evaluate what you have accomplished so far in this phase. Does your project meet or exceed your input and audio requirements? Are you dissatisfied with any of your audio music or effects? After some play testing, do you need to alter the input configuration, or are your key mappings sensible for the player?

If you decide to alter any of the game design, remember to keep your design document updated and create a new timebox with these different requirements.

CHAPTER EXERCISES

1. Create some different sound effects for your own project. Experiment with starting and stopping different audio files depending upon the state of your game, along with different sound effects depending upon what action is occurring.

SUMMARY

Although not very long, this chapter helped you visualize what is needed for loading and playing audio data, along with adding input support to your game. Feel free to spend some time going through the code along with the material from this chapter. The project is really starting to take shape now, so you should feel proud at your accomplishments so far!

One of the primary goals of most games today is the destruction of other objects or players within the game world. Processing, if one object has struck another, forms the core of what is known as collision detection, which you learn more about in the next chapter.

13

Collision Detection and Physics Techniques

Chapter Goals

- Explore simple collision detection.
- Introduce bounding box collision detection.
- Experiment with bounding cube/sphere collision detection.
- Introduce ray collision detection.
- Introduce implementing the Tokamak physics library in your application.

Within the realm of game programming, an important and crucial part of the game experience is having proper collision detection. *Collision detection* is the art and science of determining whether one object has hit another. This is a crucial aspect of the player's experience within your game world, as making the player a part of the environment helps to suspend the player's disbelief. If your collision detection is not refined, then the player could be faced with some jarring inconsistencies that will lessen the enjoyment.

PRIORITIZE SPEED

One problem with having 100-percent effective collision detection is the increased risk that your game will be very slow, because it is processing these computations during every update cycle of your game.

In the majority of game situations, the world objects will spend more time moving and updating themselves than they will colliding with each other. For this reason, most collision detection implementations start with a higher level approach to quickly test whole sections of your object or world and then proceed to gradually work downward toward a pixel-perfect solution. This can keep collision testing fast and smooth, but also allows for precise location point computing.

Axis-Aligned Bounding Box Detection

One of the first and most basic methods of collision detection is known as *Axis-Aligned Bounding Box* detection (AABB). This is the process whereby you surround your game objects with a rectangle (or cube) aligned on the x, y, and z axis. Figure 13.1 shows what this looks like.

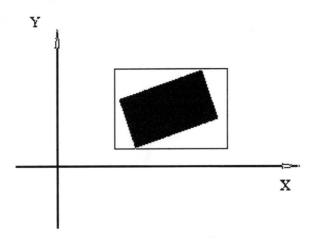

FIGURE 13.1   A 2D axis-aligned bounding box.

For a 2D AABB, you create a rectangle around your object in order to calculate the min and max vertex coordinates to use for collision detection. These two vectors help you define the AABB. Listing 13.1 demonstrates one way to calculate the min and max points.

LISTING 13.1   Calculating a 2D AABB

```
//define an AABB skeleton object
class AABB
{
```

```
public:
  Vector3 m_vecMin, m_vecMax;
  void generateBox( const Vector3& vec );

  static bool doCollision( const AABB& obj1 );
};


//given a list of vertices, go through each one to find the min and
//max points while expanding the bounding box as necessary
void AABB::generateBox(const Vector3& vec )
{
  if( vec.x < m_vecMin.x) m_vecMin.x = vec.x;
  if(vec.x > m_vecMax.x) m_vecMax.x = vec.x;

  if( vec.y < m_vecMin.y) m_vecMin.y = vec.y;
  if(vec.y > m_vecMax.y) m_vecMax.y = vec.y;
}
```

Now that you have generated your AABB for an object, you can use it to perform basic collision detection as shown in Listing 13.2.

LISTING 13.2 AABB Collision Detection

```
inline bool AABB::doCollision(const AABB& b2) const
{

  // Early-fail for nulls
  if (this->isNull() || b2.isNull())
    return false;

  if (mMaximum.x < b2.mMinimum.x)
    return false;
  if (mMaximum.y < b2.mMinimum.y)
    return false;

  if (mMinimum.x > b2.mMaximum.x)
    return false;
  if (mMinimum.y > b2.mMaximum.y)
    return false;

  // otherwise, this AABB must be intersecting
  return true;

}
```

For an axis-aligned bounding box that extends into three dimensions, you just need to add an appropriate check for the z (depth) coordinate.

Bounding Sphere Collision Detection

The axis-aligned bounding box is one collision container to surround your object in. Depending on the object in question, however, it might be necessary to provide a different approach for collision detection. Another popular method of determining when objects collide is to surround your object with an invisible sphere. Listing 13.3 defines a bounding sphere.

LISTING 13.3   Bounding Sphere

```
/**
 * This object is used as a form of collision detection. It is a
"bubble" that
 * forms a container around the object in question
 */
class PEONMAIN_API BoundingSphere
    {
    public:
       /** the center of the sphere */
       Vector3 m_vecCenter;

       /** the radius of the sphere */
       float m_fRadius;

       /**
        * This method is used for collision detection purposes.
        */
       static bool doCollision( const BoundingSphere& obj1 );

    };
```

Now that you have defined the sphere, you can use it in collision detection tests. See Listing 13.4 for an example of processing a collision.

LISTING 13.4   BoundingSphere::doCollision

```
bool BoundingSphere::doCollision(const Sphere& s) const
{
   return (s.mCenter - mCenter).length() <= (s.mRadius + mRadius);
}
```

Depending on the situation or mesh itself, bounding spheres might be more appropriate for collision tests than AABBs. One issue to keep in mind with bounding spheres, however, is that they can be controlled only by the radius of the sphere, whereas the axis-aligned bounding box has two or three axes points with which to work.

For example, surrounding a long cylindrical object such as a hammer is better suited with an AABB since you can stretch the y-axis to contain the handle of the hammer. A bounding sphere would instead sometimes produce erroneous results, since the bounding sphere would encompass an area as wide as the object is long.

PLANE COLLISIONS

In mathematics, a *plane* is defined as a section of space that is perfectly flat and extends to infinity on two dimensions. Thus far, the most obvious use of planes during collision detection calculations has been with the discussion surrounding the View Frustum culling algorithm detailed in Chapter 8, "Scene Geometry Management." The standard plane equation is defined as shown in Equation 13.1:

$$ax + by + cz = d \qquad (13.1)$$

Equation 13.1 equates to a vector representing the normal of the plane whose *x, y* and *z* components are represented by *a, b,* and *c,* respectively. The constant *d* represents the distance the plane is from the origin. Listing 13.5 provides the `Plane` object defined in Peon.

LISTING 13.5 `Plane` **CLASS**

```
namespace peon
{
  /**
  * This object is used to encapsulate some basic functionality
  * of a Plane object
  */
  class PEONMAIN_API Plane
  {
    public:
    /** Constructor */
    Plane();
    /** Destructor */
    ~Plane();
```

```
                 /** normal vector of the plane */
                 Vector3 normal;
                 /** constant defining distance from origin (0,0,0)
                 float d;
              };
      }
```

Collision of Plane versus AABB

In Chapter 8, "Scene Geometry Management," you learned how to calculate the intersection of a bounding sphere with a View Frustum plane. Another use of plane collision tests is to calculate an intersection between an axis-aligned bounding box and a plane. Listing 13.6 details how this calculation is performed.

LISTING 13.6   Plane versus AABB

```cpp
bool Plane::doAABBCollision( const AABB& box ) const
{
  //grab list of corners
  Vector3* pCorners = box.getCorners();
  Plane::Side lastSide = this.getSide( pCorners[0] );
  //test the four corners of the AABB with the plane.
  //If we are using a 3D AABB, then there should be 8 corners
  for( int corner = 1; corner < 4; ++corner )
  {
    if( this.getSide( pCorners[corner] ) != lastSide)
    {
      return true;
    }
  }
  //did not collide
  return false;
}
```

RAY COLLISIONS

Another useful mathematical entity that you can use for collision detection techniques is the *ray*. A ray contains two vectors: one to define its starting point and the other to define the direction in which the ray travels. Listing 13.7 defines the Ray object defined in the Peon toolkit.

LISTING 13.7 Ray Definition

```
Namespace peon
{
/**
* This object is used to define and encapsulate some basic
functionality
* for using Ray objects within the game world. Rays only have 2
components:
* a vector representing the origin of the Ray, and a vector to
represent
* the direction of the Ray.
*/
class PEONMAIN_API Ray
    {
    public:
/** Constructor */
Ray();
/** Destructor */
~Ray();

/** Origin of the Ray */
Vector3 vecOrigin;
/** Direction of the Ray */
Vector3 vecDirection;
};
```

Collision of Plane versus Ray

A popular use for rays is to test the distance between the ray and the plane. You first need to calculate the angle *alpha* between the normal of the plane and the ray vector by using the dot product.

NOTE

If the cosine of this angle is zero (meaning the angle is 90 degrees), then the two vectors will not cross each other.

The next step is to find the difference (*D*) between the distance between the plane and the origin and the distance of the ray from the world origin. Using trigonometry, you then can find the desired distance by dividing *D* by *alpha*. Listing 13.8 demonstrates how this can be done with the Ray object.

LISTING 13.8 Ray versus Plane Calculation

```
/**
* This method tests to see if the Ray intersects with the
* Plane object. It returns a 1 if there is an intersection
* and a 0 otherwise.
*/
int Plane::TestRayCollision(const Ray& ray,
  Vector3 collision_normal,
  float collision_distance ) const
{
  //first calculate the dot product between the direction vector of
  //the Ray, and the normal vector of this plane
  float fDotProduct = ray.vecDirection.calculateDot( this.vecNormal );

  //if the dot product calculation is invalid, then exit
  if( fDotProduct < 0.0f && fDotProduct > -0.0f )
    return 0;

  //now just calculate the distance to the collision point from
  //the given origin of the ray
  float fCollPointDistance = this.vecNormal.calculateDot(
    this.d - ray.vecOrigin)) / fDotProduct;

  //if the collision occurred behind our starting point, then exit
  if( fCollPointDistance < -ZERO )
    return 0;

  collision_normal = this.vecNormal;
  collision_distance = fCollPointDistance;

  //success, there is a collision!
  return 1;
}
```

IMPLEMENTING PHYSICS

The trend in the past decade or so for most games has been to differentiate themselves based on their graphics capabilities. Every year, titles would try to separate themselves from the pack by boasting new texture manipulation techniques, world environment appearance, or even simply by the demonstration of different weapons and their explosions within the game world. Today, however, there is more emphasis on other aspects of the game. The bleeding-edge graphics engines are more or less the same now, and so the game marketing teams no longer rely on different graphical effects to sell the product.

To fill the gap, a popular trend among most games today is the demonstration of an advanced physics library to achieve a higher level of realism. Games like *Half-Life 2* and other popular titles boast the ability to manipulate just about every object within the game world to give the player a new level of freedom and interaction. There are also some rumors surrounding the work of video hardware vendors incorporating physics techniques within upcoming graphics card architectures. If you are so mathematically inclined or do not mind spending a lot of time working with physics textbooks, then this is a very exciting time! On the other hand, if you are not so strong with math or simply do not have the time and patience to develop your own physics library from which to work, many useful choices are available on the Internet that provide a professional simulation of physics.

For the purposes of this book, you will be using the Tokamak physics library to provide a way to render realistic *rigid body* effects. Rigid body dynamics is a field of study involving the dynamic simulation of a rigid collection of points. In other words, a rigid body is a solid entity of a given size that does not alter its shape regardless of any external forces.

Using the neSimulator

For handling the calculations necessary to perform rigid body collisions, you first need to prepare your world environment. The neSimulator object from the Tokamak library is used to encapsulate the number of bodies within the simulation, along with a few other properties. It is a required object within any application using Tokamak and acts as the main access point for processing the physics in the scene. Listing 13.9 details how to initialize your world to use the neSimulator, taken from the /chapter_13/CubeSim sample found on the CD-ROM.

ON THE CD

LISTING 13.9   Initialize the neSimulator

```
bool MainApp::onLoadWorld()
{
  //first declare some Tokamak specific simulation.
  //objects. These are in MainState.h
  //neSimulator* m_pSimulation;

  //neRigidBody* m_pCubeObjects[ MAX_BODIES ];

  //define a gravity for our simulation. It can be anything!
  neV3 gravity;
  gravity.Set( 0.0f, -10.0f, 0.0f );
```

```
//The neSimulatorSizeInfo basically defines an overall "world"
//set of properties
neSimulatorSizeInfo sizeInfo;

sizeInfo.rigidBodiesCount      = MAX_BODIES;
sizeInfo.animatedBodiesCount   = NUM_BLUE_PLATFORMS;
sizeInfo.rigidParticleCount    = 0;
sizeInfo.controllersCount      = 0;

// Use the following formula to compute the number of overlapped
//pairs required:
//(num_rigid_bodies * num_animated_bodies) + num_rigid_bodies *
//(num_rigid_bodies - 1) / 2
sizeInfo.overlappedPairsCount  = (MAX_BODIES *
  NUM_BLUE_PLATFORMS) + MAX_BODIES * (MAX_BODIES - 1) / 2;
sizeInfo.geometriesCount       = MAX_BODIES +
  NUM_BLUE_PLATFORMS;
sizeInfo.constraintsCount      = 0;
sizeInfo.constraintSetsCount   = 0;
sizeInfo.constraintBufferSize  = 0;
sizeInfo.sensorsCount          = 0;
sizeInfo.terrainNodesStartCount = 0;
sizeInfo.terrainNodesGrowByCount = 0;

//Create the overall simulation using the properties structure
//you just filled in, along with the gravity you want to apply
//to the game world.
m_pSim = neSimulator::CreateSimulator(sizeInfo,NULL,&gravity );
```

Although the `neSimulator` object controls the simulation, you need to add actual objects to simulate. Entities that are able to act as rigid bodies are referenced as `neRigidBody` objects.

The first step in setting up the simulation is selecting a gravity constant that will be applied to the scene. This constant can be anything you want and is a fun way to wreak havoc with Newton's principles.

The real configuration of our simulation is done by manipulating the `neSimulatorSizeInfo` structure, which is used during the initialization of the `neSimulator` object. In Listing 13.9, you are specifying how many rigid bodies will be in the simulation. One of the other important properties to define is how many bodies can be in a collision. The SDK documentation pretty much specifies that this calculation should be as shown in Equation 13.2:

$$MAX\_BODIES * (MAX\_BODIES - 1) / 2 \qquad (13.2)$$

This calculated value is then used in the `overlappedPairsCount` property.

Finally, you initialize and create the main simulation by using the `CreateSimulator` method, which uses the `neSimulatorSizeInfo` structure as well as your gravity constant.

Working with Geometry

When you have finished initializing the container for the physics engine, you can begin to add rigid bodies to the simulation. In Listing 13.9, you used the `neSimulatorSizeInfo` structure to inform the simulation container how many objects you would be working with. For the sample you are working from, you need to generate a wall of cubes that demonstrate the ability to properly stack objects. The `neGeometry` object encapsulates every rigid body within the simulation. Listing 13.10 details the process of generating new blocks to work with along with defining the needed properties for rigid body calculations.

LISTING 13.10 Adding `neGeometry` Objects

```
neV3 cube_size;
neV3 cube_position;
neGeometry* cube_geom;
float mass = 0.1f;

//Iterate through each initial rigid body in our scene
for(int i = 0 ; i < MAX_BODIES; i++)
{
  //use the current simulation to create a new rigid body handle
  m_pCubeObj[i] = m_pSim->CreateRigidBody();

  cubeGeom = m_pCubeObj[i]->AddGeometry();

  cube_size.Set( 1.0f, 1.0f, 1.0f ); // Unit size

  cubeGeom->SetBoxSize( cube_size );


  m_pCubeObj[i]->UpdateBoundingInfo();


  m_pCubeObj[i]->SetInertiaTensor(
    neBoxInertiaTensor(
     cube_size,
     mass )
  );
```

```
//Define the mass properties for this geometry body
m_pCubeObj[i]->SetMass( mass );
//set an initial world position based on which cube object
//you are working with
if( i == 0 )
  cube_position.Set( 0.0f, 1.5f, 0.0f );
else if( i != 0 )
  cube_position.Set( 0.0f, (1.5f * (float)(i + 1)), 0.0f );

m_pCubeObj[i]->SetPos( cube_position );
}
```

Running the Simulation with Tokamak

While your simulation progresses, your rigid body objects move and interact with each other. Meanwhile, the Tokamak library is hard at work calculating any collisions. During the updating phase of your application, collision detection functions are called to determine whether there are any collisions within your game world. Listing 13.11 describes how to update the simulation.

LISTING 13.11   Updating the neSimulator

```
//TIME_INTERVAL is defined as 0.013333f
//This can be adjusted to match something from the system clock or
our
//Timer object.
m_pSim->Advance( TIME_INTERVAL, 1, NULL );
```

Rendering the Geometry

You should be used to rendering something as easy as blocks within OpenGL, but the purpose of this section is to detail how to render objects that have been put into a Tokamak simulation. Listing 13.12 describes how to loop through the block objects you are working with in the simulation.

LISTING 13.12   Rendering the neGeometry

```
Matrix44 matWorld;
Matrix44 matScale;
```

```
for( int i = 0; i < NUM_CUBES; i++ )
{
  if( m_pCubeObj[i] )
  {
      //convert the matrix format Tokamak uses to our own
      //Matrix44 format
      matWorld = NET3_TO_MATRIX44( m_pCubeObj[i]->GetTransform() );

      //demonstrate another way to render vertices, using the
      //glInterleavedArrays and specifying we're enabling
      //the normal and vector position
      glPushMatrix();
      {
          glMatrixMode( GL_MODELVIEW );
          //apply our transformation matrix calculated by
          //the physics engine
          glMultMatrixf( matWorld.m );
          //render the cube with red
          glColor3f( 1.0f, 0.0f, 0.0f );
          //specify to OpenGL that we're specifying vertex
          //information along with normals.
          glInterleavedArrays( GL_N3F_V3F, 0, m_cubeVertices );
          //render the cube!
          glDrawArrays( GL_QUADS, 0, 24 );
      }
      glPopMatrix();
  }
}
```

Cleaning Up

When you are finished with your simulation using the Tokamak library, you simply need to clean up the memory allocated by the neSimulator object. It will then internally handle the process of cleaning up any neGeometry object. Listing 13.13 demonstrates how this is done.

LISTING 13.13   Tokamak Garbage Collection

```
void MainApp::onUnloadWorld()
{
    neSimulator::DestroySimulator( m_pSim );
}
```

CHAPTER EXERCISES

1. Find and research any other collision detection techniques that you might find useful in your game engine.
2. Create some more advanced samples using the Tokamak library. One good test could be to implement an OpenGL particle system using Tokamak to surround and control each particle's interaction with the scene/simulation.

SUMMARY

You now have another key to the puzzle of game development. Although rendering your graphics, playing the audio, and processing input from the player are important aspects of a complete game, none are more important than proper collision detection. Nothing can be more frustrating for a player than to "hit" the enemy only to find that the action is not detected properly. So far, we've covered simple techniques used in 2D games, all the way up to some commonly used collision detection for 3D engines. You were finally introduced to the Tokamak physics library that enables you to surround each object within your game world by a geometry mesh. Processing these geometry collisions properly allows your scene to have a proper feel that the player will enjoy. One of the final components of any game created today is the use of networking technology to create the multiplayer experience. In the next chapter, you begin by learning the basics of network programming.

14 Introduction to Networking

Chapter Goals

- Introduce and discuss basic network fundamentals.
- Cover some networking components available for game programming.
- Introduce and cover basic socket programming concepts.

One of the most popular features available to any game on the market today is having multiplayer support. Depending upon the game, this can follow a model similar to *Battle.Net,* where the player connects to a central game server that is responsible for hosting each game. Another available option is that your game is responsible for hosting a session on your local area network or across the Internet. Properly tweaked and balanced multiplayer support can add a great layer of depth to any title.

NETWORKING BASICS

To understand network game programming and its dynamics, you need a fairly cohesive understanding of how networks themselves operate and what options are available on the PC today. Usually, when learning network programming for the first time, you are introduced to lower level concepts. However, this adds an unnecessary level of difficulty and confusion. Instead, in this chapter, you shall begin with a higher level approach and move your way downward into the grittier details.

When a situation involves two or more players in some kind of gaming environment, a final decision usually needs resolving. For example, in a competitive head-to-head (or *deathmatch*) scenario, a decision needs to be made whether player A has killed player B or vice versa. The game cannot function properly if player A receives feedback that player B is dead, and likewise player B receives the same confirmation about player A. To help manage this conflict resolution, network game communication can be architected in two ways: *client-server* or *peer-to-peer*. This is also collectively referred to as the *network topology* (or structure).

Peer-to-Peer

The *peer-to-peer* architecture is characterized by the fact that every machine in the network communicates their state to every other machine in the network. Although one machine needs to be designated as the *host*, or boss, of this network, the architecture allows a more distributed approach for each peer machine. This is outlined in Figure 14.1.

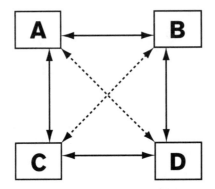

FIGURE 14.1   Peer-to-peer topology.

An advantage to this type of architecture is that if the host machine should drop from the network, it is possible for the rest of the connected machines to elect a new host to keep the session running. Machines that are involved in this network setup can also communicate directly with any other machine in the network. An obvious disadvantage to this type of networking approach is that as the number of peer machines increase in the network, so does the amount of network traffic.

NOTE

There is no set rule for the amount of peers to allow in one session. This all depends on the type of game you are creating, along with what kind of gameplay or action you are trying to simulate. The goal is to allow as many players as possible to enjoy the exciting game, while optimizing network communication. The rule of thumb is to keep the maximum number of players involved in a session in the low teens.

Client-Server

Another popular choice for network game developers is the *client-server* architecture, where one machine is designated the *server* and is responsible for listening for requests from all of the players, known as the *clients*. This is shown in Figure 14.2.

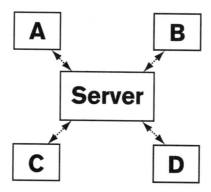

FIGURE 14.2   Client-server topology.

The server is also in charge of tracking the single, definitive state of the game world and updates the clients as necessary with this view. Clients cannot communicate with each other directly but must use the server as an intermediary messenger. This networking model allows for a much higher number of players in the game. One caveat to keep in mind is that the speed of any networked game becomes largely dependent upon the hardware (and network connection) of the server machine.

TCP versus UDP

After deciding upon the topology model to follow, the next important choice that needs to be made is the *network protocol* that is used for your game. The network protocol defines some conventions, rules, and data structures that control how the machines will exchange information over the network.

The data that needs to be sent is never sent "as is," because you want to optimize the communication exchange within the network. Instead, the networking protocol must first deconstruct the data you want to send into atomic units of information known as *packets*. Each packet contains some header information that describes the data within the packet, where it is going, and some other helpful information about the eventual reconstruction process. This stream of packets is then sent to the destination machine, each packet is then reconstructed back into the original data. The Internet operates in a nondeterministic nature so you can occasionally lose a packet or two along the way (known as *packet loss*) or can have a situation in which one packet sent later arrives before the previous packet (known as *packet ordering*). Dealing with packet loss and ordering requires some important decisions, and each protocol has their own mechanism of handling it.

The *Transmission Control Protocol/Internet Protocol* (TCP/IP) is what is known as a *streaming protocol* and is most commonly used for things like Internet browser communication, business applications, and so on. TCP functions as a reliable protocol, so the underlying network mechanism guarantees that the order of data that is sent across the network is reconstructed in the same order on the other side. Figure 14.3 details the information stored in a TCP packet header.

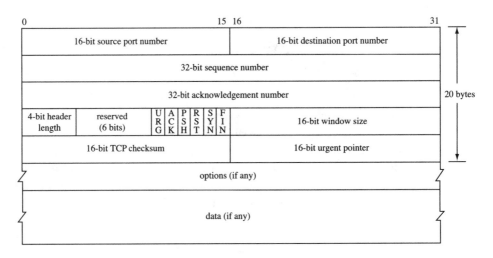

FIGURE 14.3 TCP packet header

The algorithms underneath the TCP protocol handle any packet loss or misordering by signaling the sending machine to resend the missing data stream. Some popular games using TCP as the networking protocol include Blizzard's *World of Warcraft* and EA's *Ultima Online.*

The *User Datagram Protocol* (UDP) is the other option available for network game programming. UDP is known as a connectionless and unreliable protocol, since the packets that are sent to the destination machine can be received in any order, and some might not even arrive. Figure 14.4 details the information stored in a UDP packet header.

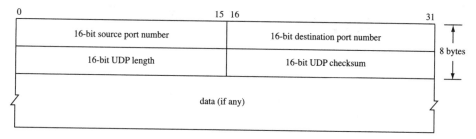

FIGURE 14.4 UDP packet header

Some popular games using UDP as the networking protocol are Id's *Quake2* and *Quake3* and NCSoft's *City of Heroes.*

The main difference between these two protocols is that when using UDP there is no packet loss algorithm or mechanism for packet recovery or ordering. If a packet of data is lost, then it is not resent by the sender machine. Because of the fact that it is a connectionless protocol, the packet header size is also slightly smaller than that of a TCP packet header size. This slightly increases the speed of UDP packets through the transmission process.

Another decision that needs to be made in the networking library is to determine how to communicate with the underlying protocol. On the Windows platform you have several choices, but there are three that are most popularly used for games: DirectPlay, Winsock, and an SDL alternative, SDL_net.

DIRECTPLAY AND WINSOCK

Introduced by Microsoft in the DirectX3.0 SDK (and subsequently overhauled and updated for the DirectX8.0 SDK), DirectPlay has existed as a *middleware* component to aid the programmer in developing network-enabled games. DirectPlay acts as an interface to the underlying network layer of the machine, taking over the tasks of socket communication and packet management. The strength of this approach is that the game programmer need not concern himself with low-level socket programming, but can instead focus efforts on communicating the various game states through a messaging approach. You simply signal to DirectPlay which type of message needs to be sent and when, and DirectPlay takes over the underlying work of queuing message requests and sending/receiving them across the network or Internet using the Winsock function calls. Although DirectPlay is a multithreaded component, it guarantees that you process only one message at a time in the message handler callback. DirectPlay also provides a throttling mechanism so that if it detects that your network traffic is getting congested, it will automatically drop unimportant messages from the network stream.

As of the Summer 2004 release of the DirectX SDK, Microsoft has chosen to deprecate the DirectPlay interfaces. Although they will still be included in the distributed runtimes for DirectX for now, they will probably disappear around the release of Windows Vista.

The alternative to using DirectPlay is to handle your networking protocols using the sockets API provided with the Winsock library. Originally based upon the BSD socket implementation on the UNIX platform, Microsoft has ported the library over to Windows while making a few additions and modifications of its own.

Winsock has become a popular networking library for the Microsoft Windows family of products, and quite a large number of multiplayer games use this API directly for network communication. One advantage to using Winsock is that you are working directly with the socket layer that DirectPlay hides from you. You can, therefore, make any optimization that is required for your own multiplayer needs.

If the eventual goal of your networking library is to function in a cross-platform environment, avoid using any of the Microsoft specific socket methods beginning with the WSA prefix. This can be accomplished with a few #define blocks along with a bit of well-structured networking objects.

SDL_NET

To round out the family of libraries available for use in SDL, the SDL_Net library provides an abstraction layer for socket programming. Because it works within the SDL framework, it is a cross-platform networking solution. Instead of dealing with sockets directly, you will instead use the SDL_Net function calls to handle your network communication. Figure 14.5 provides a basic top-level view of the SDL_Net architecture.

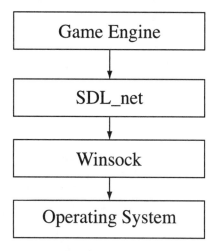

FIGURE 14.5   SDL_Net architecture

STARTING A BASIC SERVER

When starting out, server applications simply listen for incoming requests from connecting client machines. When a client attempts to make a connection, SDL_Net is notified and passes this event on to the server application, which then decides how to handle it. One approach that the server application uses to handle multiple clients is to spawn a new thread for each client. This model of client-server processing uses what are known as *blocking sockets*, which pause temporarily to wait for incoming data, connection requests, or other Winsock events. Listing 14.1 demonstrates how to prepare the server for client connections using the TCP protocol from the SDL_Net library.

LISTING 14.1   SDL_Net TCP Server

```
int main(int argc, char* argv[])
{
    //At the very least, you need to initialize the video subsystem
of SDL
```

```
if(SDL_Init( SDL_INIT_VIDEO ) < 0 )
{
  return -1;
}

// initialize SDL_net library
if( SDLNet_Init() < 0 )
{
  return -2;
}

//define a port to listen on
Uint16 port = 9000;

// Resolve the argument into an IPaddress type
IPaddress server_address;
if(SDLNet_ResolveHost(&server_address,NULL,port) < 0)
{
  return -3;
}

// open the server socket
TCPsocket server_socket;
server_socket = SDLNet_TCP_Open(&server_address);
if(!server_socket)
{
  return -4;
}

//store a client connection and the remote ip address
TCPsocket client_socket;
IPaddress* remote_address;
char message[1024];
int len;
Uint32 ipaddr;

//The general "process" here is to infinitely loop until
//a 'quit' message is received
while(1)
{
  // try to accept a connection
  client_socket = SDLNet_TCP_Accept(server_socket);
  if(!client_socket)
  {
```

```
            // no connection accepted
            SDL_Delay(100); //sleep 1/10th of a second
            continue;
        }

        // get the clients IP and port number
        remote_address = SDLNet_TCP_GetPeerAddress(client_socket);
        if(!remote_address)
        {
            continue;
        }

        // print out the clients IP and port number
        ipaddr=SDL_SwapBE32(remote_address->host);
        OutputDebugString("Accepted a connection from %d.%d.%d.%d port
%hu\n",
            ipaddr>>24,
            (ipaddr>>16)&0xff,
            (ipaddr>>8)&0xff,
            ipaddr&0xff,
            remoteip->port);

        // read the buffer from client
        len = SDLNet_TCP_Recv(client_socket,message,1024);

        //close off the client socket
        SDLNet_TCP_Close(client_socket);
        if(!len)
        {
            printf("SDLNet_TCP_Recv: %s\n",SDLNet_GetError());
             continue;
        }

        // print out the message
        printf("Received: %.*s\n",len,message);
        // if the string received is a "quit" command
        if(message[0]=='Q')
        {
            printf("Quitting on a Q received\n");
            break;
        }
    }
```

```
    // shutdown SDL_net
    SDLNet_Quit();

    // shutdown SDL
      SDL_Quit();

      return 0;
    }
```

After initializing the SDL_Net layer with the SDLNet_Init() function, the approach that you normally take with setting up a server socket is to first select a port on which to listen. This is also known as *binding*. After you have decided on a port to bind to, you must then create and fill an IPaddress structure with the proper information for your server. When this structure has been filled out by the SDL_Net library, you open the socket with the SDLNet_TCP_Open() function using the newly generated IPaddress information. If everything was initialized correctly, the application then moves into an infinite loop where it attempts to accept a socket connection from a client. If one exists, then you are reading the data sent by the client. After that is finished, the program shuts down and closes the socket from the client with the SDLNet_TCP_Close function. After the main loop is finished, the application cleans up the underlying networking objects using the SDLNet_Quit() function.

STARTING A BASIC CLIENT

Now that the server application is patiently waiting for client connections, you will be introduced to how to create a simple client and connect to the server. Listing 14.2 demonstrates how to setup a simple client using TCP sockets from the SDL_Net library.

LISTING 14.2   SDL_Net TCP Client

```
int main(int argc, char* argv[])
{
  char strError[256];
  //At the very least, initialize the video subsystem
  if(SDL_Init(SDL_INIT_VIDEO) < 0)
  {
    return -1;
  }
```

```
    // initialize SDL_net
if( SDLNet_Init() == -1 )
{
    sprintf(strError, "SDLNet_Init: %s\n",SDLNet_GetError());
    OutputDebugString(strError);
    return -2;
}

IPaddress ip;
TCPsocket sock;
char message[1024];
int len;
Uint16 port = 9000;
// Resolve the ip address taken from the command line into an
// IPaddress type
if(SDLNet_ResolveHost(&ip,argv[1],port) == -1)
{
    sprintf(strError, "SDLNet_ResolveHost:
%s\n",SDLNet_GetError());
    OutputDebugString( strError );
    return -3;
}

// open the server socket
sock = SDLNet_TCP_Open(&ip);
if(!sock)
{
    sprintf(strError, "SDLNet_TCP_Open: %s\n",SDLNet_GetError());
    OutputDebugString( strError );
    return -4;
}

// read the buffer from stdin
printf("Enter Message, or Q to make the server quit:\n");
fgets(message,1024,stdin);
len=strlen(message);

// strip the newline
message[len-1]='\0';
```

```
//if there is a message to send from the command line, then echo the
//message back to the screen as well as send it to the server
if(len)
{
    int result;

    // print out the message
    printf("Sending: %.*s\n",len,message);
    //send the message to the server
    result = SDLNet_TCP_Send(sock,message,len);
    //simple error detection
    if(result<len)
        printf("SDLNet_TCP_Send: %s\n",SDLNet_GetError());
}
//close off the socket
SDLNet_TCP_Close(sock);

// shutdown SDL_net
SDLNet_Quit();

// shutdown SDL
SDL_Quit();


    return 0;
}
```

This sample code is quite similar to Listing 14.1. The small program first initializes the networking layer with the SDLNet_Init function. After this is completed, the program is then creating a new IPaddress structure. Rather than using it for creating a server socket, however, this time around the application is attempting to generate the necessary IPaddress information using the server's IP address and port number.

When creating a local client-server application, remember that your own local IP address can either be referenced as 'localhost' or the IP address 127.0.0.1.

NOTE

After everything is properly created and initialized, the program then proceeds to send a message string to the server before closing everything down and cleaning up with the SDLNet_TCP_Close function. As in Listing 14.1, the SDLNet_Quit function performs the necessary underlying garbage collection.

Sending and Receiving Data

From within both the client and server applications created in Listing 14.1 and 14.2, you are sending data from the client to the server for processing. Before closing the connection to the client, the server displays the message received through the network.

The SDLNet_TCP_Send function is responsible for sending data using the TCP protocol from within SDL_Net. It is defined in Listing 14.3.

LISTING 14.3 SDLNet_TCP_Send Function

```
        int SDLNet_TCP_Send(
    TCPsocket sock,     //a valid TCPsocket structure
    void *data,         //pointer to the data to send
    int len)            //length (in bytes) of the data
```

For an example of how to use SDLNet_TCP_Send to transmit some data across the network, take a look at Listing 14.4.

LISTING 14.4 Using SDLNet_TCP_Send

```
    // send a string over sock
    //TCPsocket sock;
    int len,result;
    char *msg = "Timelords are from Gallifrey!";

len=strlen(msg)+1; // add one for the terminating NULL
result = SDLNet_TCP_Send(sock,msg,len);
if(result<len)
 {
    //error during send
}
```

Conversely, the SDLNet_TCP_Recv function handles receiving data from the socket. Taking a look at Listing 14.5, you can see that it has the same parameters as the SDLNet_TCP_Send function.

LISTING 14.5 SDLNet_TCP_Recv Function

```
        int SDLNet_TCP_Recv(
    TCPsocket sock,   //This is a valid connected TCPSocket
    void *data,       //pointer to the buffer that receives the data
    int maxlen)       //the maximum length (in bytes) of data to read
```

Take a look at a sample of using the SDLNet_TCP_Recv function in Listing 14.6.

LISTING 14.6 SDLNet_TCP_Recv **Sample**

```
//TCPsocket sock;
#define MAXLEN 1024
int result; //store the result of the SDL_Net operation
char msg[MAXLEN]; //buffer to store the incoming data

result = SDLNet_TCP_Recv( sock, msg, MAXLEN );
if(result <= 0)
{
  //there was an error with the transmission. Check the status
  //of the socket as it might have been invalidated.
}
```

You have now crossed the threshold of basic network programming and have created a small base to build your skills upon. There is still much to cover, but you are making good progress. Feel free to pause and review the concepts covered previously.

Non-Blocking Sockets

Until now, your server code has been demonstrating how to use *blocking sockets.* When SDL_Net works with these types of sockets, the methods used do not return until either they succeed or they fail. In effect, these are synchronous tasks. An alternative is to use *non-blocking sockets,* which are asynchronous in nature. When these types of sockets are used, any calls made to SDL_Net will return immediately, allowing the program to continue its execution. It is then up to the programmer to repeatedly use a type of polling method to find out whether the call has succeeded or failed.

One problem with using a pure non-blocking solution is that you then have to run your application in an infinite polling loop to check on any network event-related results.

Using SDLNet_CheckSockets

To benefit from non-blocking sockets without the insanity attached to having an infinite spinning loop, on the server side you can instead use the SDLNet_CheckSockets method that accepts groups of sockets to see which ones are ready for reading data, writing data, or are returning errors. Listing 14.7 demonstrates how it could be used.

LISTING 14.7   Using SDLNet_CheckSockets

```c
int main(int argc, char *argv[])
{
    IPaddress ip;
    TCPsocket sock;
    SDLNet_SocketSet set;
    char *message = NULL,*host;
    Uint32 ipaddr;
    Uint16 port = 9000;

    // initialize SDL
    if(SDL_Init(0) == -1)
    {
        printf("SDL_Init: %s\n",SDL_GetError());
        exit(1);
    }

    // initialize SDL_net
    if(SDLNet_Init() == -1)
    {
        printf("SDLNet_Init: %s\n",SDLNet_GetError());
        SDL_Quit();
        exit(2);
    }

    // Resolve the argument into an IPaddress type
    // for now use your local machine which is defined by the
    // IP address of 127.0.0.1
    if(SDLNet_ResolveHost(&ip,"127.0.0.1",port) == -1)
    {
        printf("SDLNet_ResolveHost: %s\n",SDLNet_GetError());
        SDLNet_Quit();
        SDL_Quit();
        exit(3);
    }

    // resolve the hostname for the IPaddress
    host = SDLNet_ResolveIP(&ip);
```

```
// print out the hostname we got
if(host)
    printf("Hostname    : %s\n",host);
else
    printf("Hostname    : N/A\n");

// output the port number
printf("Port        : %d\n",port);

// open the server socket
server = SDLNet_TCP_Open(&ip);
if(!server)
{
    printf("SDLNet_TCP_Open: %s\n",SDLNet_GetError());
    SDLNet_Quit();
    SDL_Quit();
    exit(4);
}

while(1)
{
    int numready,i;
    set = create_sockset();
    numready = SDLNet_CheckSockets(set, (Uint32)-1);
    if(numready == -1)
    {
        printf("SDLNet_CheckSockets: %s\n",SDLNet_GetError());
         break;
    }
    if(!numready)
        continue;
    if(SDLNet_SocketReady(server))
    {
        numready-;
        OutputDebugString("Detecting Connection...\n");
        sock = SDLNet_TCP_Accept(server);
        if(sock)
        {
            char *name = NULL;
            OutputDebugString("Accepted Connection...\n");
            if(getMsg(sock, &name))
            {
```

```
                    //In your own usage, here is where you would
instantiate

                    //your own object which would define the necessary
                    //properties of a player in your game world.
                    Client *client;
                    client = add_client(sock,name);
                    if(client)
                        do_command("WHO",client);
                }
            else
                SDLNet_TCP_Close(sock);
        }
    }
    for(i=0; numready && i<num_clients; i++)
    {
        if(SDLNet_SocketReady(clients[i].sock))
        {
            //if there is a message waiting in the queue
            if(getMsg(clients[i].sock, &message))
            {
                char *str;

                numready-;
                printf("<%s> %s\n",clients[i].name,message);
                // interpret commands
                if(message[0]=='/' && strlen(message)>1)
                {
                    //this function would be executed when
                    //the command you want to process has been
                    //passed. You would define your own do_command
                    //function perhaps using the message and the
                    //client "sender" or "target" of the command
                    do_command(message+1,&clients[i]);
                }
                else // it's a regular message
                {
                    // forward message to ALL clients...
                    str=mformat("ssss","<",clients[i].name,">
                                                ",message);

                    if(str)
                    {
```

```
                                        //This is also another function you would
                                        //create on your own. Basically you would loop
                                        //through each client in your list and send them
                                        //this message
                                            send_all(str);
                                    }
                            }
                            free(message);
                            message = NULL;
                    }
                    else
                    {
                            //remove the client from your set of client objects
                            remove_client(i);
                    }
                }
            }
        }

        // shutdown SDL_net
        SDLNet_Quit();

        // shutdown SDL
        SDL_Quit();

        return(0);
    }
```

Although Listing 14.7 looks complicated, there is not much going on to which you have not already been exposed. The process of starting up and initializing the SDL_Net library is a familiar practice by now. After the socket has finished binding to the server, it launches into an infinite loop. Within this loop, the application first creates an SDLNet_SocketSet structure, which is filled with as many sockets as there are clients already connected. When this is finished, the program then iterates through each socket within the SDLNet_SocketSet. It first inspects the socket to see whether any network activity has taken place. If a new client request is waiting, then the client is added to the socket set. The sample then proceeds to display any string data that was sent by the client sockets. After the demo exits, it shuts down the network and cleans up the allocated sockets.

TCP/IP VERSUS UDP (PART II)

As stated previously, a common and critical issue is to determine which protocol your game will be using when choosing between TCP/IP and UDP.

As outlined previously in this chapter, TCP/IP provides you with a guaranteed (reliable) packet delivery mechanism, although UDP does not. From this behavior alone, you might be tempted to always use TCP/IP to handle the network communication in your game. In a regular network or Internet application that requires this guaranteed approach to packet delivery, TCP/IP is certainly the preferred method. In the world of game programming, however, UDP is often the protocol of choice for multiplayer communication.

UDP is fast, compact, and connection-less, which lends itself to a high-performance application such as a first-person shooter or real-time strategy game. The only major drawback to using pure UDP is the fact that not only can packets arrive in any order; they can also be dropped without notification.

For regular game action, such as running through a maze or traveling through the game world, a few dropped packets will not make much of a difference. By the time the next scene of your game is processed, it is more than likely that new network messages will be received with updated information. However, there are cases in which you *must* receive the packet information. Combat is a good example. If you kill another player, then everyone in the level *must* get the information signaling that the player has died. If this message is dropped somewhere, then there could exist several ugly scenarios of a game that is now out of sync.

Some programmers might decide to implement a solution involving both protocols. This usually centers on a plan of using UDP packets for the in-game action, while relying on TCP/IP for any guaranteed messages. However, in practice, this method can generate a lot of problems depending upon the implementation. Dependent upon the network connection, the two protocols could quickly fall out of sync with each other, since the TCP/IP thread could be trying to resend a lot of packets. In short, this type of algorithm should only be attempted by advanced network programmers with a complete *zen* understanding of the two protocols and how they are processed by the operating system and socket libraries.

A common approach to this problem is to use a mechanism loosely defined as *reliable-UDP*. In a lot of ways, this approach gives you the benefits of both worlds: the speed and small overhead associated with using UDP, with, at the same time, a mechanism similar to the reliable, guaranteed delivery associated with using TCP/IP. You will learn more about using reliable-UDP in the next chapter where you add some network support to the *SuperAsteroidArena* project.

Network Address Translation

Network Address Translation (NAT) is an important issue to remember when implementing your network solution. A large number of computer users now have their own small network at home. This means that there is a mechanism in place to share the Internet connection, either with a router such as a Linksys device, a proxy server machine (either Windows or Linux), or through the Internet Connection Sharing mechanism of Windows XP. This is outlined in Figure 14.6.

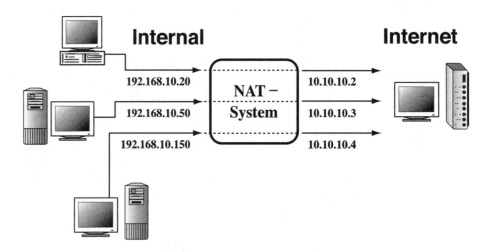

FIGURE 14.6 NAT Translation.

The purpose of these devices is to take a publicly available Internet address given to you by the Internet service provider and then filter it among the devices in your internal network. Depending upon the algorithm used by your router/proxy system, this can cause several problems, depending upon how your NAT device remembers or processes each client request.

For this reason, it is usually better to run the game server directly facing the Internet, as opposed to being hidden behind a router. This can help minimize any negative issues surrounding network communication and your NAT device.

CLIENT-SERVER PREDICTION/AUTHENTICATION

In a client-server environment, the server contains the master copy of the game world. The server is the final authority on what is and what is not allowed by the players. For this reason, it is necessary to create and establish a mechanism of action authentication in which the server must authenticate actions performed by the client.

The simplest way this can be done is to have a basic authentication scheme between the client and the server. Each time the client wants to perform an action within the game world, such as moving or firing his gun, the client must send a request to the server for its permission for the action to occur. The server then processes this request and makes a decision on whether or not the action is legal and responds to the client. Depending on the number of players in the game session, along with how often these requests are performed, this can be an acceptable method.

This, however, can slow things down considerably as the number of players increase in the game world. If you are using straight UDP for the delivery mechanism, a percentage of data can be lost between the client and server. In other words, the client might miss authentication messages from the server and vice-versa.

Client prediction, therefore, is an effort to maintain gameplay as smoothly as possible. Client prediction simply describes a technique that is used to handle any consistency problems between the client and server.

Dead-Reckoning

Dead-Reckoning is a common technique for client prediction that involves the client machine acting as a *representative* of the game server. Since the client knows the state of the game world since the last update from the server, you can then use this state to loosely authenticate client/player requests. Then when you hear back from the server, any adjustments to the players' position or movement can be made. This is an effective technique used in just about every First Person Shooter and some Massively Multiple Online Role Playing Games today.

CHAPTER EXERCISES

1. Many different open-source and low-cost commercial networking packages are available for the non-network programmer. Create a small matrix of the strengths and weaknesses of each one before making a decision on what to use.

2. Investigate other methods of client prediction and learn what is appropriate for what type of solution.

SUMMARY

You covered some basic principles behind the composition and topology design of networks, along with learning about SDL_Net and using either TCP or UDP for network communication. You learned that TCP is a guaranteed delivery mechanism, while UDP is not. You also went through some basic SDL_Net examples to learn the basics behind how a client and server communicate with each other. The chapter finished off with some discussion behind some techniques for managing legal actions within the game world. In the next chapter, you will focus a little less on networking theory and more on creating actual network code for the *SuperAsteroidArena* project.

15 Networking Timebox

Chapter Goals

- Explain UDP in greater detail.
- Introduce the ReplicaNet networking library.

Now that you have an introductory networking base of knowledge from which to work from, it is time to cover adding some networking support into the *SuperAsteroidArena* project. Network socket programming is not a topic with which most beginner (or intermediate) game developers are comfortable. To this end, you will be using a popular third-party solution known as ReplicaNet to handle network communication.

INTRODUCTION TO REPLICANET

Although you have a basic foundation of network programming from Chapter 14, "Introduction to Networking," it is another matter entirely to create a working networking solution suitable for the needs of a game. Although it might feel like you have been introduced to a lot of different topics, we have only really scratched the surface when it comes to handling game data over the Internet or LAN.

To this end, you will be using an excellent cross-platform network library called ReplicaNet, which has been designed from the ground up as a multiplayer solution for games. It satisfies the requirement of a reliable-UDP packet delivery mechanism covered in Chapter 14, "Introduction to Networking," which provides a hybrid between implementing your game using strictly either TCP or UDP. The other benefit of using this library is that it has already undergone a high level of optimization and has implemented a lot of the underlying networking code that you will not need to worry about.

Network Topology Design

Recall in the previous chapter, on the introduction to multiplayer support, that your networked game can fall under two topologies: client-server or peer-to-peer (P2P). Although both offer their own advantages and disadvantages, you will be using the peer-to-peer model for *SuperAsteroidArena*.

Usually in client-server applications, the game logic is separated such that the server contains the master record of the game world and processes every request by the client(s) to move and interact within it. The client contains the code base with all of the graphics, sound effects, and everything else that you present to the player. The logic behind this approach is that the server can just focus on processing the players and every other object in the game world, while the client represents the player's experience or view of the game world. The disadvantage of this model is that should the server leave or be disconnected from the network, then the session effectively ends.

By creating the *SuperAsteroidArena* project in a peer-to-peer design with ReplicaNet, you are able to take advantage of a networking layer that can automatically poll the network to find a new "host" node should the current server be disconnected. This is an attempt to minimize any session loss between the players in the group.

Networking Timebox

From the timebox allocated to this phase of implementation, the goal is to create a game server and add enough capabilities to any peer instance to move and shoot each other within the game world. This network design layout behind the *SuperAsteroidArena* project allows you to keep the code in one project which is used to distribute the game world objects around each peer node in the network. The client application is the one you have been working on throughout this book. It contains the graphics, sounds, and everything else presented to the player. The server application, on the other hand, is solely responsible for maintaining the main view of the game world. It does not display any graphics or play any sound effects. Because most multiplayer games support a chat feature of some kind, you will also add some basic text sending in this timebox.

MAKING ADDITIONS TO PEON

To make these networking additions to the game, you first need to create and update some components of the underlying Peon engine. This will allow you to create the necessary mechanisms to process network messages.

Creating the NetStream Object

Although you can create a small hierarchy of networking-related components in the Peon engine, you first create an object that will encapsulate both client and server processing.

When this timebox is completed, feel free to make any adjustments to the Peon networking model to fit your own multiplayer practices.

NOTE

ON THE CD

Start by working through a skeleton application that manages a peer-to-peer configuration. This chapter's code is taken from the `NetworkLayer.cpp` file in the project folder and is defined in Listing 15.1.

LISTING 15.1 `NetworkLayer.cpp`

```
bool NetworkLayer::onLoad()
{
//snip
//create a new Network instance
m_pNetwork = new NetworkLayer();
m_pNetwork->SetManualPoll();          // Make ReplicaNet use the manual
                                      // poll method.

//allow the XPsession / XPURL threads to use automatic scheduling
m_pNetwork->SetPollLayerBelow(false);
m_pNetwork->SetPollLayerBelowForXPSession(false);
m_pNetwork->SetAutomaticPollXPSession();
m_pNetwork->SetAutomaticPollXPURL();
return true;
}
```

ReplicaNet makes careful use of threads to process network events and messages. The main benefit of using ReplicaNet is that it allows you to focus more on processing network events than actually dealing with the lower level socket communication and threading.

When the network layer object is communicating properly, it will receive event notifications automatically when a player joins or leaves the game, or other objects need to be synchronized among the nodes.

Working with Message Types

When the client and server are talking to each other, you need to define what network messages you will listen for and process. These messages are almost always game-specific, which is why ReplicaNet does not try to define its own message types (beyond the extreme basics).

Instead, each object that you wish to replicate in the master database through ReplicaNet needs to have an identifier "type" attached, for easier processing on each node in the network.

For the most part, there are only two object types that you will need to use for any object that wishes to be involved in the network: `Certain()` and `Reliable()`.

The benefit of using ReplicaNet is that you can throw any kind of object into the database which will then be optimized to send under the covers. You do not need to worry about manually creating some packet objects or mechanisms to do this.

UPDATING PLAYERS

Most of the fun of multiplayer games derives from being able to challenge other human players. Although you were introduced to a few basic client predication concepts in the previous chapter, you become more familiar with them here. Since the *SuperAsteroidArena* game is meant as a small battleground, you only need to implement some basic client prediction techniques to keep the flow of the game fast and furious. To begin with, you will need to actually define your `Player` object, which represents each player in the session. Listing 15.2 demonstrates this.

LISTING 15.2   `Player` Definition from `Player.rol`

```
object Player
{
//this script defines two datablocks for the Player entity in our
//game
datablock Predict_Float;
```

```
datablock NData;
//snip!

//ensure that this object is defined using the Certain transmission
//"type" instead of Reliable(). Certain will use less bandwidth
Certain();
}
```

When you have the basic player set up and able to fly around your game world, you need a way to allow other players to join/leave your session, as well as update every player's view of the game world.

Session Hosting/Joining

During the design of the game, it was decided that the game would not start until all the players have finished joining to the session. Although there is no chat room location in the game, this would be a good place to use one. It would allow the players to communicate with each other prior to the game, allowing for much trash talk. The ReplicaNet library references other machines in the network, not by IP address, but rather using sessions. After the session starts, however, any new player attempting to connect to the session will be denied. Listing 15.3 gives a sample method of handling join requests.

LISTING 15.3   Handling Player Join Requests

```
bool NetworkLayer::joinSession(const String& strURL)
{
  m_pNetwork->SessionJoin(strURL);

  return true;

}
```

Likewise, when a player wants to leave the game, he should be allowed to drop out of the session without disrupting every other active player. Listing 15.4 shows one way to handle this.

LISTING 15.4   Handling Player Drop Requests

```
void NetworkLayer::disconnect()
{
  m_pNetwork->Disconnect();
}
```

Players Tend to Move Around

After the session begins, every player involved in the game will naturally begin to move around the game world in an attempt to win the round. The server will be the continuous authority of the game world, sending view update snapshots to every player in the game. This is a basic attempt to ensure that some of your players do not try to cheat the game.

After a player (or any other entity) is added to the master database for the session using the Publish method, the objects are updated automatically when they need to be.

When you adjust your player's position, for example, the changes are reflected at a lower level, and ReplicaNet is alerted to the fact that it needs to wake up and propagate these modifications to the master database.

Players Want to Fire

As the players move around the game world, they will also have the ability to fire laser blasts at each other in an attempt to be the last player standing. Again, you have to be somewhat careful of possible cheating attempts by clients in your session—especially when it comes to computing any change of health, positive or negative. Listing 15.5 begins some details on adding the ability to process laser blasts.

LISTING 15.5   Player Fire events

```
Projectile *proj = new Projectile();
proj->SetPosition(mPlayerConrolledPlane->GetPosition());
proj->SetRotation(mPlayerConrolledPlane->GetRotation());
proj->Publish();
```

TIMEBOX EVALUATION

You should be getting used to it by now, but again pull out your design documentation and ensure that you have completed everything assigned for this timebox. Do the multiplayer aspects meet your criteria as outlined in the document? Are you happy with the network communication layer, or is there a need to create/design a new one?

These thoughts should appear in any notes for this timebox along with any decisions that need to be made.

If you decide to alter the requirements of this timebox, do not forget to keep the design documentation updated. As you have done before, create a new timebox with your desired requirements.

CHAPTER EXERCISES

1. You have covered only one or two events involved in the *SuperAsteroidArena* game. Add some networking events to the game to create a more intimate experience for the player.
2. Add some basic chatting capabilities to the game. When the player hits a certain key, it should open a small chat window to send some text to the server, which will send it to every other player
3. Ensure the prediction techniques you implemented in the game are sufficient to handle your projected min and max number of clients joined to the session.

SUMMARY

Adding network support to any game is no trivial task and should not be taken lightly. Proper planning must be in place; be aware of the time and cost involved in doing so for any of your projects, especially if you intend to create your own socket library. Though you were able to take advantage of ReplicaNet, which is a very useful third-party networking library, there are always hurdles to face when designing games that communicate over a network. Leave some time in your project planning to properly test the networking layer if you want to add it to your game.

In the next chapter, you begin focusing on using your favorite modeling software to create and display meshes within your game world.

16 Introduction to Models

Chapter Goals

- Work with the 3DS model format.
- Introduce model animation and the MD3 format.
- Introduce and discuss the Collada initiative.

Throughout this book you have been introduced to various methods and practices of getting various game assets into the engine. You have been shown how to load texture information and how to use music and sound effects. One of the most popular remaining assets left to cover is the generation and manipulation of model objects within the game world.

MODEL GENERATION

A *model* (or mesh) represents a collection of vertices and textures to define an object within a game world. In most titles requiring 3D models and other artwork, development teams tend to establish an art *asset pipeline*. At a high level this is simply a method of organizing the communication between your programmer(s) and your artist(s). The programmers must decide on certain requirements of the art-work, such as a particular file format the models must be in, along with other details, such as any polygon count restrictions. The artists must themselves work with the game designer to create a common, unified vision that represents the designer's game world. Figure 16.1 demonstrates an overview of the model asset process.

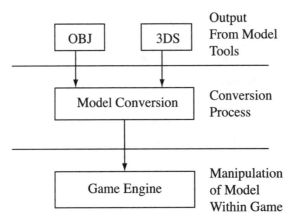

FIGURE 16.1   Model asset process.

The output mesh from the model tool must usually pass through a conversion pipeline process in which the model is converted into a format that is recognized by your engine.

UPDATING THE MESHFACTORY IN PEON

Until now you have been using the MeshFactory interface of the Peon to create sim-ple meshes for use in your scenes in order to display relatively simple objects such as a box. For the majority of the projects you work on, however, it is necessary to render some complex geometry created in external third-party modeling software such as 3DS Studio Max, Maya, or Blender. Since the design and focus of the OpenGL is solely on controlling the state machine to render primitive data, there are no methods or libraries provided by the ARB to work with model information. This is left to you to implement on your own.

A wide variety of model formats is available for use with your engine, giving you a wide array of choices for deciding which format(s) to support. For the purposes of the MeshFactory object within the Peon library, you focus on working with a popular model format: the 3DS format.

Before using a file format for your game and/or engine, be sure to look for any license restrictions surrounding it, even though the majority of formats used in modeling software are free for use in your applications. Although developed by Id Software for Quake3, for example, the MD3 animation file format used later in this chapter is free for use in your own applications, but proprietary models created by commercial games stored in this format are not.

CREATING A 3DS IMPORTER

Most of the file formats used by the modeling software are not readable by humans, so it is possible and most often necessary to develop your own code for importing model information.

In most situations, it is often necessary to first pass the model object through a piece of intermediary software, which converts it to a format used for your engine. Milkshape3D is such a tool and is available on the accompanying CD-ROM.

The 3DS file format is somewhat more advanced in that the information is stored in a binary format. You will now write a small object to import model information that is stored in the popular 3DS format.

Listing 16.1 details the new method necessary that you will need to add to the /Peon/PeonMain/include/MeshFactory.h file.

LISTING 16.1

```
namespace peon
    {
/** This structure holds the model face information */
struct sFace
{
    int vertIndex[3];
    int coordIndex[3];
};
```

```
/** This structure stores material information */
struct sMaterialInfo
{
    char   strName[255];
    char   strFile[255];
    BYTE   color[3];
    int    texureId;
    float uTile;
    float vTile;
    float uOffset;
    float vOffset;
};


struct s3DObject
{
    int   numOfVerts;
    int   numOfFaces;
    int   numTexVertex;
    int   materialID;
    bool bHasTexture;
    char strName[255];
    UINT      *pIndices;
    Vector3  *pVerts;
    Vector3  *pNormals;
    Vector2  *pTexVerts;
    sFace *pFaces;
};

struct s3DModel
{
    int numOfObjects;
    int numOfMaterials;
    vector<sMaterialInfo> pMaterials;
    vector<s3DObject> pObject;
};

/** This structure is used to load 3DS indicies which are stored as
* 4 unsigned shorts */
struct sIndices {

    unsigned short a, b, c, bVisible;
};
```

```
/** This structure is used to contain chunk information
*/
struct sChunk
{
    unsigned short int ID;
    unsigned int length;
    unsigned int bytesRead;
};

    /**
    * The purpose of this object is to load the model data contained
in
    * a given resource
    */
    class PEONMAIN_API MeshFactory : public ISingleton<MeshFactory>
    {
    //snip
public:
    /** This method is used to load a 3DS model into a
    * s3DModel object
    */
    s3DModel* loadMeshFrom3DS( const String& strFilename );

    MeshFactory();
    ~MeshFactory();
    static MeshFactory& getSingleton(void);
    static MeshFactory* getSingletonPtr(void);
private:
    int getString(char *);

    void readChunk(sChunk *);

    void processNextChunk(s3DModel *pModel, sChunk *);

    void processNextObjectChunk(s3DModel *pModel, s3DObject *pObject,
sChunk *);

    void processNextMaterialChunk(s3DModel *pModel, sChunk *);

    void readColorChunk(sMaterialInfo *pMaterial, sChunk *pChunk);

    void readVertices(s3DObject *pObject, sChunk *);
```

```
    void readVertexIndices(s3DObject *pObject, sChunk *);

    void readUVCoordinates(s3DObject *pObject, sChunk *);

    void readObjectMaterial(s3DModel *pModel, s3DObject *pObject,
sChunk *pPreviousChunk);

    void computeNormals(s3DModel *pModel);

    void unloadData();

    FILE *m_pFile;

    sChunk *m_pCurrentChunk;
    sChunk *m_pTempChunk;


    };
}
```

Loading the 3DS Model Data

Loading the actual 3DS data is not difficult. You use the MeshFactory object to process one or more model data files. Listing 16.2 begins the process of loading the data from the model file.

LISTING 16.2   Loading the Data

```
    s3dModel* MeshFactory::loadMeshFrom3DS( const String& strFileName )
    {
      s3dModel* pModel = new s3dModel();

      m_pFile = fopen(strFileName.c_str(), "rb");

      if(!m_pFile )
      {
        return NULL;
      }

      readChunk(m_pCurrentChunk);
```

```
    if (m_pCurrentChunk->ID != PRIMARY)
    {
      //unable to load the PRIMARY chunk from the file! Abort!
      return NULL;
    }

    processNextChunk(pModel, m_pCurrentChunk);

    computeNormals(pModel);

    unloadData();

    return( pModel );
}
```

Rendering the Model

Now that you have gone through the entire process of loading the model information into memory, you can easily render this data within your OpenGL application.
Listing 16.3 demonstrates how to render the 3DS data.

LISTING 16.3   Rendering Model Data

```
void s3DModel::onRender()
{

    for(int i = 0; i < this.numOfObjects; i++)
    {

        if(this.pObject.size() <= 0) break;

        s3DObject *pObject = &this.pObject[i];

        if(pObject->bHasTexture)
        {
            glEnable(GL_TEXTURE_2D);

            glColor3ub(255, 255, 255);
```

```
            glBindTexture(GL_TEXTURE_2D, TextureArray3ds[pObject-
                                                  >materialID]);
    }
    else
    {
        glDisable(GL_TEXTURE_2D);

         glColor3ub(255, 255, 255);
    }

    glBegin(GL_TRIANGLES);

    for(int j = 0; j < pObject->numOfFaces; j++)
    {

        for(int whichVertex = 0; whichVertex < 3; whichVertex++)
        {
            int index = pObject->pFaces[j].vertIndex[whichVertex];

            glNormal3f(pObject->pNormals[ index ].x, pObject->
                pNormals[ index ].y, pObject->pNormals[ index ].z);

            if(pObject->bHasTexture) {

                if(pObject->pTexVerts) {
                    glTexCoord2f(pObject->pTexVerts[ index ].x,
                                    pObject->pTexVerts[ index ].y);
                }
              } else {

                if(m3DModel.pMaterials.size() < pObject->
                                                    materialID)
                {
                    BYTE *pColor = m3DModel.pMaterials[pObject->
                                                materialID].color;

                    glColor3ub(pColor[0], pColor[1], pColor[2]);
                }
            }
```

```
                    glVertex3f(pObject->pVerts[ index ].x, pObject->
                            pVerts[ index ].y, pObject->pVerts[ index ].z);
                }
            }

        glEnd();
    }

}
```

Cleaning Up

Since you allocated quite a few data structures during the loading of your 3DS model information, you need to remember to clean this memory up when you are finished with the object. Listing 16.4 demonstrates what the onUnload method looks like.

LISTING 16.4 s3DModel::onUnload()

```
void s3DModel::onUnload()
{
    for(int i = 0; i < this.numOfObjects; i++)
    {
        PEON_DELETE_ARRAY( pObject[i].pFaces );
        PEON_DELETE_ARRAY( pObject[i].pNormals );
        PEON_DELETE_ARRAY( pObject[i].pVerts );
        PEON_DELETE_ARRAY( pObject[i].pTexVerts );
    }
}
```

MODEL ANIMATION

Although the ability to load and render static objects created with modeling software is a good addition to your game engine, another popular use of models is to create stored animations. When *Quake3* was released by Id Software, the animation format the company had created was known as the MD3 format. It defined the ability to store a model's key-frame data for a particular animation. In other words, rather than needing to generate or store every single cell of animation for your model, you can instead define a set of cells that are marked as transitional cells between animation movements. These transitional cells are known as "key-frames."

After your game engine loads the key frames involved in an animation, it then calculates some interpolation frames of animation between the key-frames, depending upon the speed of the local machine. The goal of this is to provide a smooth mechanism of model animation. If you had a faster machine, for example, then the game would automatically generate more frames of the animation to produce a clean and more realistic model. In contrast, if you had a slower machine, the game would automatically drop unneeded frames of animation in order to keep the game as near-smooth as possible.

THE MD3 FILE FORMAT

At the highest level, the MD3 file format can be broken into two segments: the header information and the model data. The header information defines the basic composition of the model, such as the number of vertices and triangle data, along with the offset into the model data where the distinct key-frames of animation are stored.

 The MD3 format has no license restrictions surrounding it. This means that you can freely use it for your own models in your games. Obviously, it does not give you license to include copyrighted MD3 models.

Listing 16.5 starts off with the top-level MD3 header information.

LISTING 16.5 sMD3Header

```
struct sMD3Header
{
   char    fileID[4];   // This stores the file ID - Must be "IDP3"
   int     version;     // This stores the file version - Must be 15
   char    strFile[68]; // This stores the name of the file
   int     numFrames;   // This stores the number of animation frames
   int     numTags;     // This stores the tag count
   int     numMeshes;   // This stores the number of sub-objects
                        // in the mesh
   int     numMaxSkins; // This stores the number of skins for
                        // the mesh
   int     headerSize;  // This stores the mesh header size
   int     tagStart;    // This stores the offset into the file
                        // for tags
```

```
    int     tagEnd;      // This stores the end offset into the file
                         // for tags
    int     fileSize;    // This stores the file size
};
```

The `fileID` attribute identifies the file being loaded as an MD3 file. It must always have a value of IDP3; otherwise, you can gracefully exit your model importing process here. The `numFrames` attribute specifies the number of animation frames contained in the model data, which is useful for calculating the offset into this data.

The next structure you will work with is the `sMD3Mesh` structure defined in Listing 16.6, which details the mesh information.

LISTING 16.6 `sMD3MeshInfo` structure

```
// This structure is used to read in the mesh data
// for the .md3 models
struct sMd3MeshInfo
{
  // This stores the mesh ID (We don't care)
  char meshID[4];

  // This stores the mesh name (We do care)
  char strName[68];

  // This stores the mesh animation frame count
  int numMeshFrames;

  // This stores the mesh skin count
  int numSkins;

  // This stores the mesh vertex count
  int numVertices;

  // This stores the mesh face count
  int numTriangles;

  // This stores the starting offset for the triangles
  int triStart;

  // This stores the header size for the mesh
  int headerSize;
```

```
// This stores the starting offset for the UV coordinates
int uvStart;

// This stores the starting offset for the vertex indices
int vertexStart;

// This stores the total mesh size
int meshSize;
};
```

Next you will learn about the tag structure used to rotate and work with child objects. Listing 16.7 details this tag information.

LISTING 16.7 sMD3TagInfo

```
struct sMd3TagInfo
{
  char     strName[64];      //This stores the name of the tag
  Vector3  vecPosition;      //This stores the translation
  float    rotation[3][3];   //Stores the 3x3 rotation
};
```

Bone information for the MD3 model format can be loaded and stored into another structure shown in Listing 16.8.

LISTING 16.8 sMd3BoneInfo

```
struct sMd3BoneInfo
{
  float    mins[3];       //This is the min (x, y, z) value for the bone
  float    maxs[3];       //This is the max (x, y, z) value for the bone
  float    position[3];   //This supposedly stores bone position
  float    scale;         //This stores the scale of the bone
  char     creator[16];   //The modeler used to create the model
};
```

The vector normals and vertex indices can be loaded and stored within a structure as outlined in Listing 16.9.

LISTING 16.9 sMd3TriangleInfo

```
struct sMd3TriangleInfo
{
  signed short  vertex[3]; //The vertex for this face
  unsigned char normal[2]; //This stores some normal values
};
```

Indexes into the vertices of the vertex and texture coordinate arrays can be loaded and stored into the structure outlined in Listing 16.10.

LISTING 16.10 sMd3FaceInfo

```
struct sMd3FaceInfo
{
  int vertexIndices[3];
};
```

U, V coordinate information, which is used for texture manipulation purposes, can be contained within a structure as shown in Listing 16.11.

LISTING 16.11 sMD3TexCoordInfo

```
struct sMd3TexCoordInfo
{
  float textureCoord[2];
};
```

Finally, the skin name is loaded and stored into a structure defined in Listing 16.12.

LISTING 16.12 sMD3SkinInfo

```
struct sMd3SkinInfo
{
  char strName[68];
};
```

ON THE CD
If you take a look in the /chapter_source/bin/media/md3 folder on the CD-ROM, you will notice that each MD3 model is defined by three segments: the head, upper body, and lower body.

Now, you will learn how to load and incorporate this data into the Peon engine in order to render and animate any MD3 file.

The `AnimatedMeshFactory`

According to the Peon design with regard to working with model information, there should be a level of abstraction between the model format (that is, MD3) and the Peon engine itself. The advantage of this approach is that you can then add support for other animated model formats without the need to hardcode anything into your engine.

Within the Peon engine, you will be working with the `AnimatedMeshFactory` object, which is an interface to the different model formats the engine can load and work with. In this case you will obviously be working with MD3 animated meshes.

The approach of the Peon engine is to first use the `AnimatedMeshFactory` object to load the data from an MD3 model. The model data is then converted into a `sMD3Model` object that can be inserted into the scene graph you have been working with throughout this book.

INTRODUCTION TO COLLADA

As you might have noticed, one of the struggles when working with assets created by modeling software is the accompanying effort to find the best way to get the content in your game engine. In some cases, this can involve using third-party tools to import the model generated by your software in order to export it in a format that your game engine supports. Each major modeling software application has its own private format, and they do not always include proper importing or exporting tools to work with. In most cases, this involves almost forcing you to use a particular asset creation tool for your modeling needs.

COLLAborative Design Activity (Collada) is a movement to establish an open sourced standard for 3D applications and their digital asset format. The popular content creation companies are participating in this initiative, bringing together people from Alias, Discreet, and Softimage, among a host of other middleware focused companies.

Some major hardware vendors such as NVidia, ATI, 3DLabs, and Sony Entertainment are also participating in this collaborative effort. The data format being designed by Collada is one using XML to describe both models and animation, but with the intention of supporting shader creation and even real-time physics. Each participant in the Collada is responsible for the implementation and support of their import and exporting tools but are all supposed to handle the same XML data structure(s). Since the specification is written in XML, you can also modify the format to your particular engine's requirements, should the need arise.

CHAPTER EXERCISES

1. Research some other common model file formats and decide whether you should write an importer for them as well. What are the limitations of the 3DS or MD3 model file formats?

SUMMARY

This chapter provided you with a brief overview on the concept of meshes and model making. When working on a game project, the decision needs to be made whether the game is going to be 2D or 3D and how best to create and load any model data. Throughout this chapter, you worked with several classes that are responsible for loading and rendering 3DS model data. You also were introduced to model animation and working with the MD3 file format into the scene graph of the Peon engine.

There are quite a number of common special effects that most game programmers want or need for their projects. In addition to working with the presentation of a background in your game world, the next chapter focuses on various effects that are used in some games today.

17 Animation and Special Effects

Chapter Goals

- Introduce and discuss billboarding.
- Introduce and discuss cube environment mapping (that is, skyboxing).
- Introduce particle systems and point sprites.
- Introduce using simple billboard animation techniques.

You have learned a great deal so far in graphics programming, so it is time to pick up the pace and introduce a few more common graphics effects found in most games today. Although these are fairly simple techniques that can be dropped into your game, they can add quite a bit of depth to the overall effect of your scene, which can impress the player even further.

BILLBOARDING

Billboarding rose to fame several years ago as a way to trick the game player into seeing a 2D effect or animation rendered in a 3D game world. *Billboarding* involves taking a 2D texture (or sprite animation) and rendering it to a quad set of vertices, which are always facing the camera.

For example, a common use for the billboarding technique is to create several frames of an explosion and load them into texture containers. Then, when the game signals the need to render an explosion, you calculate the position of the camera and render the necessary frame of explosion animation. To the viewer, this simple technique tricks him into perceiving that the explosion is happening in 3D space, no matter if they try and move the camera around it.

Understanding the View Matrix (Recap)

To understand how billboarding works, it is essential to understand the composition of the view matrix within the graphics pipeline. Equation 17.1 shows you a breakdown of the view matrix, including its vector composition, that you learned in Chapter 6, "Creating an OpenGL Renderer."

$$\begin{pmatrix} right\_vector.x & right\_vector.y & right\_vector.z & -(right\_vector \cdot eye\_vector) \\ up\_vector.x & up\_vector.y & up\_vector.z & -(up\_vector \cdot eye\_vector) \\ -look\_vector.x & -look\_vector.y & -look\_vector.z & -(look\_vector \cdot eye\_vector) \\ 0 & 0 & 0 & 1 \end{pmatrix} \quad (17.1)$$

As you can see, the right, up, and look vectors compose the top 3×3 corner of the view matrix. The final column contains the dot product calculation between the right, up, and look vectors and the eye point vector. Listing 17.1 details the start of the /chapter_17/BasicBillboard sample project, which positions the initial camera orientation.

ON THE CD

LISTING 17.1 BasicBillboard Initialization

```
//first define the starting position of the camera or view matrix
Vector3 vecEye(0.0f, 0.0f, 5.0f);    // Eye Position
Vector3 vecLook(0.0f, 0.0f, -1.0f);  // Look Vector
Vector3 vecUp(0.0f, 1.0f, 0.0f);     // Up Vector
Vector3 vecRight(1.0f, 0.0f, 0.0f);  // Right Vector
```

Extracting the Vectors

To create and work with a billboarding matrix to position your scene's objects, you first need to extract the modelview matrix from the OpenGL matrix stack. Then you align this matrix along either the x, y, or z axis before rendering the texture. Listing 17.2 details how this is done using the `generateMatrix` method of the `Billboard` object.

LISTING 17.2   void Billboard::generateMatrix(float x, float y, float z)

```
{

    float mat[16]; //our current modelview matrix
    //take a snapshot of the current modelview matrix
    glGetFloatv( GL_MODELVIEW_MATRIX, mat );

    float pi    = 3.141592654f; //pi value
    float theta = -180 * atan2f(mat[8], mat[10]) / pi;
    float d     = x*x + y*y + z*z; //magnitude of the vector(x,y,z)
    float ct    = cosf(PEON_DEGTORAD(theta));
    float st    = sinf(PEON_DEGTORAD(theta));

    // Normalize the incoming vector values which could be placed
    // into a Vector3 object
    if( d > 0 )
    {
        d = 1/d;
        x *= d;
        y *= d;
        z *= d;
    }

    //reset the matrix to the identity
    mat[ 0] = 1; mat[ 1] = 0; mat[ 2] = 0; mat[ 3] = 0;
    mat[ 4] = 0; mat[ 5] = 1; mat[ 6] = 0; mat[ 7] = 0;
    mat[ 8] = 0; mat[ 9] = 0; mat[10] = 1; mat[11] = 0;
    mat[12] = 0; mat[13] = 0; mat[14] = 0; mat[15] = 1;

    mat[0] = x*x + ct*(1-x*x) + st*0;
    mat[4] = x*y + ct*(0-x*y) + st*-z;
    mat[8] = x*z + ct*(0-x*z) + st*y;

    mat[1] = y*x + ct*(0-y*x) + st*z;
    mat[5] = y*y + ct*(1-y*y) + st*0;
    mat[9] = y*z + ct*(0-y*z) + st*-x;

    mat[2] = z*x + ct*(0-z*x) + st*-y;
    mat[6] = z*y + ct*(0-z*y) + st*x;
    mat[10]= z*z + ct*(1-z*z) + st*0;
```

```
        //apply the calculated matrix to the current stack
        glMultMatrixf( mat );
    }
```

This billboarding technique effectively produces a view matrix that is axis-aligned. The final step in this process is to compute the orientation of the bill-boarded texture with respect to the updated view matrix that you created in Listing 17.2. Listing 17.3 documents this procedure.

LISTING 17.3 Rendering the Billboard

```
void Billboard::onRender()
{
//calculate the billboard matrix around the y-axis
generateMatrix( 0.0f, 1.0f, 0.0f );

//now render a simple primitive by enabling alpha-blending
glEnable( GL_BLEND );
glBlendFunc( GL_SRC_ALPHA, GL_ONE_MINUS_SRC_ALPHA );

glEnable( GL_ALPHA_TEST );
glAlphaFunc( GL_GREATER, 0 );

//set the texture
glBindTexture( GL_TEXTURE_2D, m_pTex->getTex() );

//arbitrary polygon rendering mode here. It could be replaced
//with a GL_QUADS or GL_TRIANGLES
glBegin( GL_POLYGON );
{
  glTexCoord2f(0.0f, 0.0f);
  glVertex3f(-1.0f, -1.0f, 0.0f);

  glTexCoord2f(1.0f, 0.0f);
  glVertex3f(1.0f, -1.0f, 0.0f);

  glTexCoord2f(1.0f, 1.0f);
  glVertex3f(1.0f, 1.0f, 0.0f);

  glTexCoord2f(0.0f, 1.0f);
  glVertex3f(-1.0f, 1.0f, 0.0f);
}
glEnd();
```

```
glDisable( GL_BLEND );
glDisable( GL_ALPHA_TEST );
}
```

SKYBOXES (ENVIRONMENT MAPPING)

Another common effect within most games today is the use of a cube environment map, also known as a *skybox*. The common practice for creating a skybox is to create a cube mesh, which is then placed at the current camera position with its surface normals facing inward. You then texture-map the inward faces of this cube with whatever environment you want to present to the player: deep space, an undersea view, floating clouds, and so on.

You can use the view matrix composition of vectors presented in Equation 17.1 to create the proper orientation of the skybox.

NOTE

Because you want the background to appear as an infinite distance from the camera, you must remember to disable any depth-buffer writes before rendering and then re-enable them when you are finished.

The common practice involves the following:

- Obtaining the current view matrix and storing it
- Adjusting the matrix, so that it is centered on the camera's position
- Rendering the skybox
- Restoring the original view matrix

Listing 17.4 documents how to render the skybox around your camera's position.

LISTING 17.4   Skybox

```
void Skybox::onRender()
{
  // Bind the BACK texture of the sky map to the
  // BACK side of the cube
  glBindTexture(GL_TEXTURE_2D, m_oTexture[BACK_FACE]);
```

```
// This centers the sky box around position (m_x, m_y, m_z)
m_x = m_x - m_vecDim.x  / 2;
m_y = m_y - m_vecDim.y / 2;
m_z = m_z - m_vecDim.z / 2;

// Start drawing the side as a QUAD
glBegin(GL_QUADS);

// Assign the texture coordinates and vertices for BACK Side
glTexCoord2f(0.0f, 0.0f); glVertex3f(m_x, m_y, m_z);
glTexCoord2f(0.0f, 1.0f); glVertex3f(m_x, m_y + m_vecDim.y, m_z);
glTexCoord2f(1.0f, 1.0f); glVertex3f(m_x + m_vecDim.x, m_y +
  m_vecDim.y, m_z);
glTexCoord2f(1.0f, 0.0f); glVertex3f(m_x + m_vecDim.x, m_y,
  m_z);
glEnd();

//Bind the FRONT texture of the sky map to the FRONT
glBindTexture(GL_TEXTURE_2D, m_oTexture[FRONT_FACE]);

// Start drawing the side as a QUAD
glBegin(GL_QUADS);

// Assign the texture coordinates and vertices for the FRONT Side
glTexCoord2f(1.0f, 0.0f); glVertex3f(m_x, m_y, m_z + m_vecDim.z);
glTexCoord2f(1.0f, 1.0f); glVertex3f(m_x, m_y + m_vecDim.y, m_z +
  m_vecDim.z);
glTexCoord2f(0.0f, 1.0f); glVertex3f(m_x + m_vecDim.x, m_y +
  m_vecDim.y, m_z + m_vecDim.z);
glTexCoord2f(0.0f, 0.0f); glVertex3f(m_x + m_vecDim.x, m_y,
  m_z + m_vecDim.z);
glEnd();

// Bind the BOTTOM texture of the sky map to the BOTTOM face
glBindTexture(GL_TEXTURE_2D, m_oTexture[BOTTOM_FACE]);

// Start drawing the side as a QUAD
glBegin(GL_QUADS);

// Assign the texture coordinates and vertices for the BOTTOM
glTexCoord2f(1.0f, 0.0f); glVertex3f(m_x, m_y, m_z);
glTexCoord2f(1.0f, 1.0f); glVertex3f(m_x, m_y, m_z + m_vecDim.z);
glTexCoord2f(0.0f, 1.0f); glVertex3f(m_x + m_vecDim.x, m_y,
  m_z + m_vecDim.z);
```

```
glTexCoord2f(0.0f, 0.0f); glVertex3f(m_x + m_vecDim.x, m_y,
  m_z);
glEnd();

// Bind the TOP texture of the sky map to the TOP
glBindTexture(GL_TEXTURE_2D, m_oTexture[TOP_FACE]);

// Start drawing the side as a QUAD
glBegin(GL_QUADS);

// Assign the texture coordinates and vertices for the TOP Side
glTexCoord2f(1.0f, 1.0f); glVertex3f(m_x, m_y + m_vecDim.y, m_z);
glTexCoord2f(1.0f, 0.0f); glVertex3f(m_x, m_y + m_vecDim.y, m_z +
  m_vecDim.z);
glTexCoord2f(0.0f, 0.0f); glVertex3f(m_x + m_vecDim.x, m_y +
  m_vecDim.y, m_z + m_vecDim.z);
glTexCoord2f(0.0f, 1.0f); glVertex3f(m_x + m_vecDim.x, m_y +
  m_vecDim.y, m_z);
glEnd();

// Bind the LEFT texture of the sky map to the LEFT
glBindTexture(GL_TEXTURE_2D, m_oTexture[LEFT_FACE]);

// Start drawing the side as a QUAD
glBegin(GL_QUADS);

// Assign the texture coordinates and vertices for the LEFT
glTexCoord2f(1.0f, 0.0f); glVertex3f(m_x, m_y, m_z);
glTexCoord2f(0.0f, 0.0f); glVertex3f(m_x, m_y, m_z + m_vecDim.z);
glTexCoord2f(0.0f, 1.0f); glVertex3f(m_x, m_y + m_vecDim.y,
  m_z + m_vecDim.z);
glTexCoord2f(1.0f, 1.0f); glVertex3f(m_x, m_y + m_vecDim.y, m_z);
glEnd();

// Bind the RIGHT texture of the sky map to the RIGHT face
glBindTexture(GL_TEXTURE_2D, m_oTexture[RIGHT_FACE]);

// Start drawing the side as a QUAD
glBegin(GL_QUADS);

// Assign the texture coordinates and vertices for the RIGHT Side
glTexCoord2f(0.0f, 0.0f); glVertex3f(m_x + m_vecDim.x, m_y, m_z);
glTexCoord2f(1.0f, 0.0f); glVertex3f(m_x + m_vecDim.x, m_y,
  m_z + m_vecDim.z);
```

```
glTexCoord2f(1.0f, 1.0f); glVertex3f(m_x + m_vecDim.x, m_y +
   m_vecDim.y, m_z + m_vecDim.z);
glTexCoord2f(0.0f, 1.0f); glVertex3f(m_x + m_vecDim.x, m_y +
   m_vecDim.y, m_z);
glEnd();

}
```

After you have launched the skybox demo, you should be able to use the mouse to look around the various sides.

OBJECT PICKING/SELECTION

Another common problem among most game programmers is the necessity to map the current player's cursor to data within the game world. In other words, how do you detect whether the player has selected a particular unit within your world? This is known as *picking*.

Because of your introduction and expertise using the bounding boxes to detect collisions between objects within your game world, you can leverage this technique to detect a collision (that is, selection) by the mouse. Since each object should have its own bounding box within your scene, you simply need to cast (or project) a ray from the current mouse position into the game world. Should this ray collide with an object, then you can generate some feedback to the player that this particular unit has been selected.

NOTE

If your game requires much more precision in object selection, such as the ability to select an object's appendage, and so on, then other solutions should be explored. You could use the ray-to-bounding box collision detection approach to define a general area and then create more detailed tests after you have determined that the mouse has selected something within this general region.

Although there are many approaches to this type of algorithm, OpenGL provides a mechanism for this selection process. Known as a *selection buffer*, it can be used to specify some OpenGL commands to process the scene.

Listing 17.5 provides a mechanism to perform mouse selection.

LISTING 17.5   Mouse Picking

```
#define SUN 101
#define MOON 102
#define EARTH 103
```

```
    //snip
    //within the event queue, listen for the mouse button click.
Override the
    //onMouseEvent function
    void MainApp::onMouseEvent( SDL_Event* pEvent)
  {
      if(pEvent->type == SDL_MOUSEBUTTONDOWN)
      {
        // Here we pass in the cursors X and Y co-ordinates to test an
        //object under the mouse.
        obj_ID = testObjectID(pEvent->button.x,pEvent->button.y);
        sprintf(strTemp, "Position of click and ObjID: (x,y):(%d, %d) :
(%d)", pEvent->button.x,pEvent->button.y, obj_ID);
        m_strPos = strTemp;

        //the obj_ID records what was generated by the hit test.
        switch( obj_ID )
        {
          case MOON:
            m_strChosen = "Moon";
          break;
          case SUN:
            m_strChosen = "Sun";
          break;
          case EARTH:
            m_strChosen = "Earth";
          break;
        }

      }


  int MainApp::testObjectID(int x, int y)
  {
     int window_width = peon::EngineCore::getSingleton().
       getRenderer()->getWidth();
     int window_height = peon::EngineCore::getSingleton().
       getRenderer()->getHeight();

     //This will hold the sum total of objects clicked on
     int objectsFound = 0;
     //This array will store our viewport coordinates
```

```
int    viewportCoords[4] = {0};
  //Handle to our selection buffer
  unsigned int selectBuffer[32] = {0};

  //Setup the selection buffer to accept object ID's
  glSelectBuffer(32, selectBuffer);

  //Get the current viewport coordinates
  glGetIntegerv(GL_VIEWPORT, viewportCoords);

  //switch the matrix stack to PROJECTION
glMatrixMode(GL_PROJECTION);
  //save the current projection matrix
glPushMatrix();
  //switch the rendering mode to GL_SELECT. This flag allows
  //you to render the objects (like normal), but will not write
  //the output to the frame buffer
glRenderMode(GL_SELECT);
  //reset the projection matrix
glLoadIdentity();

  //use the gluPickMatrix method to take a snapshot of the current
  //clipping region and convert it to an orthogonal unit cube
  //which makes hit testing much easier
glPickMatrix(x, viewportCoords[3] - y, 2, 2, viewportCoords);


gluPerspective(45.0f,(float)window_width/(float)window_height,1.0f,100.
0f);

  glMatrixMode(GL_MODELVIEW);
                              // Go back into our model view matrix


  m_bToggle = true;


  onRenderWorld();
  // Now we render into our selective
                              //mode to pinpoint clicked objects


  m_bToggle = false;
```

```
objectsFound = glRenderMode(GL_RENDER);    // Return to render mode
                                           // and get the number of objects found

glMatrixMode(GL_PROJECTION);                 // Put our projection
                                             // matrix back to normal.
glPopMatrix();                               // Stop effecting our
                                             // projection matrix

glMatrixMode(GL_MODELVIEW);                  // Go back to our normal
                                             // model view matrix

  if (objectsFound > 0)
  {
     unsigned int lowestDepth = selectBuffer[1];

     int selectedObject = selectBuffer[3];

     for(int i = 1; i < objectsFound; i++)
     {
       if(selectBuffer[(i * 4) + 1] < lowestDepth)
       {
         // Set the current lowest depth
         lowestDepth = selectBuffer[(i * 4) + 1];

         // Set the current object ID
         selectedObject = selectBuffer[(i * 4) + 3];
       }
     }

     // Return the selected object
     return selectedObject;
  }

  // didn't click on any objects so return 0
  return 0;
}
```

Finally you need to learn about the rendering method for the selection buffer, as you need to surround each individual object in the scene with a Name value that can be queried by OpenGL.

Listing 17.6 details how this is done using the OpenGL name stack.

LISTING 17.6 Using `glLoadName`

```
glInitNames();
glPushName( 0 ); //push at least one name on the stack
//for the EARTH object
glLoadName( EARTH );
glPushMatrix();
glLoadIdentity();
glTranslate(0.0f, 0.0f, -10.0f);
//render EARTH
glPopMatrix();
//do the same for the MOON and the SUN
```

PARTICLE SYSTEMS

Another standard effect among most games today is the use of *particle systems*. A particle system is a way of organizing and managing a system of particles. These particles can be just about anything you want them to be: smoke, gas, water, fire, rain, lightning, laser bursts, and snow are just a small list of the effects that you can create and render within a scene. Depending upon the level of realism you are attempting to create, these particles can also be controlled by forces of gravity, other particles, or perhaps even other affecting agents you want to simulate, such as a magnetic coil or an unlicensed nuclear accelerator. Listing 17.7 defines the basic Particle entity with which you will be working.

LISTING 17.7 Particle

```
namespace peon
{
  struct PEONMAIN_API Particle
  {
    bool    m_bActive;     // are we active?
    Vector3 m_vecCurPos;   // Current position of particle
    Vector3 m_vecCurVel;   // Current velocity of particle
    float   m_fInitTime;   // Time of creation of particle
  };
}
```

The next task is to create and define a particle emitter object, which is solely responsible for acting as the manager to a host of `Particle` entities. This manager will then be responsible for creating, updating, rendering, and destroying these particles. Listing 17.8 outlines the particle emitter.

LISTING 17.8 ParticleEmitter.h

```
namespace peon
{
  /**
  * This object is used to encapsulate a tiny particle emitter
system for
  * the developer to use with Peon.
  */
  class PEONMAIN_API ParticleEmitter
  {
  public:
   /** constructor */
   ParticleEmitter();

   /** destructor */
   ~ParticleEmitter();

   /** list of currently active particles */
   std::list<Particle*>   m_oActiveList;

   /** list of not-so-active particles */
   std::list<Particle*>   m_oFreeList;

    int      m_iActiveCount;
   float      m_fCurrentTime;
   float      m_fLastUpdate;

   SceneTexture* m_pTexture;
   bool      m_bUsePointSprites;

   // Particle Attributes
   int      m_iMaxParticles;
   int      m_iNumToRelease;
   float      m_fReleaseInterval;
   float      m_fLifeCycle;
   float      m_fSize;
   Vector3    m_vecPosition;
   Vector3    m_vecVelocity;
   Vector3    m_vecGravity;
   float      m_fVelocityVar;
  };
}
```

There are probably many other properties that the `ParticleEmitter` could store, but this is a good starting point to learn about particle systems.

 For simplicity's sake, the member variables of the `ParticleEmitter` are defined within a `public` access block in order to trim the amount of methods you would need to create to get/set each member variable.

Updating the Emitter

After you have created a `ParticleEmitter` instance and defined a location within the game world to place it, you need to have the container of `Particle` objects update itself every frame of the game. You can do this to keep the particle animation smooth, along with handling how long each particle should last before "dying" (that is, being marked as inactive). Listing 17.9 demonstrates the updating procedure of the `ParticleEmitter`.

LISTING 17.9 `ParticleEmitter::updateEmitter(float fElapsedTime)`

```
void ParticleEmitter::updateEmitter( float fElapsedTime )
{
  Particle  *pParticle;
  Vector3 vecOldPosition;

  m_fCurrentTime += fElapsedTime;

  for(std::list<Particle*>::iterator it = m_oActiveList.begin();
    it != m_oActiveList.end();
    it++)
  {

    //get our particle
    pParticle = (Particle*)it;

    if(pParticle->m_bActive)
    {

      // Calculate new position
      float fTimePassed  = m_fCurrentTime - pParticle->m_fInitTime;
```

```
                  if( fTimePassed >= m_fLifeCycle )
                  {
                    // Time is up, put the particle back on the free list...
                    m_oFreeList.push_back( pParticle );

                    —m_iActiveCount;
                  }
                  else
                  {
                    // Update particle position and velocity

                    // Update velocity with respect to Gravity (Constant
                    // Accelaration)
                    pParticle->m_vecCurVel += m_vecGravity * fElapsedTime;

                    // Finally, update position with respect to velocity
                    vecOldPosition = pParticle->m_vecCurPos;
                    pParticle->m_vecCurPos += pParticle->m_vecCurVel *
                      fElpasedTime;


                  }
          }
```

Rendering the Emitter

Now that the particles contained in the ParticleEmitter object are updating themselves, you need to render them within the game world. Listing 17.10 demonstrates
one way to accomplish this where you loop through each Particle object. If it is
marked as active, then render it; otherwise ignore it.

LISTING 17.10 ParticleEmitter::onRender()

```
      void ParticleEmitter::onRender()
      {
        //first set our particle texture
        glBindTexture( GL_TEXTURE_2D, m_pTexture->getTex() );
```

```
                  Particle* pParticle;
                  for(std::list<Particle*>::iterator it = m_oActiveList.begin();
                    it != m_oActiveList.end();
                    it++)
                  {
                    pParticle = (Particle*)it;
                    if(pParticle->m_bActive)
                    {
                      glPushMatrix();
                      glLoadIdentity();
                      glTranslatef( pParticle->m_vecCurPos.x,
                        pParticle->m_vecCurPos.y, pParticle->m_vecCurPos.z );

                      glBegin(GL_QUADS);
            glTexCoord2f(0.0f, 0.0f); glVertex3f(-1.0f, -1.0f,  1.0f);
            glTexCoord2f(1.0f, 0.0f); glVertex3f( 1.0f, -1.0f,  1.0f);
            glTexCoord2f(1.0f, 1.0f); glVertex3f( 1.0f,  1.0f,  1.0f);
            glTexCoord2f(0.0f, 1.0f); glVertex3f(-1.0f,  1.0f,  1.0f);
                      glEnd();
                        glPopMatrix();
                    }
                  }
                }
```

Particle System II: Point Sprites

Depending upon the video hardware you have available, you might also be able to take advantage of the point sprites extension, ARB_point_sprite. Point sprites are hardware accelerated billboards, which can be textured and are meant for particle systems, since you do not need to send the quad vertex data to the pipeline. Instead, you only need to send the vertex position of the particle, and the GPU will handle the necessary math to properly view align it.

You must first query the hardware to see whether the point sprite functionality is accessible, as with every other OpenGL extension. Listing 17.11 demonstrates how this is done.

LISTING 17.11 Point Sprite Extension Querying

```
        PFNGLPOINTPARAMETERFARBPROC  glPointParameterfARB  = NULL;
        PFNGLPOINTPARAMETERFVARBPROC glPointParameterfvARB = NULL;
        m_bUsePointSprites = true;
```

```
//First check the renderer to see if the extension is supported
if( !pRenderer->isExtensionSupported( "GL_ARB_point_parameters" ) )
{
  //it's not, so let our internal variable reflect this
  m_bUsePointSprites = false;
}
else
{
  //Our hardware supports point sprites. Load the proper
  //function pointers from the provided vendor DLL
  glPointParameterfARB  = (PFNGLPOINTPARAMETERFARBPROC)
    SDL_GL_GetProcAddress("glPointParameterfARB");

  glPointParameterfvARB = (PFNGLPOINTPARAMETERFVARBPROC)
    SDL_GL_GetProcAddress("glPointParameterfvARB");

  //If there was a problem grabbing these methods from the
  //vendor supplied DLL, then disable the use of point sprites
  if( !glPointParameterfARB || !glPointParameterfvARB )
  {
    m_bUsePointSprites = false;
  }
}
```

Now that you have verified whether the ARB_point_sprite extension exists, you can modify the render method of the ParticleEmitter object to take advantage of this capability. Listing 17.12 provides some additional details.

LISTING 17.12 Modification to ParticleEmitter::render()

```
void ParticleEmitter::render()
{

  // Query for the max point size supported by the hardware
  glGetFloatv( GL_POINT_SIZE_MAX_ARB, &m_fMaxPointSize );

  // This is how our point sprite's size will be modified by
  // distance from the viewer.
  float attenuation[] =  { 1.0f, 0.0f, 0.01f };
  glPointParameterfvARB(
GL_POINT_DISTANCE_ATTENUATION_ARB,attenuation );
```

```
// The alpha of a point is calculated to allow the fading of
//points instead of shrinking them past a defined threshold size.
//The threshold is defined by GL_POINT_FADE_THRESHOLD_SIZE_ARB
//and is not clamped to the minimum and maximum point sizes.
glPointParameterfARB( GL_POINT_FADE_THRESHOLD_SIZE_ARB, 60.0f );

glPointParameterfARB( GL_POINT_SIZE_MIN_ARB, 1.0f );
glPointParameterfARB( GL_POINT_SIZE_MAX_ARB, m_fMaxPointSize );

// Specify point sprite texture coordinate replacement mode for
// each texture unit
glTexEnvf( GL_POINT_SPRITE_ARB, GL_COORD_REPLACE_ARB, GL_TRUE );

//enable the point sprite extension
glEnable( GL_POINT_SPRITE_ARB );

glPointSize( m_fSize );

//for particle rendering using point sprites, you need to
//use a different primitive: the GL_POINT
glBegin( GL_POINTS );
{
  Particle* pParticle;
  for(std::list<Particle*>::iterator it = m_oActiveList.begin();
    it != m_oActiveList.end();
    it++)
  {
    pParticle = (Particle*)it;
    if(pParticle->m_bActive)
    {
      //Just supply the vertex to OpenGL. Since it is working
      //in GL_POINTS mode, then each vertex will be automatically
      //view-aligned by the OpenGL point sprite extensions
      glVertex3f( pParticle->m_vecCurPos.x,
                  pParticle->m_vecCurPos.y,
                  pParticle->m_vecCurPos.z );

    }
  }
glEnd();
//disable the point sprite extension
glDisable( GL_POINT_SPRITE_ARB );
  }
}
```

BILLBOARD ANIMATION

Another popular tool among game programmers is to create the illusion of *billboard animation*. For most purposes, this is where you take a texture containing the cells of animation for the billboard object in the scene, such as a character walking, running, or jumping, and then you display this frame to the player. This same feat can also be accomplished by loading up individual textures containing the sprite information, and then proceeding to cycle through them at a specific time interval. Rendering explosions is a good example of sprite animation and one that also fits in with the *SuperAsteroidArena* project.

The first step in adding the ability to display animation on a billboard surface is to derive a new instance of the ISGNode entity. As with the other objects you have created in this chapter, you are doing this to provide you with the ability to insert the AnimatedBillboard object into your scene graph. Listing 17.13 details the header file from which you will be working.

LISTING 17.13 AnimatedBillboard.h

```
namespace peon
{
/** This object is responsible for displaying some frames of animation
* to the player.
*/
class PEONMAIN_API AnimatedBillboard
{
public:
/** std vector container for storing our frame data */
std::vector<AnimatedFrame*> m_oFrames;

public:
/** Constructor */
AnimatedBillboard();

/** Destructor */
virtual ~AnimatedBillboard();

};
}
```

This new entity is a manager object that is responsible for containing the frames of textures contained in your animation. The AnimatedBillboard entity exhibits the same behavior as the Billboard object with the added ability of loading and displaying the frames of animation. These frames can be contained in a small object called AnimatedFrame. Listing 17.14 provides further details.

LISTING 17.14 AnimatedFrame.h

```
namespace peon
{
/**
* This object is used for storing a "frame" of animation from a given
* texture
*/class PEONMAIN_API AnimatedFrame
{
Public:
SceneTexture* m_pTexture;
float m_fTime;
public:
/** Constructor */
AnimatedFrame();

/** Destructor */
virtual ~AnimatedFrame();
};
}
```

The new AnimatedFrame object shown in Listing 17.14 presents a way to handle
the rendering of an animation onto the billboard. You create an instance of the
AnimatedFrame object for each frame of animation. The only other property of this
object that you need to manipulate is the timing variable m_rTimeToDisplay. This
is just a float value that is used when the computer needs to evaluate how long to
present this frame of animation.

Loading New Frames

Now that you have the AnimatedFrame object defined, you will then need to create a
way to contain them. STL is more than capable of this task, and so you can use the
STL linked list container to store each frame of your animated sprite. Listing 17.15
demonstrates how this can be accomplished.

LISTING 17.15 Loading New AnimatedFrame Frames

```
bool loadFrame(const peon::String& strFilename, float fTime)
{
  AnimatedFrame *pFrame = new AnimatedFrame();

  // create a texture for this frame
  pFrame->m_pTexture = peon::EngineCore::getSingleton().
    getRenderer()->loadTexture(strFilename);
```

```
                    // add to vector
                    pFrame->m_fTime = fTime;

                    m_oFrames.push_back(pFrame);

                    return true;

                }
```

Updating Frames

To create the illusion of animation, you need to consider how to time the process of displaying the texture containing the desired frame. To make things simpler, you use a variable within the AnimatedFrame interface as a crude timer for judging how long you should be rendering this particular frame to the player. With each update cycle of this object, you simply subtract the current frame's elapsed time from the AnimatedFrame's time marker. When it has dropped below zero, you update the linked list container to iterate to the next AnimatedFrame object. Listing 17.16 provides a code example of this.

LISTING 17.16   AnimatedFrame::onUpdate()

```
void AnimatedFrame::onUpdate( float elapsed_time )
{
  //only bother to update things if we are in fact "running"
  //an animation
  if( m_bIsRunning )
  {
    //update the time with our elapsed time
    m_fTotalTime += elapsed_time;
    //make sure that our current frame is valid.
    //Meaning that our time length for the entire
    //animation has not elapsed
    if( getCurrentFrame() > (int)m_oFrames.size() )
    {
      //halt animation immediately
      stopAnimation();
    }
  }
}
```

You have seen the rendering code before, as you are simply setting the necessary texture handle within the OpenGL pipeline and then rendering a quad at the sprite's location in the game world.

CREATING A SHOCKWAVE

A particularly fantastic effect used in some games is the proper use of a shockwave. Within most science fiction movies, a shockwave is usually rendered as a wave of energy that surges outward whenever a large object is obliterated. Figure 17.1 presents the texture used for the shockwave.

FIGURE 17.1 Shockwave texture.

The basic algorithm that you will learn for manipulating the shockwave is to first generate a mesh of triangles that form a ring. When you want to animate the shockwave outward (or inward), you just need to expand or contract the vertices in this ring.

Listing 17.17 details the Shockwave header file.

LISTING 17.17 Shockwave Object Header

```cpp
namespace peon
{
  /**
   * This object is used to represent a shockwave effect in space.
   */
  class PEONMAIN_API Shockwave
  {
  public:
    Shockwave();
    ~Shockwave();

    bool m_bIsRunning;
    SceneTexture* m_pTexture;
    Vector3 m_vecPos;
    int m_iNumDivisions;
    float m_fThickness;
    float m_fLifetime;
    float m_fAge;
    float m_fExpandRate;
```

```
        float m_fSize;
        float m_fScale;
        int m_iNumVerts;

        //snip
    };
}
```

Initializing the Shockwave

The only slightly difficult task of using a Shockwave object in your game is the proper way to create one. Listing 17.18 demonstrates how this is done.

LISTING 17.18

```
    bool Shockwave::load(float fSize, float fThickness, int
iNumDivisions,
    float fExpandRate, float fLifetime)
  {
    m_iNumDivisions = iNumDivisions;
    m_fSize = fSize;
    m_fThickness = fThickness;
    m_fExpandRate = fExpandRate;
    m_fLifetime = fLifetime;

    //we are rendering the primitives using the Quad primitive type (4
    //verts per square). If we were to switch to GL_TRIANGLES, then
    //change this value to 6 since it takes 6 vertices for one square
    m_iNumVerts = iNumDivisions * 4;

    m_pParticles = new ParticleVtx[m_iNumVerts];

    m_fAge = 0.0f;
    m_fScale = 0.0f;

    // calculate number of vertices
    float fStep = 360.0f / iNumDivisions;

    int i = 0;
    for (float q=0.0f; q < 360.0f; q+= fStep)
    {
      // calculate x1,y1, x2,y2, x3,y3 and x4,y4 points
      float x1 = m_fSize * cosf(PEON_DEGTORAD(q));
```

```
          float y1 = m_fSize * sinf(PEON_DEGTORAD(q));
          float x2 = (m_fSize-m_fThickness) * cosf(PEON_DEGTORAD(q));
          float y2 = (m_fSize-m_fThickness) * sinf(PEON_DEGTORAD(q));

          float x3 = m_fSize * cosf(PEON_DEGTORAD(q+fStep));
          float y3 = m_fSize * sinf(PEON_DEGTORAD(q+fStep));
          float x4 = (m_fSize-m_fThickness) * cosf(PEON_DEGTORAD(q+fStep));
          float y4 = (m_fSize-m_fThickness) * sinf(PEON_DEGTORAD(q+fStep));

          m_pParticles[i] = ParticleVtx( x2, y2, -1.0f, 0.0f, 0.0f, 1.0f,
255,
            255, 255, 255, 0.0f, 1.0f);
          i++;

          m_pParticles[i] = ParticleVtx( x1, y1, -1.0f, 0.0f, 0.0f, 1.0f,
255,
            255, 255, 255, 0.0f, 0.0f);

          i++;

          m_pParticles[i] = ParticleVtx( x3, y3, -1.0f, 0.0f, 0.0f, 1.0f,
255,
            255, 255, 255, 1.0f, 0.0f);

          i++;

          m_pParticles[i] = ParticleVtx( x4, y4, -1.0f, 0.0f, 0.0f, 1.0f,
255,
            255, 255, 255, 1.0f, 1.0f);

          i++;

      }

      m_bIsRunning = false;

      return true;
  }
```

Updating the Shockwave

Most of the difficult work was done during the initialization of the Shockwave object. When you want to update the explosion ring, you only need to loop through each vertex in the shockwave mesh. As each vertex expands outward, you scale each vertex while also adjusting the alpha channel value of the ring to slowly fade it over time. Listing 17.19 details how this is done.

LISTING 17.19   Updating the Shockwave

```
void Shockwave::onUpdate( float fElapsedTime )
{
  if(!m_bIsRunning)
    return;

  m_fScale += m_fExpandRate * fElapsedTime;
  m_fAge += fElapsedTime;
  int iAlpha = 0;
  iAlpha = (int)(255.0f - ( 255.0f * (m_fAge/m_fLifetime)));

  for( int i = 0; i < m_iNumVerts; i++)
  {
    m_pParticles[i].m_a = iAlpha;
  }

  if (m_fAge > m_fLifetime) stop();

}
```

Rendering the Shockwave

The algorithm for rendering the shockwave ring is simple as well. You just need to cycle through each vertex of the ring and render it with the shockwave texture. Take note that you are using the alpha channel color information to properly fade out the rings of the shockwave as it progresses through space. Listing 17.20 details how this is accomplished.

LISTING 17.20   Shockwave Render Method

```
void Shockwave::onRender()
{
  if(!m_bIsRunning)
    return;

  glDisable( GL_DEPTH_TEST );
  glEnable( GL_BLEND );
  glBlendFunc( GL_SRC_ALPHA, GL_ONE_MINUS_SRC_ALPHA );
```

```
    glBindTexture( GL_TEXTURE_2D, m_pTexture->getTex() );

    glPushMatrix();
    glLoadIdentity();
    glTranslatef(m_vecPos.x, m_vecPos.y, m_vecPos.z);
    glScalef( m_fScale, 1.0f, m_fScale );

    glBegin( GL_QUADS );

    ParticleVtx* p;
    for(int i = 0; i < m_iNumVerts; i++)
    {
      p = &m_pParticles[i];

      glColor4b( p->m_r, p->m_g, p->m_b, p->m_a );

      glTexCoord2f( p->m_tu, p->m_tv);
      glNormal3f( p->m_nx, p->m_ny, p->m_nz );
      glVertex3f( p->m_x, p->m_y, p->m_z );

    }

    glEnd();
    glPopMatrix();
    glDisable( GL_BLEND );
    glEnable( GL_DEPTH_TEST );

    }
```

TAKING A SCREEN SHOT

In most games today there is almost nothing as useful as the ability to capture and store screen data during the runtime of the game. Not only does it allow the player to rapidly capture moments in the game they would want to preserve or send to their friends, but it also provides you with another helpful support mechanism tool. Listing 17.21 documents one way to implement preserving the current state of the OpenGL context into a BMP image file.

LISTING 17.21   Storing the current scene into a BMP

```
void SceneRenderer::getScreenCapture()
{
  SDL_Surface *temp;
  unsigned char *pixels;
  int i;

  //use a static variable as a counter for naming
  //the file. You could always just keep calling the saved
  //screenshot the same name, but what if players wanted
  //to put together a slide-show to show off your game?
  static int file_count = 0;

  TCHAR strFileName[MAX_PATH];
  sprintf(strFileName, "screen_capture_%d.bmp", file_count);

  //Create an SDL software surface matching the OpenGL context
  //surface
  temp = SDL_CreateRGBSurface(SDL_SWSURFACE, m_pOGLSurface->w,
    m_pOGLSurface->h, 24,

#if SDL_BYTEORDER == SDL_LIL_ENDIAN
    0x000000FF, 0x0000FF00, 0x00FF0000, 0
#else
    0x00FF0000, 0x0000FF00, 0x000000FF, 0
#endif
  );

  if (temp == NULL)
    return;

  pixels = new unsigned char[3 * m_pOGLSurface->w * m_pOGLSurface-
>h];
  if (pixels == NULL)
  {
    SDL_FreeSurface(temp);
    return;
  }
```

```
//use glReadPixels to blast the pixels from OpenGL into the newly
//created array
glReadPixels(0, 0, m_pOGLSurface->w, m_pOGLSurface->h, GL_RGB,
  GL_UNSIGNED_BYTE, pixels);

//loop through the array to dump everything into our SDL
//surface
for (i=0; i<m_pOGLSurface->h; i++)
memcpy(((char *) temp->pixels) + temp->pitch * i,
    pixels + 3*m_pOGLSurface->w * (m_pOGLSurface->h-i-1),
    m_pOGLSurface->w*3);

//We are done with the pixel array. Clean it up
PEON_DELETE_ARRAY( pixels );

//Use some SDL "stock" functions to save the bitmap and
//free the associated surface
SDL_SaveBMP(temp, strFileName);
SDL_FreeSurface(temp);

file_count++;

}
```

CHAPTER EXERCISES

1. Experiment with the AnimatedBillboard object and see whether you can derive it from the Billboard entity.
2. Although point sprites are an eye-pleasing addition to your particle emitter, they can cause some performance drain on some hardware even when the extension is supported. Be sure to have a backup in place should the hardware not support the extension, or only support the extension at a minimal level.
3. Experiment with new properties for each Particle object used in the emitter. One trick is to define two colors for each Particle. One color is used when the Particle is first emitted and is slowly interpolated with the second *Finish* color.

SUMMARY

This chapter covered a lot of ground with respect to a small sample of the common effects and techniques seen in many games today. You started off by learning how to create and use billboards within your game. You then discussed the environment mapping technique of presenting the background to the player, whereby you wrap the sides of the camera's view space with some textures. You also learned how to create a simple particle system that also has the ability to support the point sprite extension available in OpenGL.

Of the recent developments in graphics programming, none are more significant to games developers than the introduction and use of vertex and fragment programs. Developed to fit within the model of the programmable pipeline, the shader technology allows you to surpass some of the shortcomings of the fixed function graphics pipeline. You will learn more of this in the next chapter.

18

Introduction to the OpenGL Shading Language (GLSL)

Chapter Goals

- Describe how the programmable pipeline alters the Fixed Function Pipeline model.
- Introduce and describe basic pixel and fragment shader technologies.
- Introduce using the GLSL library.
- Describe and document the process of implementing fragment and vertex programs in your applications.
- Add GLSL support to Peon.

As you learned in Chapter 5, "Graphics Programming Mathematics," the Fixed Function Pipeline system has been the process used since the introduction of the graphics pipeline approach of 3D technology. In the early days of 3D programming, the FFP was perfectly suited for the applications that were developed at the time.

The FFP model can run into complications and limitations, however, as hardware vendors continually attempt to add more features accessible to the graphics programmer. There is also the added complexity of ensuring proper stability and performance with the existing OpenGL state machine. As a result of these limitations, the combination of academic research and hardware vendor participation brought about an alteration to the pipeline design to also allow OpenGL to inject pre-transformed and lit vertices directly into the last stage of the FFP.

With many recent breakthroughs in video hardware technology, you are able to take advantage of the hardware's own CPU, known as the GPU or *Graphics Processing Unit*, to crunch through scene vertices at incredible rates as well as create your own imaginative effects.

SOME HISTORY OF SHADING LANGUAGES

Beginning with the earlier DirectX8.0 version of the SDK by Microsoft, the vertex and pixel shader implementations needed to be coded in straight assembly language and allowed up to 128 instructions to be executed on a single vertex. Although this allowed the shaders to move through the programmable pipeline as quickly as possible, it was highly error-prone. Bugs were often difficult to track down, not to mention that the only shading capability OpenGL hardware had was through some vendor-specific extensions. Another difficulty surrounding the earlier shader implementations was that it was very difficult to see the results of your shaders without having to recompile your code base.

Listing 18.1 demonstrates an older VS1.0 vertex shader script which highlights this point nicely.

LISTING 18.1   An Early VS1.0 Vertex Shader for DirectX8.0

```
vs.1.0
dp4   oPos.x , v0 , c0    // Transform the x component
dp4   oPos.y , v0 , c1    // Transform the y component
dp4   oPos.z , v0 , c2    // Transform the z component
dp4   oPos.w , v0 , c3    // Transform the w component

mov   oD0   , v5          // Apply the original color specified
```

The DirectX team were well aware of these difficulties around shader programming, and so with the recent release of the DirectX9 SDK, Microsoft introduced the *High Level Shading Language* (HLSL), which created a higher level approach to programming shaders. No longer did the developer need to create and debug pages of assembler; the HLSL allowed for a cleaner approach to programming the GPU. Listing 18.2 provides a snapshot of some HLSL code from the SDK, which is far more readable and faster to debug.

LISTING 18.2   BasicHLSL.fx

```
// Transform the position from object space to homogeneous
// projection space
Output.Position = mul(vAnimatedPos, g_mWorldViewProjection);
```

```
// Transform the normal from object space to world space
vNormalWorldSpace = normalize(mul(vNormal, (float3x3)g_mWorld));
// normal (world space)

// Compute simple directional lighting equation
float3 vTotalLightDiffuse = float3(0,0,0);
for(int i=0; i<nNumLights; i++ )
    vTotalLightDiffuse += g_LightDiffuse[i] *
    max(0,dot(vNormalWorldSpace, g_LightDir[i]));

Output.Diffuse.rgb = g_MaterialDiffuseColor * vTotalLightDiffuse +
                     g_MaterialAmbientColor * g_LightAmbient;
Output.Diffuse.a = 1.0f;

Output.TextureUV = vTexCoord0;
```

When you could be working with shaders reaching 40–50 instructions, this code clarity can really benefit your application.

Cg

NVidia has also developed a specification and implementation of its own shading language known as Cg, or *C for Graphics*. The purpose of this API is to abstract vertex and pixel shader technology one level higher, allowing you to run them in both Direct3D and OpenGL implementations. Additionally, you do not need to create different shader module files for each different specification of the pixel and vertex shader. Although the first version of Cg really only ran on NVidia video hardware, the company has put a lot of effort and resources into making the implementation compatible with ATI-based cards. It gives you an ample introduction to creating and using shader technology interfaces, while also providing you with the ability to render your modules using either OpenGL or Direct3D.

The OpenGL Shading Language (GLSL)

The OpenGL ARB released the programmable pipeline specifications of its own for the OpenGL in the 1.5 specification. It allowed the OpenGL developer to access vertex shaders (known as *vertex programs*) and pixel shaders (known as *fragment programs*) through the extension mechanism using a language syntax and construction similar to that of assembler. It was not until the OpenGL 2.0 specification, however, that these vertex and fragment program extensions were officially renamed to be incorporated into the OpenGL Shading Language (GLSL). The GLSL is a higher level approach to developing shaders for OpenGL rendering using a syntax and language construction similar to C/C++. As with the HLSL from Microsoft, this makes shader programming far easier to create and debug. Listing 18.3 demonstrates some sample GLSL vertex program script.

LISTING 18.3 Sample Vertex Program Script

```
// entry point for the vertex shader program
void main( void )
{
  // calculate the resultant vertex position
  gl_Position = gl_ModelViewProjectionMatrix * gl_Vertex;

  // assign the texture coordinate tu the texture information
  gl_TexCoord[0] = gl_MultiTexCoord0;
  //assign the front facing color of this vertex to the
  //diffuse color that we know about
  gl_FrontColor = gl_Color;

}
```

With the OpenGL ARB and other hardware vendors such as 3Dlabs, ATI, and NVidia working hard to continually improve and provide support for the GLSL in their hardware drivers, this book focuses on using this API for shader programming and effects.

The Vertex Processor

The vertex processor encapsulates your vertex shaders. The input for a vertex shader is very flexible. The specification allows you to input vertex data such as the position, normals, texture, and color information, among others. Matrices and lighting/material settings can be passed into the vertex processor as well. Although you do not need to handle every input in your shader code, you need to remember that you cannot return vertices that need to pass back through the FFP to undergo any additional transform or lighting operations. The whole point of the GLSL design prevents this from happening.

Each vertex shader is also executed per vertex in the scene. There is no way to determine how many vertices are left, for example, but the vertex shader does have access to the OpenGL state mechanism. At a bare minimum, the vertex shader is responsible for outputting one variable, glPosition, which is usually the transformed position of the vertex given the modelview and projection matrices. There are also far fewer vertices that pass through the programmable pipeline than fragment programs, so this can be one area of optimization should you run into some scene troubles. The vertex shader also has access to the scene geometry.

The Fragment Processor

The fragment processor (also known as the pixel shader) is responsible for processing inputs such as any pixel lighting operation or calculating color or texture coordinates per pixel, and so on. Similarly to the vertex processor, the fragment processor replaces all of the Fixed Function Pipeline's functionality; therefore, you must develop all of the code for processing each fragment. Texture data for a fragment cannot be written but are expensive read-only calls. Any depth or stencil buffer operations are performed after the fragment is injected back into the pipeline. The z-buffer does perform some early culling calculations before the fragment enters the processor, however, in order to drop fragments that fail the test.

If the computation requires extensive calculations, then you should probably implement it as a fragment program. If the shader requires more geometric or graphic calculations, then try to keep it a vertex program.

GLSL Data Types

Under the GLSL, there are several data types at your disposal, as shown in Table 18.1.

TABLE 18.1 Data Types

Data Type	Description
int	Integer data type
float	Float data type
bool	Boolean data type
vec2, vec3, and vec4	Two-, three-, and four-dimensional float vector
ivec2, ivec3, and ivec4	Two-, three- and four-dimensional integer vector
bvec2, bvec3, and bvec4	Two-, three-, and four-dimensional Boolean vector
mat2, mat3, and mat4	2×2, 3×3, and 4×4 dimensional float matrices
Sampler1D, sampler2D, and sampler3D	One-, two-, and three-dimensional texture handles
samplerCube	Cubemap texture handle
Sampler1DShadow, sampler2DShadow	One- and two-dimensional depth component texture handles

Shader Inputs and Outputs

When working with GLSL shaders, you have access to three types of variables in your shader programs: uniform, attribute, and varying. All three of these input and output types must be declared globally in your shader programs; it is not permissible to declare any of these within shader functions.

Uniform variable types are values that are static and do not change during a rendering process. An example of this would be the position of the light source. Uniforms are a read-only variable type and are available in both vertex and fragment shader programs.

Attribute variables are only available within the vertex shader program. They are dynamic input variables that can change with each vertex that is being processed by the shader. The vertex position or normal vector is a good example of an attribute variable. This type of variable is read-only as well.

Varying variable types represent data that is passed from the output of the vertex shader to the input of the fragment program. Within the vertex shader, these types of variables are both read and write. In the fragment shader program, however, these variable types are read-only.

Built-In Types

The GLSL specification provides you with some built-in attributes—uniform and varying types that are accessible from your shader programs. There is a complete listing within the specification, but some of the more common types are listed in Table 18.2.

TABLE 18.2   Built-In Types

Attribute Data Type	Description
gl_Vertex	4D vector type representing the vertex position
gl_Normal	3D vector type representing the vertex normal
gl_Color	4D vector type representing the vertex diffuse color
gl_MultiTexCoord0– gl_MultiTexCoord7	4D vector representing the texture coordinates for texture units zero to seven

Be sure to check with the GLSL specification for other built-in attribute data types at your disposal.

Table 18.3 lists some of the built-in uniform types available from your shader programs.

TABLE 18.3   Built-In Uniform Data Types

Uniform Data Type	Description
gl_ModelViewMatrix	4×4 matrix representing the model-view matrix
gl_ModelViewProjectionMatrix	4×4 matrix representing the model-view-projection matrix
gl_ProjectionMatrix	4×4 matrix representing the projection matrix

Be sure to check with the GLSL specification for other built-in uniform data types at your disposal.

OpenGL Shading Language Syntax

GLSL has similar syntax to that of C/C++ with a few minor differences. Always browse the latest copy of the specification to familiarize yourself with any language restrictions. The language is also 100 percent type safe, which means that you are unable to perform an assignment of a float to an int variable, for example. Listing 18.4 provides clarification.

LISTING 18.4   Type-Safe Clarification

```
/* illegal since the value assigned is an int not a float */
float current_color = 1;

/* this is legal as the value assigned is the same as the
declaration */
float next_color = 0.5;
```

When working with either the vector or matrix data types, they can only be filled with data during construction of the variable. Listing 18.5 provides more detail.

LISTING 18.5   Vector/Matrix Declarations

```
/* the following is a legal declaration for a vector */
vec3 explosion_vector = vec3( 0.0, 1.0, 0.5);

/* the following is a legal declaration for a mat3 */
mat3 explosion_mat = mat3( 1.0, 0.0, 0.0,
                           0.0, 1.0, 0.0,
                           0.0, 0.0, 1.0 )
```

The same rules apply to mathematical operations using each of these data types. For example, vector multiplication is component-wise, which follows the normal convention of multiplying two vectors. Listing 18.6 provides some sample operations.

LISTING 18.6   Sample Operations

```
vec3 vec_one = vec3( 1.0, 0.0, 0.5 )
vec3 vec_two = vec3( 0.0, 1.0, 4.0 )
/* the following operation will return a vec3 of ( 0.0,0.0,2.0 )*/
vec3 vec_three = vec_one * vec_two

/* The following matrix times vector multiplication will produce a
vector*/
gl_Position = gl_modelViewProjectionMatrix * gl_Vertex
```

There are some standard built-in operations that should be used. Table 18.4 provides a sampling of these operations.

TABLE 18.4   Built-In Operations

Function	Description
Length	Determines the length of a vector
Distance	Determines the distance between two vectors
Dot	The dot product operation
Cross	The cross-product operation
Normalize	Normalize a vector

NOTE

> *Be sure to check with the GLSL specification for other built-in operations at your disposal.*

Checking for Shader Support

By querying the OpenGL Extension mechanism that you learned about in Chapter 7, "More OpenGL Techniques," it is a trivial task to verify whether your OpenGL device is capable of shader processing. You just need to ensure that the `GL_ARB_vertex_shader`, `GL_ARB_fragment_shader`, `GL_ARB_shader_objects`, and the `GL_ARB_shading_language_100` extensions are supported as demonstrated in Listing 18.7.

LISTING 18.7   Shader Support Using Extension Querying

```
// GL_ARB_shader_objects
//Since we're working with GLSL through the extension mechanism,
//you will need to store some function pointers. (You can cut
//and copy these directly from the glext.h header!)
PFNGLCREATEPROGRAMOBJECTARBPROC    glCreateProgramObjectARB  = NULL;
PFNGLDELETEOBJECTARBPROC           glDeleteObjectARB         = NULL;
PFNGLUSEPROGRAMOBJECTARBPROC       glUseProgramObjectARB     = NULL;
PFNGLCREATESHADEROBJECTARBPROC     glCreateShaderObjectARB   = NULL;
PFNGLSHADERSOURCEARBPROC           glShaderSourceARB         = NULL;
PFNGLCOMPILESHADERARBPROC          glCompileShaderARB        = NULL;
PFNGLGETOBJECTPARAMETERIVARBPROC glGetObjectParameterivARB = NULL;
PFNGLATTACHOBJECTARBPROC           glAttachObjectARB         = NULL;
PFNGLGETINFOLOGARBPROC             glGetInfoLogARB           = NULL;
PFNGLLINKPROGRAMARBPROC            glLinkProgramARB          = NULL;
PFNGLGETUNIFORMLOCATIONARBPROC     glGetUniformLocationARB   = NULL;
PFNGLUNIFORM4FARBPROC              glUniform4fARB            = NULL;
PFNGLUNIFORM1IARBPROC              glUniform1iARB            = NULL;

//check if the proper shader extension is supported. There are
//many to choose from, but a good starting point is the
//GL_ARB_shading_language_100 string
if(!pRenderer->isExtensionSupported("GL_ARB_shading_language_100")
)
{
    //this hardware doesn't support shader tech.
    //usually you would provide a workaround
    return false;
}else
{
```

```
//The video hardware supports the GLSL extensions. There
//are a lot of function pointers to grab here, so it might
//not be a bad idea to stuff them into an object that
//automatically loads with the SceneRenderer that you
//never have to worry about again.
glCreateProgramObjectARB = (PFNGLCREATEPROGRAMOBJECTARBPROC)
    SDL_GL_GetProcAddress("glCreateProgramObjectARB");

glDeleteObjectARB        = (PFNGLDELETEOBJECTARBPROC)
    SDL_GL_GetProcAddress("glDeleteObjectARB");

glUseProgramObjectARB    = (PFNGLUSEPROGRAMOBJECTARBPROC)
    SDL_GL_GetProcAddress("glUseProgramObjectARB");

glCreateShaderObjectARB  = (PFNGLCREATESHADEROBJECTARBPROC)
    SDL_GL_GetProcAddress("glCreateShaderObjectARB");

glShaderSourceARB        = (PFNGLSHADERSOURCEARBPROC)
    SDL_GL_GetProcAddress("glShaderSourceARB");

glCompileShaderARB       = (PFNGLCOMPILESHADERARBPROC)
    SDL_GL_GetProcAddress("glCompileShaderARB");

glGetObjectParameterivARB = (PFNGLGETOBJECTPARAMETERIVARBPROC)
    SDL_GL_GetProcAddress("glGetObjectParameterivARB");

glAttachObjectARB        = (PFNGLATTACHOBJECTARBPROC)
    SDL_GL_GetProcAddress("glAttachObjectARB");

glGetInfoLogARB          = (PFNGLGETINFOLOGARBPROC)
    SDL_GL_GetProcAddress("glGetInfoLogARB");

glLinkProgramARB         = (PFNGLLINKPROGRAMARBPROC)
    SDL_GL_GetProcAddress("glLinkProgramARB");

glGetUniformLocationARB  = (PFNGLGETUNIFORMLOCATIONARBPROC)
    SDL_GL_GetProcAddress("glGetUniformLocationARB");

glUniform4fARB           = (PFNGLUNIFORM4FARBPROC)
    SDL_GL_GetProcAddress("glUniform4fARB");

glUniform1iARB           = (PFNGLUNIFORM1IARBPROC)
    SDL_GL_GetProcAddress("glUniform1iARB");
```

```
    return true;


}
```

Your shader programs are created and written similarly to the C language and are then compiled and linked into your application by the OpenGL context before they can be used in a scene.

While you can create as many shaders as you want, every shader program must have one and only one main *function defined for a vertex and fragment shader.*

When using vertex and fragment programs in OpenGL, there are three steps before you can begin rendering your shaders:

1. Loading the shader source into a shader object
2. Compiling the shader object
3. Linking the shader to part of the rendering pipeline

Loading the Shader Source

There are a few procedures to follow to load and use a shader container object that encapsulates either the vertex or fragment shader code. Listing 18.8 provides an example of preparing a shader for use.

LISTING 18.8   Loading a Shader

```
GLhandleARB hVertexShader; //the handle object to your shader
char strLog[4096]; //string to contain any log output
const char *vertexShaderStrings[1];

//load the shader object container specifying you are
//using it to contain vertex shader code
hVertexShader = glCreateShaderObjectARB( GL_VERTEX_SHADER_ARB );

//read in the contents of the shader file itself..simply dump
//the string contents of the file into a pointer
unsigned char *vertexShaderAssembly =
  readShaderFile( "vertex_shader.vert" );

vertexShaderStrings[0] = (char*)vertexShaderAssembly;

glShaderSourceARB( hVertexShader, 1, vertexShaderStrings, NULL );
glCompileShaderARB( hVertexShader);
```

```
delete vertexShaderAssembly;

//check the log status of the vertex shader handle for any
//errors during the compilation process
glGetObjectParameterivARB( hVertexShader,
  GL_OBJECT_COMPILE_STATUS_ARB,
  &bVertCompiled );
if( !bVertCompiled )
{
  //use glGetInfoLog to grab the log contents
  glGetInfoLogARB(g_vertexShader, sizeof(strLog), NULL, strLog);

  //spit it out to the debugger
  OutputDebugString(strLog);
  return false;
}
```

Creating a Shader Program

The shader program encapsulates one or more shader objects within the OpenGL context. You can have more than one program accessible during the runtime of your application and are allowed to switch between them at your leisure. Listing 18.9 demonstrates how to load a shader program, which then attaches the compiled vertex shader object you loaded in Listing 18.8.

LISTING 18.9   Shader Program

```
programObj = glCreateProgramObjectARB();
glAttachObjectARB( programObj, hVertexShader );

//link the program which means the shaders must be compiled
//by this point
glLinkProgramARB( programObj );
glGetObjectParameterivARB( programObj,
  GL_OBJECT_LINK_STATUS_ARB,
  &bLinked );

if( !bLinked )
{
  glGetInfoLogARB( programObj, sizeof(strLog), NULL, strLog );

  OutputDebugString( strLog );
  return false;
}
```

```
//finally use this program object
glUseProgramObjectARB( programObj );
```

The Shader InfoLog

Although there is a continuing effort to release shading tools that include debugging capabilities, there is no equivalent of something as handy as a `printf` statement within shader programs. You are not left completely in the dark for shader debugging, however, as you do have the capabilities of the `InfoLog` object to record the status of certain shader commands.

Be warned—there is no official specification for the InfoLog format, so different vendor OpenGL runtimes might generate different logging messages.

NOTE

You used the InfoLog in Listings 18.8 and 18.9, but another example is demonstrated in Listing 18.10.

LISTING 18.10   Another InfoLog Example

```
//This method is responsible for printing the contents of
//the InfoLog
void printInfoLog(GLhandleARB obj)
{
  int infologLength = 0;
  int charsWritten  = 0;
  char *infoLog;

  glGetObjectParameterivARB(obj,
    GL_OBJECT_INFO_LOG_LENGTH_ARB,
    &infologLength);

  if (infologLength > 0)
  {
    infoLog = (char *)malloc(infologLength);
    glGetInfoLogARB(obj, infologLength,
      &charsWritten, infoLog);
    printf("%s\n",infoLog);
    free(infoLog);
  }

}
```

Uniform and Attribute Variables

Currently, OpenGL shaders have access to the internal OpenGL state. For example, if you were to set some lighting parameters within OpenGL before calling your shader, you can then reference these same lighting parameters within the shader module. Although it is possible to use this technique as a rudimentary form of parameter passing, it is not very intuitive and can be quite painful.

Instead, OpenGL allows you to specify some values within your application, which can communicate directly with the shader. The uniform variable specifier was created for this very purpose. The uniform value property is read-only and is the same across every vertex that passes through the shader. Listing 18.11 demonstrates this.

LISTING 18.11   Sample Vertex Shader Script

```
//This is defined within the vertex shader script itself
//BasicShader.vert

//declare a uniform value to contain your scaling factor
uniform float fScale;
void main()
{
  //assign the current vertex to the a object
  vec4 a = gl_Vertex;
  a.x = a.x * 0.5;
  a.y = a.y * 0.5;
  a.z = a.z * fScale; //multiply the a scaling factor with fScale

  //the final position of this vertex is the modelview matrix
  //multiplied with the projection matrix and the a vector
  gl_Position = gl_ModelViewProjectionMatrix * a;

}
```

You are able to control the value of the parameter used in the shader inside your own application with the glUniformf*ARB() family of methods.

Contrary to the Uniform variable, the Attribute variables are used to set individual settings for each vertex that passes through the pipeline. Within the vertex shader, however, the Attribute variable is read-only and cannot be modified.

Rendering with Shaders

Now that you finally have your vertex and fragment shader programs loaded and ready for use, it is a trivial matter to enable them during the rendering process. You simply need to surround any of your `glBegin`/`glEnd` pair blocks with the pair of `glUseProgramObjectARB`/`glUseProgramObjectARB()` commands. Listing 18.12 demonstrates how this can be implemented for your application.

LISTING 18.12   Using Shaders

```
glUseProgramObjectARB( m_programObj );

//bind the texture to texture unit 0 for the shader program
glUniform1iARB( m_location_testTexture, 0 );

//use interleaved arrays to demonstrate yet another way
//to render a quad
glInterleavedArrays( GL_T2F_C3F_V3F, 0, m_quadVertices );
glDrawArrays( GL_QUADS, 0, 4 );

//finished. Unlink the shader program
glUseProgramObjectARB( NULL );
```

Shader Object Cleanup

When you are finished working with the shader objects, you need to deallocate any remaining objects as shown in Listing 18.13.

LISTING 18.13   Shader Garbage Collection

```
glDeleteObjectARB( m_hVertexShader );
glDeleteObjectARB( m_programObj );
```

SHADER VALIDATION USING GLSLVALIDATE

Before you begin to debug any problems with a GLSL vertex or fragment program, it can help tremendously to first ensure that your shaders are conforming to the GLSL standards outlined by the ARB. To this end, 3Dlabs has created and released the GLSLvalidate tool, which will process your shader scripts to validate them. Available on the CD-ROM, you simply launch the binary to install the application. After you start the application, you are able to load any vertex and fragment script to ensure its validity. Figure 18.1 demonstrates some sample output.

ON THE CD

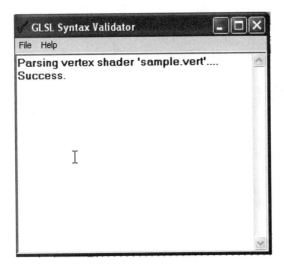

FIGURE 18.1   GLSLvalidate output.

CHAPTER EXERCISES

1. In some game engines today, the graphics pipelines are completely shader driven in order to render the game world. Discuss any tradeoffs between the Fixed Function Pipeline and the programmable pipeline and possible support issues this might entail.

2. Create another vertex and fragment shader within the SimpleShader sample used in this chapter, along with another mesh in the scene. Designate a key to flip back and forth between shader objects for each mesh during program execution. This demonstrates how quick and easy shaders are for "skinning" the same vertices with different shader effects.

3. Create another mesh within the scene in the program developed in the previous exercise (to bring your total to three meshes). Now within the application, render one mesh with one shader object, another mesh with the second shader object, and the last mesh in the scene without any vertex or shaders defined at all.

SUMMARY

Although it is still a relatively new field of graphics programming, pixel and vertex shader technology is rapidly becoming a new wave of development power for the games programmer. Although there are a myriad of shading technologies available to the developer, you were introduced to the OpenGL Shading Language, a higher level shader language added to the OpenGL 2.0 specification. You learned how to create, load, and manipulate the shader objects to bypass the Fixed Function Pipeline with the goal of creating your own transform and lighting operations. In the next chapter, you will take a look at Lua, which is a scripting language capable of extending your game and engine design.

19 Introduction to Scripting

Chapter Goals

- Introduce scripting.
- Discuss Lua.

One aspect of game programming that is becoming extremely popular is creating the illusion of a near-interactive environment to enhance the player's experience. Often this illusion is in the form of scripted events that heighten the player's perception of involvement with the game world. This involves a delicate balance of making the player feel a part of the action, while at the same time avoiding too much scripting, which only serves to alienate the player by making him feel that he has no virtual freedom in the game world.

INTRODUCTION TO SCRIPTING

The concept of scripting elements within the game world has been around for several years and helps stretch the usefulness and life span of both the game engine and any game built upon the engine.

An important team involved in the game creation process is the *design team*, which could be (but is not restricted to) the level designer, map designer, and so on for your game world. This team is crucial for creating the overall environment in which the game will take place and includes handling any contact between the player and any monster, or the player and the interaction with the game world itself.

For example, the game world is a dungeon of some kind built to be very creepy and generally unpleasant for the player. After a particularly nasty encounter with a monster, the hurt player enters a room containing a fountain and some crates with an exit on the far side. The level designer creating this room has poisoned the water but has hidden a water purification potion in one of the crates. If the player should find the specific crate and use the potion on the fountain, the water is purified and will heal the player if drunk. Otherwise, the player will die if they drink the poisoned water.

All of these events and encounters are usually accomplished with the help of a scripting library attached to the game engine. During the development of the game, the level designers are given a list of commands and/or a common language that the engine will understand and process with the help of the scripting engine. The immediate advantage to this approach is that if there needs to be any playability tweaking or other alterations to the design of a location or encounter, the designer can make the change to the appropriate script file and can re-run the game. A full recompile of the engine or game itself is avoided.

INTRODUCTION TO LUA

Initiated in 1993 by a team of developers from Brazil, Lua was created from the start to be implemented as a scripting solution capable of running on multiple platforms. Lua enables you to quickly implement a scripting language solution to affect just about anything in the game engine and has been used for a host of commercial game projects, such as Lucasarts' *Escape from Monkey Island* adventure game, Blizzard's *World of Warcraft,* and Bioware's *Baldur's Gate* series of games, among others.

Lua does not execute the scripts you enter directly, but first runs them through an interpreter that compiles them into a bytecode language, which is then executed by the Lua virtual machine.

The `lua_state` variable is central to the scripting engine and contains the current state of the Lua interpreter. You create a new `lua_state` reference with a call to the `lua_open` function as outlined in Listing 19.1.

LISTING 19.1   Using `lua_open`

```
#include <SDL.h>

extern "C"
{
  #include <lua.h>
}

int main(int argc, char* argv[ ])
{
   lua_State* lua_vm = lua_open(0);

   if(NULL == lua_vm)
   {
    //serious problem, exit program
    return -1;
   }

   return 0;
}
```

Lua was written to be ANSI C compliant, so the compiler will automatically mangle the names of any function based on the C calling convention. To link properly, you need to, therefore, surround the Lua header file with the `extern "C"` *macro.*

After you have finished with the Lua scripting library, you need to close and release the allocated heap memory taken by the `lua_State` reference. This is done with the `lua_close` method as demonstrated in Listing 19.2.

LISTING 19.2   Using `lua_close`

```
#include <SDL.h>

extern "C"
{
  #include <lua.h>
}

int main(int argc, char* argv[ ])
{
  lua_State* lua_vm = lua_open(0);
```

```
    if(NULL == lua_vm)
    {
      //serious problem, exit program
      return -1;
    }

    //do our script processing here.
    //now we are finished, close off Lua
    Lua_close( lua_vm );

    return 0;
}
```

Using the Interpreter

Now that you have created and initialized the Lua interpreter, you can begin to use it for something useful within the game engine. Another important function is the lua_dostring method, which is the common method of passing commands to the Lua interpreter.

In order to properly interpret any script you feed into the engine, you still need to initialize a few other Lua-specific libraries. The Lua documentation explains this in further detail, but you can see how this is done by taking a look at Listing 19.3.

LISTING 19.3 More Lua Initialization

```
#include <SDL.h>

extern "C"
{
  #include <lua.h>
  #include <lualib.h>
}

int main(int argc, char* argv[ ])
{
  lua_State* lua_vm = lua_open(0);

  if(NULL == lua_vm)
  {
    //serious problem, exit program
    return -1;
  }
```

```
        Lua_baselibopen( lua_vm );
        Lua_iolibopen( lua_vm );
        Lua_strlibopen( lua_vm );
        Lua_mathlibopen( lua_vm );

        //do our script processing here.
        //now we are finished, close off Lua
        Lua_close( lua_vm );

        return 0;
    }
```

You can now take advantage of some helpful Lua functions.

A SIMPLE SCRIPT

You can create a simple script to demonstrate Lua's power and flexibility. The print method of the Lua library is a good starting point for this demonstration, and Listing 19.5 shows some code.

LISTING 19.5   Simple Script

```
    //snip

    Lua_baselibopen( lua_vm );
    Lua_iolibopen( lua_vm );
    Lua_strlibopen( lua_vm );
    Lua_mathlibopen( lua_vm );

    //do our script processing here.
    std::string strScript = "a = 2 + 2;\nprint( a );\n";

    Lua_dostring( lua_vm , strScript.c_str() );

        //now we are finished, close off Lua
        Lua_close( lua_vm );

        return 0;
    }
```

When you compile and launch the program, you will see a simple command window with the result of "4".

A Simple Script File

Processing script commands within the code base can be enough depending upon the project, but in order to create a flexible and extendible engine, you should be able to process script commands contained within a file.

Using the `lua_dofile` function, you can accomplish the same output as the previous `Simple Script` program, but instead of hardcoding the value of the `strScript` variable, the input comes from a scripting file as shown in Listing 19.6.

LISTING 19.6 A Simple Script File

```
//snip
Lua_baselibopen( lua_vm );
Lua_iolibopen( lua_vm );
Lua_strlibopen( lua_vm );
Lua_mathlibopen( lua_vm );

//do our script processing here.
Lua_dofile( lua_vm, "./simple_script.lua" );

//now we are finished, close off Lua
Lua_close( lua_vm );
```

Within your favorite text editor, you can create the `simple_script.lua` file to just contain the text shown in Listing 19.7.

LISTING 19.7 Simple_Script.lua

```
—comment lines start with double-hyphens
—This script is just responsible for adding two
—numbers and displaying the sum
X = 10;
Y = 30;
Z = X + Y;
Print( "x + y = " .. Z );
```

Although this is an extremely handy component to add to your engine repertoire, there remains a problem: the scripting code is completely wide open and visible to everyone who downloads your game.

INTRODUCING LUAC

Another component of the Lua distribution is the bytecode compiler known as Luac. Similar in nature to the Java compiler, when it is used to compile a Lua script file, it will convert the contents from a human readable format into a bytecode representation that can then be fed back into the Lua interpreter. This can be accomplished as demonstrated in Listing 19.8.

LISTING 19.8   Using Luac

```
Luac —o Simple_Script.bin Simple_Script.lua
```

In the `Simple_Script` program you can now simply specify this new file created by Luac, instead of the `Simple_Script.lua` file.

When you create the script files as either text or with the Luac compiler, you can use any file extension you want to. It is not necessary to name them *.lua.

NOTE

Lua Stack

Now, you can begin to understand Lua data types allowed in script. Since Lua is a scripting language, you do not have the same data types that exist in the C/C++ realm. There are no `ints`, `char`, or `float` data types to use, since this would then be moving away from the flexibility associated with a scripting language.

Instead, Lua has a generic multipurpose data type called a *variant*. This means that the value of the variant is defined by the data it contains. The variant can contain a number, string, function, userdata, table, or simply a null value. Since it can contain many different types of data, you need a way to extract this information within your C/C++ engine after it has passed through the Lua interpreter. This is accomplished by pushing the variant onto the Lua stack, which you then process within the engine. Several of these conversion methods are outlined in Listing 19.9.

LISTING 19.9   Lua Conversion Functions

```
double lua_tonumber( lua_State* state, int index );
const char* lua_tostring( lua_State* state, int index );
size_t lua_strlen( lua_State* state, int index );
lua_CFunction lua_tocfunction( lua_State* state, int index );
void* lua_touserdata( lua_State* state, int index );
```

All of these Lua conversion functions require two parameters: the State instance and an index value. The following details what is involved.

State: The lua_State reference.

Index: This value can be positive or negative and represents an index into the Lua stack. A positive value represents that you are specifying an absolute position within the stack, beginning from 1. A negative index implies an offset from the top of the stack.

Calling a Lua Function

Part of the real power and flexibility of a scripting language comes from the ability to call scripting methods from the compile engine base. This then gives you the ability to both extend the engine as well as to make it easier to debug any level design features. Listing 19.10 demonstrates how to call a Lua function from your application.

LISTING 19.10   Calling a Lua Function

```
//snip
//execute your script
lua_dofile( oLuaState, "mult_function.lua" );

// Call the special wrapper function, which will look-up and call
//the Lua function for us.
int nAnswer = mult_numbers( oLuaState, 9, 6 );

// Output the return value returned by the Lua function
cout << "The ultimate answer of life, the universe and everything
  is: " << nAnswer << endl;
```

Listing 19.11 defines the mult_function.lua scripting code.

LISTING 19.11   mult_function.lua

```
— Define a simple Lua function that takes two arguments and mults
— them together

function mult_numbers( arg1, arg2 )

print( "arg1 = ", arg1 )
print( "arg2 = ", arg2 )
```

```
return arg1 * arg2

end
```

USING LUA TO POSITION OBJECTS

A common practice for using Lua in a game engine is for object positioning. This can be either for initial object placement during program initialization, or perhaps after a major event occurs in the game world. The goal of incorporating this type of scripting in your game projects should be apparent: avoiding long recompiles. As has been previously mentioned within this chapter, using script for certain aspects of your game should greatly reduce the amount of time spent debugging objects in your game world. It is also much easier to test game play, when you can make quick and rapid changes to the world while avoiding a long recompile of the project. You will work from the /chapter_19/BasicLuaPosition sample that demonstrates one way to achieve this effect of object placement shown in Listing 19.12.

LISTING 19.12   LOADING THE SCRIPT

```
bool MainApp::onLoadWorld()
{
m_pLuaVM = lua_open();
if(NULL == m_pLuaVM)
{
//serious problem, exit program
return false;
}
lua_baselibopen( m_pLuaVM );
lua_iolibopen( m_pLuaVM );
lua_strlibopen( m_pLuaVM );
lua_mathlibopen( m_pLuaVM );
// Execute the script
lua_dofile( m_pLuaVM, "data\\calculate_position.lua" );
//initialize our position variables
m_fZRotation = 0.0f;
m_fYRotation = 0.0f;
m_fXPosition = 0.0f;
}
```

There should be nothing new in Listing 19.12. You are initializing the Lua libraries within the onLoadWorld method of the application class. If the loading is successful, Lua then proceeds to attempt to load your script file. Listing 19.13 provides the `calculate_position.lua` script that is used in the sample.

LISTING 19.13 Calculate_Position.lua

```lua
- This small lua sample demonstrates one sort-a practical way to use
- scripting. We merely pass in two numbers, our current x position and
- our elapsed time variable. I think the rest is self-explanatory
- The only important thing is to return the new xposition
function calculatePosition( arg1, arg2 )
        temp = 1.0
    if arg1 > 5.2 then
            arg1 = -5.2
        end
        - 5.0 is the speed that our object is moving..change at your
leisure! :)
    arg1 = arg1 + (temp * 5.0 * arg2)
    return arg1
end
```

Updating the Object Position

Now that the Lua script is loaded and ready to go within your game, you can go through the process of updating these world objects using the Lua engine. The `calculatePosition` function is already defined in Listing 19.13, so you just need to reference the method in the script from the `onUpdateWorld` phase of your application's processing shown in Listing 19.14.

LISTING 19.14 onUpdateWorld

```cpp
void MainApp::onUpdateWorld( float fElapsedTime )
{
m_fXPosition = calculatePosition( m_pLuaVM, m_fXPosition, fElapsedTime
);
m_fZRotation += 8.0f * fElapsedTime;
m_fYRotation += 8.0f * fElapsedTime;
}
```

The rendering code for the objects in this sample has been seen many times before, so it does not need to be displayed here again.

CHAPTER EXERCISES

1. Create another Lua script to perform simple vector calculations.
2. Create a Lua script to multiply two matrices of uniform size.
3. A popular use of scripting is for specifying which resources to load into your game during startup. Create an object for the Peon engine to allow you to specify which texture resources you need to load into your game during initialization.
4. Expand upon the object(s) created in the third exercise to load other properties and resources such as audio files.

SUMMARY

One of the more popular features of game engines today is how they handle scripting elements of the game design. You discussed how proper object scripting within the game world can really open up the possibilities encountered by the player. You were then introduced to the Lua scripting library, which launches a small virtual machine to process any scripting commands. By gaining more experience with the Lua language, you have the ability to add some helpful scripting interfaces to both your game engine and the *SuperAsteroidArena* project.

In the next chapter, you will take the knowledge gained from the previous chapters in order to add more substance to your *SuperAsteroidArena* project.

20 | Polish Timebox

Chapter Goals

- Demonstrate how to add some simple effects to the project.
- Discuss how to implement some basic Lua scripting support to the project.

There are still some finishing touches and polish that you can apply to *SuperAsteroidArena*; in this chapter you incorporate some of the topics you have covered over the previous few chapters with respect to scripting support, animation, effects, and even some GLSL.

TIMEBOX GOALS

After taking a look at the timebox goals for this stage of the project, you are aiming to add a few more effects and/or eye candy to the game to add some extra punch to the *SuperAsteroidArena* experience. To take advantage of the Lua scripting language, you will need to create an object that will load and process Lua scripts. Another goal of this timebox is to add GLSL support to the project. In this case, you should make a shader object, which is fully optional depending upon the video hardware available.

ADDING SCRIPTING SUPPORT

After being introduced to the Lua scripting library in Chapter 19, "Introduction to Scripting," you will now add some basic scripting support to the *SuperAsteroidArena* project. These components will provide you with some capabilities to script different events in the game, allowing you to debug problems far more easily, along with all the other benefits that scripting gives you.

For the Peon library, you will create a small bare-bones object to handle some Lua script processing. Listing 20.1 provides the detailed header information located in the /Peon/PeonMain/include folder.

LISTING 20.1 ScriptEngine

```
namespace peon
{
/**
* This object is used for some basic Lua script support in our engine.
It
* just encapsulates
* The whole process of loading the Lua function pointers, as well as
* handling the scripts that
* the user will wish to load for their scene.
*/
class PEONMAIN_API ScriptEngine : public ISingleton<ScriptEngine>
{
public:
/**Constructor */
ScriptEngine();
/**Destructor*/
~ScriptEngine();
/** Grab a reference to our object */
static ScriptEngine& getSingleton(void);
/** Grab our singleton instance pointer */
static ScriptEngine* getSingletonPtr(void);
};
}
```

ADDING SHADER SUPPORT

In this phase of the project implementation, you will add some basic GLSL support to the *SuperAsteroidArena* project. The framework should be as light as possible to allow you to add your own vertex and fragment shader scripts at your leisure, giving you the ability to organize the objects as you see fit. For the moment, it is easiest to create another Singleton object, which can be globally accessible to access any shader scripts you might create for the game.

This object is designed this way on purpose. For the outline and design of your own game, you might not want to even take advantage of shader scripting. Listing 20.2 covers the ShaderEngine module in further detail.

LISTING 20.2 ShaderEngine

```
namespace peon
{
/**
* This object is used for some basic GLSL script support in our engine. It
* just encapsulates
* The whole process of loading the GLSL function pointers, as well as
* handling the scripts that
* the user will wish to load for their scene.
*/
class PEONMAIN_API ShaderEngine : public ISingleton<ShaderEngine>
{
public:
/**Constructor */
ShaderEngine();
/**Destructor*/
~ShaderEngine();
/** Grab a reference to our object */
static ShaderEngine& getSingleton(void);
/** Grab our singleton instance pointer */
static ShaderEngine* getSingletonPtr(void);
};
}
```

TIMEBOX EVALUATION

Since you are now completing this timebox of the project, you should sit down with your design documentation and evaluate this stage. Are you happy with the design of the game so far and how it is evolving? Make sure that you do not get trapped into a never-ending cycle of simply adding nice-looking effects to your game. Critically evaluate each one to decide whether it belongs with the rest of the game. Otherwise, create a list of effects or other related issues which might fit more into a "Version 2.0," or even a sequel of the game.

CHAPTER EXERCISES

1. Take a look at the ScriptEngine object and see what else can be defined by scripts in your game. (Not only can your art and audio resources be scripted, but so can just about everything else related to your game logic.)
2. Investigate the ShaderEngine Singleton object to see how you can best leverage shader technology in your environment. Some new AAA games under development have dropped FFP programming completely and explicitly use shaders, but there is no need to be so "radical" in your approach.

SUMMARY

You can always add minor tweaks to your project. Either you might decide that a certain effect does not look quite right, or perhaps your enemy monsters are too difficult in some situations. This chapter provided some insight and discussion as to how you might choose to implement some of the topics you have covered in the previous chapters. Feel free to experiment on your own to either create a really snazzy look to your game, or perhaps to even give it a retro feel.

In the next chapter, you are presented with more information and suggestions on adding some finishing touches to your game project.

21 Finishing Tips and Tricks

Chapter Goals

- Review a small and simple list of suggestions to add polish to your game.
- Review some tips to create your installation script.
- Conduct beta testing.
- Create the *User Instruction Manual*.

Now that you have either finished your game or are in the process of doing so, there are always the little details that will spring up near the end of your project. In strict software engineering terms, this is the dreaded 90/10 rule that states that the last 10 percent of the project will consume 90 percent of your efforts. You need to keep your design document nearby, as you should be doing only some final gameplay tweaking. Now is definitely not the time to add any new features, unless it is deemed critical.

SIMPLE SUGGESTIONS

After you have created a version of your game that is ready for a final testing process, it is important to cover the aspects involved in the presentation of the game itself. Although there are only a small set of suggestions here, an endless amount of small things can contribute to the overall polish of the game. For most projects, the final touches are the most time consuming, but they also provide a higher quality presentation to the player and can potentially increase sales.

It sometimes helps to take a few days off within this phase, in order to come back to your game with a fresh outlook. You might have been staring at the same game for so long that you miss small but important details that a fresh perspective can spot. The following is just a list of suggestions to watch for. They may or may not apply, depending upon your game.

Besides the obvious steps of making sure that the menu and GUI systems are functioning properly, you should also ensure that there are some audio and visual feedbacks to accompany it. For example, is there a small clicking sound to let the player know that a menu option has been selected? Do you have any type of high-lighting around the chosen menu option itself? Are any other sound effects provided when you switch between menu options? Is the menu or GUI font appropriate for the overall style and presentation of the game? Are all of the font characters legible? Are there any spelling mistakes in any of the game text?

Game state transition effects are also an important consideration. When your game moves between a title screen and the main menu, for example, do you present a progress bar for the player to signal that the game has not crashed but is simply loading resources? Although there can be a danger of presenting too much feedback, it is also critical to keep reassuring the player that the game is still running and functioning properly despite any long load times. Some players can be very impatient, and if things are not continually updating, then they might choose to end the application out of a perceived frustration that nothing is happening with your game.

Another important consideration is how the game processes the player's input. In the past, the Esc key was used in a game to exit the application. However, in most games today, the Esc key either brings up an in-game menu and/or console, or is simply used to back up to the previous dialog controls from within a GUI system. A detail that some games overlook is the ability to configure the game's input to whatever the player chooses. Nothing can derail a player's enjoyment like an an-noying or strange key mapping that cannot be changed. Some basic play testing, though, should bring to the forefront any strange key mappings.

If you are only processing keyboard input for the game, then do not forget to hide the mouse cursor. A good rule of thumb is that if the player can see it, they should be able to use it.

Another basic area of final touches revolves around video settings. Can the player switch among different resolutions or change between windowed and full-screen display modes? Can the player select between different levels of realism for the game depending upon their video hardware (that is, disable/enable certain effects, and so on)?

All of these suggestions are just that: suggestions. Many might apply to your game, many might not. It is important to remain objective about your game and to learn to differentiate between good (or bad) feedback from your testers. They can help pinpoint any problems with either your game or user interface design.

GAME PLAY TESTING

While you have been testing the game during each iteration of your project, the focus has been more on the technical aspects of the game. You need some other players involved to find out how well or poorly the overall game plays and feels. Does it meet the original game requirements outlined in your design document? Is the game fun (yes, this is still an important question)?

It is important to obtain some feedback from some impartial testers on your game project, especially if you plan on ever attempting to sell it. Table 21.1 provides some simple survey material that you can gather from your testing group, which can help iron out any last-minute problems with the game.

These sample questions were graciously offered from Mike Summers of Blue Bug Games and were used in their title, Add'Em Up.

TABLE 21.1   Some Sample Gameplay Survey Questions

1. What kind of computer are you using? Operating System, Processor Speed, Ram?
2. If you didn't know how to play the game before, was it easy to learn how? Were the instructions easy to find and understand? If not, what could be improved?
3. Were you able to easily navigate around? Was it easy to start? Quit?
4. Now that the game is more complete, would you recommend it to a friend? Why, or why not?
5. Any other comments? Please be as detailed and specific as possible.

Using feedback and survey questions from your testers is a great way to gauge the status of your game.

INSTALLATION SCRIPTS

There comes a point in time when you want to release the project to either an external group of beta testers, or to the public itself. Part of this process involves creating an installation routine for the player to execute to properly set up the assets and binaries required. Although we touched upon this in Chapter 1, "Game Technologies," this phase is critical to the overall appearance of the game. To distribute an archive of your game (for example, in ZIP or RAR form) is quite unacceptable and can quickly lead to other avenues of frustration for the player. For example, they might not understand what an archive is or what to do with it; the game might be required to decompress in a specific folder; their firewall software might block it by default, and so on.

To create an installation package for your project does not necessarily need to be difficult. Although there are many fine packages and utilities available on the Internet, the package used for this book is the InnoSetup tool. This free installation creation utility conforms to other commercial installation packages' look and feel, so it should not present anything strange or alien to the end user.

Using InnoSetup

ON THE CD

After you have launched the InnoSetup installation located on the CD-ROM, you can create a small script to put together the project. If you open the *SuperAsteroidArena.iss* file, you can view how the installation script looks for *SuperAsteroidArena*, as shown in Listing 21.1.

LISTING 21.1 SuperAsteroidArena.iss

```
;SuperAsteroidArena installation script v1.0

[Setup]
AppName=SuperAsteroidArena
AppVerName=SuperAsteroidArena version 1.5
DefaultDirName={pf}\SuperAsteroidArena
DefaultGroupName=Wazoo Enterprises Inc.
UninstallDisplayIcon={app}\SuperAsteroidArena.exe
Compression=lzma
SolidCompression=yes

[Files]
Source: "SuperAA.exe"; DestDir: "{app}"
Source: "*.dll"; DestDir: "{app}"
Source: "Readme.txt"; DestDir: "{app}"; Flags: isreadme
```

```
[Icons]
Name: "{group}\SuperAsteroidArena"; Filename: "{app}\SuperAA.exe"

[Code]
function InitializeUninstall(): Boolean;
begin
  Result := MsgBox('InitializeUninstall:' #13#13 'Uninstall is
      initializing. Do you really want to start Uninstall?',
      mbConfirmation, MB_YESNO) = idYes;
  if Result = False then
    MsgBox('InitializeUninstall:' #13#13 'Ok, bye bye.',
      mbInformation, MB_OK);
end;

procedure DeinitializeUninstall();
begin
  MsgBox('DeinitializeUninstall:' #13#13 'Bye bye!', mbInformation,
    MB_OK);
end;

procedure CurUninstallStepChanged(CurUninstallStep:
    TUninstallStep);
begin
case CurUninstallStep of usUninstall:
  begin
    MsgBox('CurUninstallStepChanged:' #13#13 'Uninstall is about to
      start.', mbInformation, MB_OK)
    // ...insert code to perform pre-uninstall tasks here...
  end;

  usPostUninstall:
  begin
    MsgBox('CurUninstallStepChanged:' #13#13 'Uninstall just
      finished.', mbInformation, MB_OK);
    // ...insert code to perform post-uninstall tasks here...
  end;
end;
end;
```

You are simply putting some default locations where the project will be installed after the setup binary is launched by the player. Obviously, the player will be able to change these default settings, but it is nice to provide some common locations. (For example, by default your game should be put into the `c:\Program`

`Files\<company>\<game>` location on the player's hard drive and maybe not just `c:\<game>`). Although it has been stated before, it is worth walking through some existing popular installs to verify what default locations/settings other game companies are using. In Listing 21.1 you are providing a logic path for the (off chance) that the player will want to uninstall your product.

Although nobody wants to think of someone uninstalling a game they spent a long time developing, be gracious and make sure that the script removes everything installed by your game.

For further details, simply check with the detailed help available for InnoSetup.

BETA TESTING OR QUALITY ASSURANCE TESTING

Assuming that you have your own internal quality assurance (QA) testing procedures during the lifecycle of your game, you might also want to recruit a final QA group from within either a chosen favorite community of game developers on the Internet, or some friends, relatives, or even neighbors. Whatever the case, by the time the project reaches the beta testing phase, you should have pretty much discovered and either noted or fixed any critical bugs within the project. Beyond the stability of the game itself, you also need to ensure you are testing the actual gameplay as outlined previously. It is important to keep in mind the targeted audience and to convey this to any group of beta testers. This communication is vital, as it can help test the gameplay and experience of the game along with helping you discern what your testers are reporting to you.

For example, a game you are developing has the targeted game demographic as the typical player who enjoys a fairly light role-playing game with simplistic battle controls, similar to a game like *Diablo*. Upon the initial (disappointing) feedback from beta testers, you quickly realize that some of the players are avid fans of first-person shooters and others enjoy a more relaxed type of puzzle game. Hence, they might find the pace of your game quite slow or quite fast. After this is realized and your target audience communicated to the testing group, you might find the quality of feedback to be much improved.

To minimize any mixed-message communication between you and the beta testers, you should first ensure that they are somewhat fans of the type of game you are sending them. The benefit of this is that they can help compare the product to what they are currently enjoying, which can help pinpoint any gameplay or presentation issues.

USER INSTRUCTION MANUAL

With the amount of effort that you have put into creating your game throughout this book, please do not simply stick your keyboard commands into a plain text file and include it with your game as your user manual. Along with the installation of your game, another important consideration is providing some instructions for the player. Surely you have purchased a game in the past, only to be extremely disappointed with the instruction manual that came with it. Some companies treat the instruction manual as an afterthought, but there are also a lot of good user instruction manuals out there, which can help to add definite depth to your game. Imagine spending a few years of your life creating a fantastic role-playing game with a huge amount of artwork, only to put the game instructions in a readme file. It sounds crazy, but there are still companies that go to these extremes.

Another pitfall that some games experience is that the user instruction manual (or player's manual) is generated fairly early on in the project. This is a risky venture, as a game is more than likely to change or evolve a few times during the project, which can outdate older documentation.

Now that you are nearing the end of the *SuperAsteroidArena* project, you should be able to create an interesting user manual that is available for the player. It is enough for most projects to generate your user instruction manual in PDF format that you can distribute with your game.

Most installation procedures these days give the player the choice to view the instruction manual during the last step of the setup dialog.

Another use of the manual is to provide the player with first-level support. In other words, it should not only detail any system or operating system requirements, it should also contain a section describing any general technical support problems that 90 percent of your customers might experience. It is also very important to keep the technical verbiage as layman as possible. There is no point in providing support documentation that the intended audience cannot read or understand.

Although it is a common stereotype, design the technical support for your parents. They might not understand how to use 90 or so percent of the computer, but they should not have to in order to enjoy your game. The documentation should be easy to access, and they should be able to solve any basic problems that might arise when playing your game.

User Manual Checklist

In order to help you with the user instruction manual, it would help to have a small checklist to ensure that most of the bases are covered in your support. The most important thing to remember is to keep your target audience in mind throughout the entire manual.

System requirements: In a few lines, detail the system requirements to play your game. Keep your audience in mind here; if you are creating a puzzle game for everyone to enjoy, then avoid listing too many details. Just listing a system capable of running Windows 2000 with a 1 GHz machine and 64 MB of RAM is probably sufficient. On the other hand, if you are writing a manual for a game targeting the hardcore user crowd, go ahead and list any DirectX requirements, along with any minimum video driver versions, and so on. Most of the hardcore gamer crowd is already familiar with this technical verbiage.

Background: Although not critical for your user manual, you might want to include a background for your player to understand the environment of the game. This is part of the hook you need to generate interest in your game, which is hopefully enough to make a sale. Provide some interesting details about the game setting, but avoid writing another chapter of the *Lord of the Rings*. Just as a suggestion, keep it as precise as possible, but loose enough to demonstrate how fun and energetic the game is.

Technical support: Another important area of the instruction manual is the technical support area. Again, remember that this manual is the first level of support provided for your customer. The more the manual can help the player troubleshoot a technical problem, the less effort is required by the player to contact you. Any common problems experienced by your testers could probably go here, which also includes any common difficulties or issues noted during the setup process.

Further support: Although search engines such as Google have entered the general lexicon, do not force the player to hunt for your support area. In the user manual, provide a clear Web site point of contact or at least a toll-free phone number and email address that the player can use for any further difficulties with the game.

Although the instruction manual for *SuperAsteroidArena* is not intended as the *de facto* standard of game instruction creation, it can be a helpful starting point for your own projects. It is included on the CD-ROM, so feel free to read through it at your leisure for more help in creating your own.

ON THE CD

GAME ASSET COMPRESSION/ENCRYPTION

One of the primary considerations of some developers or companies is the worry or fear that the assets included with the game will be tampered with or stolen by other companies. Depending on the project, these game assets can cost a company a fair share of money; so it might be worth trying to taking steps to prevent them from being modified or manipulated by a curious player. One such approach is to create your own binary storage format for your levels, sound effects, music, and/or artwork. This way, you can pack together every asset of the game into one single large binary file that you then use by manipulating pointer references to this giant blob of data. This is definitely not a very basic approach and can be more troublesome than it is worth. If your file offset calculations are wrong, for example, then some asset might not load or be presented properly. If the file becomes corrupted, then it also pretty much destroys the access to every other asset.

Another concern is the total size of your project that is available for the public. Although you might have a broadband connection to the Internet and be capable of downloading a demo version of a game, which can exceed 100 MB in size, an average gamer interested in your product might not. They might have a dialup connection to the Internet and would never be interested in something exceeding 10-12 MB or so in size.

One solution that most developers use to satisfy these requirements to encrypt their game assets and/or compress the size of their product are third-party tools. One such popular utility to perform this manipulation is the Molebox runtime packer, which is included on the book's CD-ROM in the /tools_install folder.

ON THE CD

REGISTRATION/PATCH/UPDATING MECHANISM

Although you will strive to produce the highest quality code base you can put together for the game, there will almost always be necessary updates for your product. Perhaps you find and fix some critical bugs within the software, or you would like to distribute additional content to the player.

NOTE

This area of discussion is worth sitting down and analyzing the best approach for your product and company. It is another situation in which there is no right or wrong answer, simply the approach which you feel more comfortable supporting.

Although we touched upon creating differences between the demo and registered versions of your game back in Chapter 2, "Design Fundamentals," you will need to contemplate more about how you want to distribute your game. Some companies take the approach of a registration key to unlock the registered version of the game. In this scenario, your demo version of the game in fact contains the entire product. After the player pays for the registered version of your game, you would then send them a registration key, which will unlock the rest of the game.

Another approach taken by some developers is to create two distributions of the game; one for the demo version and one for the registered version. In this scenario, after the player registers the product, you might send him a login and password to a secure download location on your website.

The updating process needs to be considered as well. There are several approaches that one might take, and this is by no means a complete list.

Create a patch: In this case, you would put together a small patch file for the player to download from your Web site. Depending upon the information gathered by the purchase process, you would either email everyone who bought the game or would display this update on the product's Web site. The player would then download the patch and launch it on their system to update the game.

Auto-patching: In this case, your application would first make a version check with some kind of resource on your company's Web site. This verification check would then inspect the version of the software available on your Web site to the version the player has installed on their machine. If they differ, then the game will either automatically prompt the player to install it or will perform this task without player intervention.

Do not forget that not everyone is permanently attached to the Internet. The customer might want to launch your game from their notebook device, which may be offline. Make sure you take this into account when creating a patch/update process.

FINAL THINGS TO REMEMBER

One of the aims of this book was to present you with a *gestalt* approach to creating a game. As you should have learned, there is more involved than simply rendering an explosion or playing a sound effect. Creating a game is a much more holistic venture and can help broaden not only your resume, but your experience in all of these different areas.

Where you go after this book is up to you. The world of game programming is vast and continually evolving. Keep reading whatever you can on game development, keep practicing manipulating your game world objects to produce your design vision, and above all: *KEEP PLAYING.*

CHAPTER EXERCISES

1. Although you are close to the end, an almost insurmountable number of issues can pop up during the last few stages. Do not forget to have your exit strategy defined so that you can draw the line on when your project is finished.

2. A worthwhile investment for your project might be a project tracking tool of some kind that can store any bug reports or incident issues that your beta testers experience. With the help of Google, research a few such products and decide whether you need them or not. Otherwise, if you have sufficient knowledge of spreadsheet applications, you can use these to generate a matrix of bugs and incidents.

SUMMARY

You have come a long way with the creation of the Peon engine project, as well as your *SuperAsteroidArena* game. Not to be forgotten, there are quite a lot of little things that can add more polish to your project, making it more appealing for the player. You have only touched on a list of bare essentials, but there is definitely an infinite amount of other polish techniques that you can apply to any game. You have also been introduced to the creation of installation scripts to create install packages for your project, as well as discussing some simple beta testing techniques and processes for finding as many gameplay issues as possible during these final stages before a release. You were also introduced to generating a quality user instruction manual that should provide the player with enough information to really minimize any problems he could experience just starting your game, along with some clear details on how to play the game itself.

Appendix

A

Setting Up the SDL and the Compiler

Before you can start executing any of the code in this book, you need to set up your favorite compiler. With the vast amount of different compilers and IDE tools available for developers today, we decided to use three environments for this book. For the most part, you simply need to configure the IDE properly in order to find the header and library files for SDL.

INSTALLING SDL

SDL is contained on the book's CD-ROM; to install SDLs, unzip it to your favorite library location on your machine. Unless otherwise noted, the default location for the SDL is C:\SDL.

The required subprojects of SDL_Image, SDL_Mixer, and SDL_Net have all been included for your convenience in the SDL folders. To compile and link your SDL projects properly, you need to ensure to link with the following libraries: `SDL.lib`, `SDLmain.lib`, `SDL_image.lib`, `SDL_mixer.lib`, `opengl32lib`, and `glu32.lib`.

MICROSOFT VISUAL STUDIO 6.0

The Visual Studio 6.0 IDE is starting to show its age among the other compilers available for Windows, but it is still a very popular choice for game developers. It is a very lightweight IDE compared to that of the .NET 2003/2005 products because it contains no capabilities of compiling .NET-managed applications, among some of the other features that the newer versions offer.

To compile and run your SDL applications using this IDE, you need to specify in the default list of header and library files where the SDL directory is located. This is done using the Tools->Options menus.

If you are using the Studio 6.0 product, please add the STLPort project headers and library path included on the CD-ROM. The version of STL that ships with the IDE has been proven to contain several memory leaks and other performance-related issues. Another option is to download and install the latest version of the Platform SDK.

MICROSOFT VISUAL STUDIO .NET 2003

SDL will compile and run just fine from the .NET 2003 product. You just need to specify the location of the SDL header and library path. The version of the STL that ships with this product is acceptable, so you do not need to use the STLPort libraries.

MICROSOFT VISUAL STUDIO .NET 2005

As of this writing, this IDE is the very latest from the Visual Studio team at Microsoft. It is a free download (so far) from the *http://labs.microsoft.com* Web site. After it is downloaded and installed, you need to configure the IDE with the location of the

header and SDL library files, following the same procedure that you used for the .NET Studio 2003 product. More detailed instructions are included on the CD-ROM.

Appendix

B

Debugging Tools

Through the past several years, the amount and quality of resources available to game developers has increased at a fairly linear rate. However, with this increase in the quantity of resources, there has also been a corresponding increase in the complexity of the hardware and systems involved; Windows XP is definitely a more complex operating system than Windows 3.11. As you create and develop new modules within your game or game engine, you are also potentially introducing new bugs to the system that need to be taken care of.

These are just some small methods available to you, which rely mostly upon the Visual Studio family of development products.

OUTPUTDEBUGSTRING

A commonly used technique for debugging code is to use a `printf` or other such statement to log a known state or message to the debugging console. For game programming on the Windows platform, you can use the `OutputDebugString` method to accomplish the same thing. Any text that you output with this method will be displayed in the Debug Window of a Visual Studio IDE.

Usually when developing an application, most programmers by default build and link their application code to the debug libraries in order to ensure that application code is functioning as expected. When they are ready to publish or release the application, the developer usually switches the project to build and link the application using the runtime libraries, which are optimized in both speed and size. When you switch the compiler to build release mode binaries, the compiler will ignore `OutputDebugString` statements. This saves you the time and hassle of having to go through your code to manually remove each statement.

Listing B.1 has an example of using the `OutputDebugString` function call.

LISTING B.1   Using `OutputDebugString`

```
OutputDebugString("It was a bad call Ripley. A bad call.");
//The above string *could* be also written with compiler
preprocessor
//commands as:
#ifdef _DEBUG //if our debug mode is enabled
  printf("It was a bad call Ripley. A bad call.");
#endif
```

ASSERT

The old standby for developers, the `assert` method, can also be used to quickly test just about anything. The common approach is to use `assert` to find out whether an interface or component is `NULL` before you attempt to use it, as shown in Listing B.2.

LISTING B.2   Using `assert`

```
//our objA is our player and we need to test if he is going to
//collide with objB which is a Rover bent on capturing you!
assert( objA != NULL ); //Number 6
assert( objB != NULL ); //The Rover

//both objects are valid, so it's safe to throw them into
//the collision detection method. Does No. 6 escape?
bool bRet = DoObjectsCollide( objA, objB );
```

GDEBUGGER

ON THE CD

A popular tool for debugging the current state of the OpenGL pipeline is the gDEBugger tool from Graphic Remedy. An evaluation copy is included on the CD-ROM. Until now, graphics programmers on the Windows platform had no specific tools with which to really debug OpenGL commands. OpenGL developers could only look with envy to their Direct3D brethren who were able to view snapshots and state parameters of the Direct3D pipeline with the D3DSpy and the PIX utility. Graphic Remedy has entered the scene, providing a long-awaited solution for OpenGL programmers: the ability to use a proxy interface between the OpenGL32.DLL and the OpenGL DLL ICD provided by the video hardware vendor. One popular way to use the gDEBugger tool is to step through the OpenGL commands in a given scene. This allows you to step through any OpenGL-specific statements to help troubleshoot any problems. With the other advanced OpenGL debugging services this tool offers, it is well worth evaluating for yourself for debugging your own OpenGL projects.

GLSL VALIDATION TOOL

When working with GLSL vertex and fragment programs, anything to help code and debug shader scripts is more than welcome. 3Dlabs has put together a front-end shader script verification tool called the GLSL Validator. It is a simple utility to test your shader scripts before loading them into your programs. It is also available on the CD-ROM. You just launch the application and load your shader or fragment programs into the IDE. The validator will then process the script to ensure validity with the current specification.

ON THE CD

Appendix

C ASCII Table

No game programming book is complete without a chart of the American Standard Code for Information Interchange (ASCII), shown in Figure C.1.

Ctrl	Dec	Hex	Char	Code	Dec	Hex	Char	Dec	Hex	Char	Dec	Hex	Char
^@	0	00		NUL	32	20		64	40	@	96	60	`
^A	1	01		SOH	33	21	!	65	41	A	97	61	a
^B	2	02		STX	34	22	"	66	42	B	98	62	b
^C	3	03		ETX	35	23	#	67	43	C	99	63	c
^D	4	04		EOT	36	24	$	68	44	D	100	64	d
^E	5	05		ENQ	37	25	%	69	45	E	101	65	e
^F	6	06		ACK	38	26	&	70	46	F	102	66	f
^G	7	07		BEL	39	27	'	71	47	G	103	67	g
^H	8	08		BS	40	28	(	72	48	H	104	68	h
^I	9	09		HT	41	29	)	73	49	I	105	69	i
^J	10	0A		LF	42	2A	*	74	4A	J	106	6A	j
^K	11	0B		VT	43	2B	+	75	4B	K	107	6B	k
^L	12	0C		FF	44	2C	,	76	4C	L	108	6C	l
^M	13	0D		CR	45	2D	-	77	4D	M	109	6D	m
^N	14	0E		SO	46	2E	.	78	4E	N	110	6E	n
^O	15	0F		SI	47	2F	/	79	4F	O	111	6F	o
^P	16	10		DLE	48	30	0	80	50	P	112	70	p
^Q	17	11		DC1	49	31	1	81	51	Q	113	71	q
^R	18	12		DC2	50	32	2	82	52	R	114	72	r
^S	19	13		DC3	51	33	3	83	53	S	115	73	s
^T	20	14		DC4	52	34	4	84	54	T	116	74	t
^U	21	15		NAK	53	35	5	85	55	U	117	75	u
^V	22	16		SYN	54	36	6	86	56	V	118	76	v
^W	23	17		ETB	55	37	7	87	57	W	119	77	w
^X	24	18		CAN	56	38	8	88	58	X	120	78	x
^Y	25	19		EM	57	39	9	89	59	Y	121	79	y
^Z	26	1A		SUB	58	3A	:	90	5A	Z	122	7A	z
^[	27	1B		ESC	59	3B	;	91	5B	[	123	7B	{
^\	28	1C		FS	60	3C	<	92	5C	\	124	7C	|
^]	29	1D		GS	61	3D	=	93	5D	]	125	7D	}
^^	30	1E	▲	RS	62	3E	>	94	5E	^	126	7E	~
^-	31	1F	▼	US	63	3F	?	95	5F	_	127	7F	⌂*

* ASCII code 127 has the code DEL. Under MS-DOS, this code has the same effect as ASCII 8 (BS). The DEL code can be generated by the CTRL + BKSP key.

FIGURE C.1 ASCII chart.

Appendix
D
Windows Vista and OpenGL

As of this book's writing, Microsoft is working harder than ever in anticipation of the release of the recently named Windows Vista, known previously as *Windows Longhorn*. Microsoft is planning two release candidate versions of Vista throughout 2006 and a target release date of the final version to the public in December 2006.

Among the other new features of Vista, the user interface for the operating system has been completely revamped from previous versions of Windows. Working under the code name of *Aero*, the new user interface experience is intended to be cleaner and more aesthetically pleasing than ever before. The critical runtime component of the Aero engine is the Direct3D interface, which handles the majority of the rendering of the entire desktop and its features.

On August 6, 2005, Microsoft announced that for OpenGL applications to function under Aero, OpenGL functionality will be implemented on top of DirectX, using Direct3D to translate and process OpenGL commands. As a result of this proxy between these two technologies, Microsoft states that OpenGL performance could be impacted by as much as 50 percent.

As of this writing, no official response has been heard from any of the major video hardware vendors on the issue. Randi Rost, a 3DLabs employee, is on record as making the following statement concerning this announcement by Microsoft:

"Accelerated OpenGL drivers will be available under Windows Vista. 3Dlabs and other vendors will provide OpenGL drivers that will take full advantage of the underlying features and performance of the graphics hardware. However, the current plan for Windows Vista is that as soon as an application accesses the graphics hardware through an accelerated OpenGL driver, the Windows Vista composited desktop is turned off. The result will be that the windows on the screen will be turned opaque. Applications that are running full-screen will not be affected. To preserve the desktop appearance, you can make your application utilize Microsoft's OpenGL implementation, which is layered on top of DirectX. The Microsoft OpenGL implementation is based on OpenGL 1.4 and the layering on top of DirectX can result in reduced performance. 3Dlabs is continuing to work with

Microsoft in an effort to provide a fully composited desktop along with fully accelerated OpenGL for Windows Vista."

According to the official OpenGL Web site, *http://www.opengl.org,* and information gleaned from other hardware vendors, the technical know-how already exists to provide an ICD solution. They stress, however, that communication between Microsoft and the vendors is critical for its success. If it is not too late by the time of this book's printing, be sure to contact your hardware vendor about this problem and urge them to keep attempting this communication with Microsoft.

To be clear, this is not about OpenGL being better than Direct3D; they are two very powerful graphics APIs that both have their uses in any application. However, this limitation under Aero represents a lack of choice available to the developer for any Vista application.

Some pundits in the industry also fear that if this limitation persists through to the official release of Windows Vista, then it could severely curtail any games development on other platforms such as MacOS or Linux. Their reasoning is that most game development companies use the cross-platform OpenGL to target both the Windows and MacOS user base. Without the availability of OpenGL, most companies will revert to programming strictly in Direct3D.

About the CD-ROM

The CD-ROM included with this book has been organized into an easy-to-browse structure. The content of each folder is noted here, along with instructions on setting up the CD-ROM.

/Chapter_Source: This folder contains some subfolders for the source code to this book:

Chapter_xx: This subfolder contains any chapter-specific code that is further organized and subdivided into respective chapters.

Bin: This folder contains the compiled binaries of each chapter sample.

/Peon: This folder contains the development tree for the Peon main engine project.

/tools_install/: This top-level folder contains the third-party tools useful for the game developer.

Paint Shop Pro: This folder contains the evaluation version of one of the most common paint tools for creating your own 2D textures for use on any meshes within the game.

Audacity-win-1.2.3.exe: This is the Audacity tool useful for editing sound effect files.

cvsnt-2.5.01.1976.msi: This is the setup binary for the popular Concurrent Versioning System for Windows.

Doxygen-1.4.3-setup.exe: This is the popular Doxygen tool that generates helpful documentation in HTML format.

3D Studio Max: This folder contains a 30-day evaluation version of the popular 3D modeling studio.

TortoiseCVS-1.8.13.exe: This is the setup binary for the Windows explorer plugin, TortoiseCVS.

NSIS: This folder contains the Nullsoft Scriptable Install Software application to compile your installation scripts.

OpenAL: This folder contains the OpenAL SDK from Creative Labs.

Lua: This folder contains the Lua script interpreter library.

/ **game_source:**   This folder contains some publicly available source code that has been released by commercial developers.

/quake2:   This is the source code to Quake2 by Id Software.

/quake3:   This is the source code to Quake3 by Id Software.

REQUIRED SOFTWARE

In order to compile the source code contained within this book, you need to use a compiler compatible with Windows. The source code to this book has been written, compiled, and tested with Visual Studio 6.0 SP6 and Visual Studio .NET 2003, but it might be possible to export the projects to any other commonly used IDE that supports the SDL. The solution files contained in the source code are for Visual Studio 6.0 and .NET 2003.

SYSTEM REQUIREMENTS

Although more is always better for game programming, the game and source code will require at least a CPU capable of 1GHz with a minimum of 256 MB RAM. Since you are using OpenGL, ensure that you are running with the latest drivers installed from your video hardware's vendor's site.

INSTALLATION

For most of the default installations, you simply need to launch the appropriate setup.exe or .msi installation file.

AUTHOR SUPPORT

The Web site for this book, *http://book.wazooinc.com,* contains the most up-to-date errata and bug fixes for this book, as well as a link to some forums to post any problems or difficulties with compiling and using the source code. If you are experiencing any problems compiling the source code or sample applications within this book, please make sure that you have downloaded the latest version of the code base from the Web site.

F

Further Resources

The field of knowledge on game programming is rather large and expansive, ranging from the most basic of beginner material to the most advanced theory. Games involve the use of art, sound, mathematics, graphic effects, networking theory, and a host of other areas of knowledge.

Along with a good search engine, the following Web sites might help when you encounter some sticking points in your projects. This is by no means a complete listing, but it does contain some great starting points that you might not find directly through your search. These sites are also not in any specific ranking or preference.

For your convenience, these links also appear on the "homepage" for the book contained on the included CD-ROM.

LICENSE SPECIFIC

http://www.opensource.org—The home page for all your Open Source license needs
http://www.creativecommons.org—The site for creating a Creative Commons license

OPENGL SPECIFIC

http://www.opengl.org—The home page of the OpenGL
http://nehe.gamedev.net—A site containing many OpenGL tutorials ranging from beginning to intermediate/advanced material
http://www.ati.com/developer/index.html—Developer site at ATI
http://developer.nvidia.com/page/home.html—Developer site at NVidia
http://developer.3dlabs.com/—Developer site at 3Dlabs

SDL SPECIFIC

http://www.libsdl.org—The home page for the SDL toolkit
http://www.libsdl.org/projects/SDL_image—Home page for the SDL_image add on
http://www.libsdl.org/projects/SDL_mixer—Home page for the SDL_mixer add on
http://www.libsdl.org/projects/SDL_net—Home page for the SDL_net add on
http://sol.gfxile.net/gp/—Sol's SDL tutorials, which are loaded with SDL information

DIRECTX SPECIFIC

http://msdn.microsoft.com/directx—The home page for DirectX

AUDIO PROGRAMMING

http://www.openal.org—The home page for the OpenAL API
http://developer.creative.com/landing.asp?cat=1&sbcat=31&top=38—The OpenAL resource page at Creative Labs
http://developer.nvidia.com/object/nvidia_audio_sdk.html—An audio resource page at NVidia
http://www.fmod.org—The home page of the FMOD library
http://www.harmony-central.com/Computer/Programming/—A full page of audio programming information and links
http://www.codeguru.com/Cpp/G-M/multimedia/—Some useful audio programming information at CodeGuru
http://www.codeproject.com/audio/—More useful audio programming information and source code at CodeProject

GAME DESIGN

http://www.vancouver.wsu.edu/fac/peabody/game-book/Coverpage.html—A repost of some older design material written by Chris Crawford
http://www.gamedev.net/reference/list.asp?categoryid=23—A great collection of material gathered at GameDev
http://civ.idc.cs.chalmers.se/projects/gamepatterns/—A collection and site dedicated to recording useful design patterns for games

http://www.cs.queensu.ca/~dalamb/Games/design/design.html—Designing Games FAQs from the rec.games.design newsgroup
http://www.ludism.org/gamedesign/—The Game Design WIKI site

NETWORK PROGRAMMING

http://www.ecst.csuchico.edu/~beej/guide/net/html/—Beej's Guide to Network Programming, which is one of the great foundation pieces written on network programming
http://www.flipcode.com/articles/network_part01.shtml—An introductory series of tutorials at FlipCode
http://www.gamedev.net/reference/list.asp?categoryid=30—More information and articles on network multiplayer implementation at GameDev
http://tangentsoft.net/wskfaq/—The Winsock Programmer's FAQ home page
http://msdn.microsoft.com/library/default.asp?url=/library/en-us/dnanchor/html/ntwrkprot.asp—Networking Protocols section of the MSDN
http://enet.bespin.org—The home page for the ENET socket library, which provides a thin layer for reliable UDP
http://www.rakkarsoft.com—The home page for the RakNet multiplayer library
http://www.hawksoft.com/hawknl/—The HawkNL multiplayer game library
http://www.replicanet.com/—The home page for the ReplicaNet networking library

SCENE GRAPHS

http://www.openscenegraph.org—The home page to the OpenSceneGraph SDK
http://www.ogre3d.org—A popular open source 3D engine that also uses a scene graph for scene processing
http://irrlicht.sourceforge.net—Another popular 3D engine with source code that uses a scene graph

AGILE SPECIFIC

http://www.agilealliance.org/home—The Agile Alliance home page. This should be the first stop when investigating this design approach.
http://www.agilemodeling.com/—The Agile Modeling home page, a site dedicated to documenting effective practices for Agile modeling.

GAME PORTAL SITES

http://www.bigfishgames.com—BigFishGames

http://www.realarcade.com—The RealArcade site

http://www.reflexive.net—Another portal

http://www.popcap.com—One of the most popular game portal sites

http://www.garagegames.com—Another portal (and developer resources) by the same people who make Torque

Index